MR WONDERFUL SEEKS IMMORTALITY

THE DIARY OF A RESTLESS MAN

Mr Wonderful seeks Immortality

The Diary of a Restless Man

SilverWood

Published in 2014 by SilverWood Books Ltd

SilverWood Books
30 Queen Charlotte Street, Bristol, BS1 4HJ
www.silverwoodbooks.co.uk

ISBN 978-1-78132-197-3 (paperback)
ISBN 978-1-78132-198-0 (ebook)

British Library Cataloguing in Publication Data
A CIP catalogue record for this book is available from the British Library

Set in Sabon, Univers and Compass TRF by SilverWood Books
Printed on responsibly sourced paper

When the virus of restlessness takes possession of a man, he justifies his waywardness by some compulsion beyond his own control. My compulsion has been to place myself beside a river, the trout and salmon being a subsidiary attraction to the beauty of a flowing stream. The search for rivers in strange places has taken me around the world, although this 'travelogue with incidents' along the way is not a fishing book.

Nonetheless, I dedicate it to the Atlantic salmon because I admire its struggle for survival so much more than the selfishness of man.

Contents

[Editor's note: John, please don't try to slip these in.]

1

Cambridge

It all began in Cambridge. We were gathered there for what is known as the Alumni Weekend when a thousand elderly graduates return to hear lectures from the great minds of the twenty-first century.

It is fifty years since I left this place without the intention or desire ever to return. Indeed, in my memoir, *Here Today, Gone Tomorrow* (Politico's Publishing, 2002), I described my time as an undergraduate as 'the three most wasted years of my life'; wasted by me, of course. I found the place claustrophobic and too detached. I had wanted to get on with my life in the real world outside.

But now I have returned to my old college, Trinity, for the Annual Luncheon and we are being addressed by the Master of the College – Martin Rees – a rather great man. He might claim, if he were not so modest, to be possibly the country's leading scientist – President of the Royal Society, Astronomer Royal, Reith Lecturer. In a very busy life, he finds time to think and write about the future.

'We are meeting here,' says Martin Rees at lunch, 'in probably a more intellectually fruitful place than any other patch of ground in the whole world.' For this is the college of Isaac Newton, Francis Bacon and Charles Darwin. A former Master of the College, Rab Butler, used to boast that Trinity had more Nobel prize-winners than the whole of France – a questionable assertion, but one made, characteristically, to make a point.

Trinity is the largest and richest college in Cambridge, and possibly Oxford, too. Famed today for science and mathematics, it is a long time since it produced a succession of prime ministers – that privilege has passed to Oxford. It retains a sort of tenuous relationship with the great and the good, but what distinguishes it from many equally worthy peers is that its riches make it utterly independent, particularly of interfering governments. After fifty years of absence, I realise now, belatedly, that I am proud to have been an undergraduate at Trinity.

My next-door neighbour at the luncheon is the former Bursar of the college, the sponsor of the Cambridge Science Park – the source of much of Trinity's wealth. He whispers to me, 'Have you read Martin Rees's book?' 'No,' I reply. 'Then you must do so,' he says. 'It is called *Our Final Century: Will Civilisation Survive the Twenty-first Century?*' I do read it and it sets me off on a voyage of exploration.

Looking back on that Alumni weekend I realise that something was stirring in my brain because I chose to attend two lectures; one was entitled 'Why Life Needs Death' and the other was called 'The Big Bang – The History of the Universe in 60 Minutes'. Am I beginning to dwell on mortality? Hardly surprising as I have reached the age of eighty.

The first lecturer appears from behind a curtain. He is a very gaunt professor with rimless glasses and a strong Scottish accent. He is delightful and very eccentric. Actually, he has made a massive contribution to medicine, so we dote on him for his achievements, but even more for his eccentric charm.

He conducts the lecture about cell growth and replacement as if he is Napoleon fighting the Battle of Austerlitz – it is a huge battle between two opposing forces.

We start quite simply with a visual aid, a large screen showing a diagram entitled 'Cell death in the development of a mouse's paw', followed by 'Cell death in a mouse's mammary glands'. But when we move on with a huge diagram headed 'Phagocytosis of Apoptotic Thymocytes by Macrophages' I begin to lose him, and by the time the screen is covered in a vastly complicated diagram of living and dying cells I am lost. And when he introduces a new group of 'very clever molecular beings that biologists called viruses' I give up. I ask my doctor neighbour whether he understood it. I understood the first third of the lecture, he says, and I more or less followed the rest of it. I am impressed.

Our second lecturer, discussing 'The Big Bang – The History of the Universe in 60 Minutes', puts an image of his best-selling book on the screen. His book, he says, should not be confused with a similar title called *The Big Bang: The Only Sex Manual You Will Ever Need*. I am beginning to understand 'Creation' already. We work our way through several theories of Creation – omitting the Book of Genesis – from the theory fiercely defended by Fred Hoyle that the Universe has always been with us, it is infinite, to the more modern belief that the Universe is finite, it was created at a particular moment of time, 'a day without a yesterday' etc. I shall come back to Fred Hoyle.

When asked in questions what came before the Big Bang, Another Bang, a Big Bump or a Big Something, our lecturer confessed that there were many unanswered questions. He ended with a quote from Einstein: 'The most incomprehensible thing about the Universe is that it is comprehensible.' Is it? Here I have to disagree with Einstein. It was so *in*comprehensible to me that it gave me confidence in the Book of Genesis, which contains a very sound view of Creation.

Following a further lecture on the great philosophers Russell, Wittgenstein, Ramsay and Francis Bacon – all Trinity men – I came to a startling conclusion. Science exists but it is full of contradictions –philosophy exists and is a contradiction. Science is an invention of the human mind – better to rely on faith; or should we call it religious conviction? I somehow trust philosophers much more than scientists – apart from anything else they have less scope for destroying the human race. It brings me back to Martin Rees's book *Our Final Century*.

2

Mr Wonderful

I owe it to the loyal readers of my earlier book *Mr Wonderful Takes a Cruise* (Ebury Press, 2004) to explain this sequel. More than 10,000 people read the first *Mr Wonderful* – and a further half a million plus will have glanced at it when it was serialised in the *Daily Mail*. I hope that my books are easy reading, so people do not need the intellectual rigour required to read the *Daily Mail*. The earlier book found its name from the Mr Wonderful tea dances and it began as follows:

> I was born before the invention of the pill, television, dishwashers, disposable nappies and New Labour. In those days a 'chip' was a fried potato. We had 'crumpet' for tea. 'Grass' was mown. 'Coke' was something you put on the fire. A 'joint' was a piece of meat that you ate for Sunday lunch and 'gay' people were the life and soul of the party, not members of the Cabinet.

Ten years have passed since the first *Mr Wonderful* was published and the English language has changed further – as have the habits of its citizens; this is illustrated in the following chapters headed 'Oiks' and 'Jordan's Wedding'. As I head into my eighties I look forward with the same sense of 'curiosity' (which, incidentally, is the name of the Mars probe, maybe my next journey) that led me to cruise the Norwegian fjords with my wife.

On that occasion I applied myself to an Olympian programme of preparation for the cruise by learning to dance, swim and play bridge. In fact the Norwegian ferry had no ballroom, bridge sessions or swimming pool, but the rigorous training programme for the Norway cruise should stand me in good stead for the next one.

The adventures in the book which cover the globe conclude with a passage through the ice at the top of the world from Alaska to Greenland. After the last cruise, my wife has refused to join me. She hates the sea – and she finds the company of her grandchildren more congenial than the rich widows and divorcees who will share my passage, and hopefully my company, as we progress through the Arctic – the hereditary home of the mosquito.

This trip in a modern Ark in preparation for another biblical Flood, well nigh predicted by the global warming addicts, will be the culmination of my attempt to secure my immortality in the likely event that civilisation will not survive the twenty-first century – more of this to come.

As my visit to Cambridge made clear, I have become preoccupied with this mortality business. It is not that I have any great concerns about my forthcoming demise; it is just that I do not want my genes, which go back, no doubt, to some primal swamp which I once shared with the mosquitoes, to disappear with the collapse of civilisation.

I share the view of Martin Rees that the days of this world could well be numbered, primarily because of the uncontrolled advance of science – and the possibility that we will all be done in by some mad scientist, or by an act of bio-terrorism. This led me to travel all over the world, as described in this book, in order to find a location in which I can establish a survival community. Following the dire warnings of Nevil Shute in his book *On the Beach* I commenced my search in the Southern Hemisphere. I first looked for a suitable site in Punta Arenas, in Chilean Patagonia, and then in Stewart Island, off the southernmost shore of New Zealand.

But my preference has always been for the Northern Hemisphere; I think it may have something to do with my Scandinavian genes.

Although I admired the natives of Patagonia – or what is left of them after successive Spanish pogroms – and the attractive New Zealanders – the descendants of English convicts and local Maori girls – I have this preference for northern blondes, particularly the women of Norway, Iceland, Spitzbergen, Arctic Russia, and, not to be excluded, England. This preference has recently been fortified by a succession of Olympian gold medallists like Jessica Ennis and Laura Trott.

In anticipation of another 'Flood' I have long given thought to keeping my boat (*Forget Me Not III*), mentioned in *Mr Wonderful Takes a Cruise*, at Cadogan Pier on The Embankment of the River Thames. My home in Chelsea nearby cannot be more than a few feet above the sea levels in the North Sea. We would clearly be under water if, as many scientists predict, the melting of the Greenland and Antarctic ice caps were to raise sea levels to a currently unprecedented level. During the Ice Age sea levels were some 400 feet lower than today. What if the doomsters were to be proved right and it was all to go into reverse with a sudden change in world climate? This could happen if another portion of the Antarctic Ice Cap were to break free and if the Greenland Ice Cap were to slide at an accelerating pace into the sea. The Bering Land Bridge linking Russia with America, through which humans and animals migrated into the American continent, disappeared under the sea as the glaciers melted in earlier times.

I have never been much concerned about New York and Tokyo, but Chelsea is another matter. I live there. I have kept a rubber dinghy on the top floor of my house as a precaution in case a tidal surge up the River Thames overwhelms the Thames Barrier. Would I have time to escape to my boat at Cadogan Pier? But, worse still, what happens if we have another biblical Flood and it rains 'for forty days and forty nights upon the earth'? In such a scenario neither my dinghy nor my boat would be adequate to house my family – or members of my survival community – for the necessary period of time. I therefore had recourse to the Bible – Genesis 6.5 – to learn what Noah would have done.

> And God saw that the wickedness of man was great in the earth... and he said I will destroy man whom I have created... but Noah found grace in the eyes of the Lord... make thee an ark of gopher wood, said the Lord... And behold I, even I, do bring a flood of water to the earth to destroy all flesh... [But] come thou Noah and all thy house with the ark... and every clean beast thou shalt take to thee by sevens... and the beasts that are not clean by two... And the rain was upon the earth forty days and forty nights... And all flesh died that moved upon the earth... And it came to pass in the six hundredth and first year, the face of the ground was dry... And God spoke unto Noah saying... be fruitful and multiply... go forth off the ark thou and thy wife, and thy sons, and thy sons wives with thee... I establish my covenant with you and with your seed after you... forever.

Now there can be little doubt about 'the wickedness of man' today – look at all those bankers' bonuses. It would not be a surprise if God vented his anger again on the earth. How, then, were we to prepare ourselves for a watery Armageddon, part of the global warming nightmare?

Had I been alive at the time I would have suggested to Noah that before embarking on the Ark he should consider some mechanism to mitigate the Flood, for instance: there was the EU Emissions Trading Scheme (ETS), the Carbon Development Mechanism (CDM), the Carbon Pollution Reduction Scheme (CPRS). All of them, I would have told Noah, would mitigate Catastrophic Anthropogenic Global Warming (CAGW). But I suspect Noah would have regarded all of these palliatives as futile, expensive and self-serving for scientists and politicians – and that he would choose the route of adaptation by embarking on the Ark. In this way he would hope to avoid extinction – and he would be right.

It was at this moment that I received an invitation to dine on a private yacht, albeit one that weighed 44,000 tons and contained 165 luxury apartments. The yacht was called *The World* and was moored temporarily at Greenwich Pier, on its peripatetic journey around the world. This was to be my Ark.

The billionaire owners of the apartments on the 'yacht' were greatly concerned, as I am, with their personal survival if sea levels rose or a tsunami were to destroy their nest eggs in low-lying Wall Street or the City of London. Perhaps more immediate was the need to be as far away as possible from the jurisdiction of the US Revenue Department, the IRS, and our own Inland Revenue. The owners believed in their naiveté that, had Noah been alive today, after the triumph of science and capitalism over Creation he would have invited them on board instead of a collection of animals; although in anarchist circles, the billionaires themselves, particularly Russian ones, might be described as animals. Noah would, of course, have paired them off with their wives and mistresses. Thus we would be back to a survival community, not in the Southern Hemisphere, but in the Ark – *The World* at sea.

This is how I came to be aboard *The World* when it cruised the Arctic from Northern Alaska across the top of Canada to Greenland. It met all the requirements of a survival location without the discomforts, boredom and isolation of Punta Arenas or Stewart Island. I had no doubt that an invitation to such a luxury yacht would produce a great rush of enthusiastic totty to share with me the hazards of the Arctic cruise. I remember vividly my lunch at Club 55 on Pampellone Beach near St Tropez, described in *Mr Wonderful Takes a Cruise*, when the owners of large yachts at anchor in the bay invited the beach beauties out of their boutiques to 'come on board'. The advanced age, ugliness and squalor of the rich punters caused no check to the fortune hunters on the beach. Of course, the Arctic is one thing and Pampellone Beach another, but money talks.

So, in August 2012 I set off via Iceland, Seattle and Anchorage to Nome, the northernmost port in Alaska, to join this ship – *The World*.

3

Our Final Century

The end of the world has been promised by Jews, Christians, Muslims and assorted nutters with sandwich boards for as long as intelligent life has existed. Today the sandwich boards display the message 'Woe, the end is nigh from global warming'.

Yet for the past two hundred years we have enjoyed unprecedented progress, driven by scientific and technological innovation. We have not gained prosperity by working harder, but because clever people have invented steam engines, antibiotics, micro-processors, the internet; but only recently clever people have developed the means and knowledge to destroy the world – that is new in human history. And only recently has science created life out of a computer to produce the first man-made living organism.

Agriculture supported perhaps three hundred million people in the world during Roman times; in the nineteenth century it fed over one billion. The best estimates suggest that it will need to support over nine billion people by 2020. It is likely that more than half of them will live in towns. Roughly sixty billion human beings have preceded us over tens of thousands of years. If that is so, 10 per cent of the humans who have ever lived are alive today. The birth rate may be falling world wide, but not quite yet. Despite the strictures of the Catholic Church, the birth rate in Brazil has halved; but greater medical knowledge is extending lifespan, particularly in the developed world, and, so far, pandemics like HIV-Aids have not seriously impacted on population growth, which must be expected to produce another two billion people in the world by 2020.

Children born today might expect to live at least thirty years longer than their Victorian ancestors, forty-five years longer than their medieval ancestors and more than fifty-five years longer than their Stone Age precursors. So, why, with this unparalleled progress in the world, should some fear another Dark Age for their grandchildren? Nuclear devastation, another Chernobyl and Hiroshima can kill millions, but only modern science, not a rise in temperature, can destroy life on earth, just as it has taught us, quite recently to create life on earth out of a computer.

Apart from the dangers now existing from further scientific innovation, the three foundations of our current prosperity have been fossil fuels, particularly oil, the harnessing of water, and antibiotics. Yet fossil fuels are now condemned. It is foolish.

It is oil that has made the 'green revolution' in agriculture a possibility; it is agricultural chemicals that have supported the growth of population in India and China. It is oil that has fuelled the distribution of vital supplies of food, as well as the more frivolous pleasures of driving cars and flying in aeroplanes. Some claim, foolishly, that world supplies of oil are under pressure, as China and other developing nations have joined the race for industrial pre-eminence. Other sources of energy – hydrogen, nuclear, wave, solar or wind power – offer some alternatives to keep progress moving forward, but will not replace the need for fossil fuels.

Water is even more important for survival than oil. Is it a diminishing resource or not? One of the best films of recent times, *Manon des Sources*, concerns the struggle for water on a micro-scale in rural France. Divisions over water taken from the River Jordan; and extraction from the water-table world wide have been excessive as world population growth has demanded it. A warning for the world is the great salt pans in Iraq where the first human beings grew their crops in the valley of the two rivers, the Tigris and Euphrates.

Increasing tension over water has a sort of inevitability in a world possessing nuclear weapons. But condensation from warming may increase precipitation.

Finally, just as science today can develop strains of bacteria that are immune to antibiotics, such bacteria are in fact emerging naturally as an outcome of Darwinian selection. A growing number of hospital wards are infected by bacteria which are resistant even to Vancomycin, the antibiotic of last resort. Has the unprecedented advance against the killers of the past, measles and smallpox, been beaten by the ability of 'bugs' to mutate and win the final contest?

None of these scenarios depresses me, because this small book is about adaptation, although I am concerned for the future of my grandchildren – the prospect for their future seems quite uncertain. Somehow the United Kingdom will survive another Dark Age and the latest scare, global warming, may be on their side. If water can be successfully harnessed in the west of England, a rise in temperature should enable new protein crops like soya to be grown, just as the maize we grow today on my farm was unthinkable fifty years ago. It may be true that carbon dioxide in the atmosphere has caused global warming to increase, but I am conscious that Anglo-Saxon England grew prosperous after a Dark Age of freezing winters, precisely because of a global warming of the kind that is predicted today. I write this gloomy chapter, too, in Punta Arenas in Chilean Patagonia, where the gap in the ozone layer over wider Antarctica seems to be closing again. An awful lot of nonsense is talked by politicians about climate change, egged on by a scientific unanimity. *Where opinion is unanimous on almost any subject, you can expect it to be the by-product of fashion, not truth.*

However, I have to return to a more serious concern for the future of humankind posited so brilliantly in the book that I have referred to already – *Our Final Century* by Martin Rees. On page 74 there is the startling statement: 'I staked a thousand dollars on

'It's a bit heavy, John.'

a bet: that by the year 2020 an instance of bio-error or bio-terror will have killed a million people.' This is not the utterance of a sandwich board aficionado, but an openly expressed statement by the former President of the Royal Society. What causes him to write such a provocative and unsettling book when those of us who have met him know that he is a very human optimist?

As an astronomer he covers the traditional dangers of earthquake, hurricane, volcanic eruption and asteroid impact of the kind which killed the dinosaurs sixty-five million years ago. These natural hazards will always be with us. He passes over the dangers of nuclear Armageddon in the post-war world. Here I must interpose a personal note. As Defence Secretary during the Cold War, I was conscious of the awesome destructive power of our independent nuclear deterrent, Trident, with its separately targeted warheads. I always knew that there were no circumstances whatsoever in which I could have given an order to release a strategic weapon and the dilemmas for those in power are well set out in my memoir *Here Today, Gone Tomorrow* (see page 217). But I was never equally certain about my colleagues. It was these very uncertainties that made our weapon such an awesome deterrent against war – especially nuclear war. We must keep a viable Trident system; it is our country's single most important protection against a threat to our future. Now this weapon, albeit in a far less sophisticated form, lies in the hands of at least ten other countries.

But the most extreme dangers to life today seem to lie in particle accelerator experiments, in genetics, robotics and nano-technology. In some areas of physics and biotechnology there can be no absolute certainty, particularly as future years pass by, that some experiment will not lead to a runaway disaster. An estimate by scientists at CERN in Geneva, Europe's biggest European accelerator (which creates an intense concentration of energy by accelerating atoms at enormous speeds close to that of light, and crashing them together) was that the risk of a catastrophe of life-destroying proportions was no more than one in fifty million. But someone wins the UK National Lottery with a chance of one in fourteen million. So the chance of destroying life on earth is less than winning the National Lottery. The risks were deemed to be infinitesimal, but were they zero?

After fifty years and £10 billion, the scientists have at last discovered the Higgs boson, 'the God particle', but the physicists still do not understand it.

The Big Bang didn't produce a completely safe, stable universe, but one which scientists describe as being in a false vacuum state. 'The near criticality of the Universe is the most important thing we have learned from the discovery of the Higgs boson so far' (Gian Giudice of CERN).

A few scientists (Joseph Lykken of the Fermi National Accelerator Laboratory, for instance) say that the Large Hadron Collider could produce a bubble of a different vacuum which will then expand at the speed of light, destroying everything; obliterating the workings of reality.

We have 'dark energy sucking the galaxies from the sky, greenhouse gas catastrophes, comets and asteroids boiling the oceans, apocalyptic volcano eruptions and plagues'.

We now know that a nuclear weapon cannot trigger a nuclear chain reaction, but the scientists at Los Alamos in 1942 were not absolutely certain. We survived – and won the war. Is that somehow different from experiences in pure science?

What is thought-provoking for Martin Rees is that the worldwide attempt to enforce the import and use of illegal drugs is hopelessly failing. What better chance is there to control the dangerous excesses flowing from bio-technology? The deciphering of the human genome allows science to be misused to create new agents of mass destruction. All over the world there are people with the expertise to undertake genetic manipulation and cultivate micro-

The Meaning of Life – or the **end** of it.

organisms. The genetic blueprint of large numbers of viruses is stored in databases accessible to scientists on the internet.

Looking further ahead, possibly rather fancifully, what are the consequences when computers and robots surpass human capabilities? Surely that may happen in my grandchildren's lifetime. Things happen fast. There is more processing power in a computer game console today than was available to the Apollo astronauts when landing on the moon.

The problem is that self-restraint seems inconceivable for scientists with a narrow focus on some area of pure science; it is even more difficult to locate and control some loner, some fanatic or social misfit with the mindset of those who now design computer viruses. What can a layman do except maintain a Zen detachment while the scientists play with their toys.

4

Men

Then, a visit by one of our neighbours in Cornwall gave me a new slant on this 'immortality' business. We were visited by a delightful friend of ours, an aristocratic widow in her eighties called Lady Vyvyan. I told her about our forthcoming visit to South America and she responded with a description of her travels to Europe in her camper van.

'I go everywhere,' she said, 'in my camper van. I like going on my own. It gives me such freedom and flexibility.'

'Isn't it lonely or dangerous on your own?' I asked.

'No,' she said, 'I am always accompanied by a man.'

'Oh, how interesting,' I said. 'You have a walker, then, is that right? Or is he your toyboy?'

'Oh no,' she replied, 'he's made of plastic. He is a blow-up man. When I go to bed at night in my camper van, I take out a bicycle pump and pump him up. I then sit him in the double bunk for all to see. He is much better company than a real man. The local police have fully endorsed this practice – they strongly recommend a blow-up man, so that he can be seen by potential rapists and intruders.'

'How tall is he?' I asked.

'Oh, he is only available in a sitting position,' she replied. 'He has no private parts.'

'How very dull,' I said, 'where did you get him; from a sex shop, I presume?'

'No,' said our widow, 'the blow-up man was recommended to me on the BBC. I got him by mail order from the BBC: the only problem is that he is vulnerable to puncture and he gets full of holes. All the time I have the embarrassment of asking some other tourist for his bicycle repair kit. Fortunately, observers, burglars and rapists do not get close enough to examine my man's skin – they see him sitting on my double bunk and do the bunk themselves.'

The more I thought about her, the more I began to wonder what men were for these days. They were always fighting one another and causing trouble. With the withdrawal of the press gangs in the nineteenth century there was no way of forcing them into employment. Too many men just hung around on welfare benefits, joining gangs, and were utterly useless to society. If my widow friend was right she could replace a male companion as her protector with a blow-up male replica – even man's traditional role as a defender of the female sex was redundant.

It was clear that Darwin's theory of natural selection may be working its way through to the elimination of the male sex altogether. Do we need men any more? We hear endless statements about global warming and its dangers, but nothing about the much more serious problem – the declining sperm count of men all over the developed world. I feel a quiver of concern about the fertility of the younger generation when their sperm count is said to have reduced by 30 per cent in the past twenty years. It is no laughing matter, even though the press joke about it with headlines such as 'Try twice as hard in the sack, fellas' or 'Cigs and booze blamed as more men are firing blanks'. The NHS is crowded out by male obesity, but also requests for IVF treatment. Is natural selection creating a new race of hermaphrodites? Admittedly, men's role in producing children is rather perfunctory, but up to now men have been considered necessary for the perpetuation of life on earth.

I examined the latest scientific data on the fertility of male fish in dozens of rivers, published by the Environment Agency. Up to half the fish in some rivers can no longer produce sperm because of the feminising effect of chemicals in the water, in particular sewage effluent containing hormone residues from the Pill. It would be ironic if the Pill was causing short-term security for women, but terminal impotence in men.

According to the Environment Agency male roach and gudgeon are developing deformities in their sexual organs and some are producing eggs rather than semen in their testes. If fish are on their way to becoming hermaphrodite, why not us?

The only bright side in this story is that old men like me might have a function again; the government may ask us poor pensioners to save the world with a request that the more potent males of an earlier generation contribute to a global sperm bank. The sperm would be held at the Royal Botanic Garden's Millennium Seed Bank in the vaults at Wakehurst Place, West Sussex.

We know that women are better educated, more intelligent and better able to handle pain than men. Some women like having men around to change the light bulbs and mend fuses. Men don't talk all night about nail varnish, designer labels, shoes and hair so they have some residual value, even for women. Men have never played a very prominent part in the baby business – unlike state nurseries which have replaced motherhood for today's career girls – but they were valuable for a very short bit of assistance in the procreative process. But if they cannot do better than a plastic blow-up replica as a defender of the female sex, and are unable to make a short contribution to a woman's world when it comes to producing babies, then let's get rid of them. It would be a more peaceful world. Darwin is on the march again. Or maybe, now that we can create life out of a computer, men are redundant anyhow. Prince Charles prattles on about extinction of the species, but he has not yet talked about the coming extinction of man.

So, if my attempt to establish a survival community in the Southern Hemisphere were to fail, I might achieve immortality by storing my sperm in the vaults at Wakehurst Place.

5

A Nervous Breakdown

So far this narrative has been relatively sane [Editor's note: Has it?], but the author of this book is not always sane, as readers of *Mr Wonderful Takes a Cruise* will testify. I have a habit of spiralling into fantasy and all this doom and gloom became too much for me, especially when a wretched pollster came knocking on my door and I was challenged about the latest disaster scenario – global warming. I took myself off to meditation at a Buddhist retreat. Basically I am an optimist because I have an unswerving belief that the human race and the animal kingdom will adapt itself to whatever disaster comes along. We survived the Ice Age, challenge from the Neanderthals and recently in this country we have survived New Labour. We will surely overcome the problems caused by climate change, probably by adaptation.

But there did come a moment when I came to doubt, like Martin Rees, whether civilisation can survive the twenty-first century. Nuclear devastation, bio-terrorism, asteroid impact, chlamydia, genetic cloning, rogue nano-machines, extra-terrestrial viruses; even political correctness, the Health & Safety Executive and the European Union! Can we survive all these things? It is quite a menu.

In my earlier book I examined all the great religious of the world, Christianity, Islam, Buddhism, Hinduism, but none of them seemed to offer the certainty of life after death or much hope for immortality.

I had some excitement when I discovered Thor, the son of Odin, who gave his name, via the Romans, to Thursday. As a descendant of Vikings, here was a god that might give me an afterlife. As the God of Thunder, he travels about the clouds in a carriage drawn by two goats. He is foremost among the gods to the common man. He is the God of Fertility, and he drinks a lot of mjod (beer), he is righteous and has a violent temper... I was much attracted to him. But I discovered that in Viking mythology 'in the time of Ragnarök' (the end of the world) Thor dies in a battle with a gigantic worm called Midgard – so that put me back to where I began, the genes of my descendants.

But how was I to protect my genes from the catalogue of pending disaster mentioned above if some warehouseman were to destroy the Millennium Seed Bank? I therefore alighted on the concept of a survival community located somewhere in the Southern Hemisphere like Patagonia or Stewart Island; both are as near as you can get to Antarctica. This whole idea was provoked, as I have said already, by Nevil Shute's famous book *On the Beach* where a nuclear cloud wipes out the Northern Hemisphere.

I took myself to both these places and the stopovers on the way. I describe my journeys in this book. But who was I to take with me? My children would never come; I would need some pretty interesting people if I was to sustain this survival business.

I was inspired by a former Poet Laureate, John Betjeman, who declared in his last years that the only thing he regretted in his life was that he had not had enough sex. He had plenty, but not enough. What man can ever have enough? It is either a desert or a tsunami of sexual encounters.

Another Poet Laureate, Ted Hughes, a good friend of mine whom I accompanied on many fishing expeditions, came somewhere between a desert and a tsunami himself, but he veered rather heavily towards the tsunami end of the spectrum. I remember seeing several poetry-loving groupies at his Memorial Service in

Westminster Abbey on his final journey to Poets' Corner.

Then in my confused state I thought that I should examine Creation. It might give me some guide to immortality. I tested it when I visited Cambridge and attended lectures on 'Life Needs Death' and 'The Big Bang'. But I don't think either of these lectures provided a convincing explanation for the beginning of life on earth. If Darwin was right when he enunciated the process of natural selection, I must take the right kind of people to my survival community, a good example of modern youth for instance, and I describe how I made this search, and considered taking a 'celebrity'.

I tell you with all these unanswered questions that I nearly became a fundamentalist like my Victorian grandparents and George W. Bush. Neither acknowledged Darwin:... 'a madman,' they said. They believed, and they may have been right, that every word written in the Bible, from Creation in the Book of Genesis to the ravings of St John the Divine in the Book of Revelation, was the revealed truth. They believed also that the world woke up one morning to find Adam and Eve in the Garden of Eden, illegal aliens from outer space. 'In the beginning God created heaven and earth... and God said let there be light and there was light.'

I noted that Pope John Paul II seemed to have been a keen supporter of Darwinism but then Pope Benedict XVI, before he packed in the job, tipped the scales back to the Book of Genesis by speaking warmly of the concept of 'intelligent design'.

In fact, the Book of Genesis may need reinterpretation anyhow because God has acquired a new competitor. Not long ago, in a Californian laboratory, man created new life out of a computer. A bacterial genome was sequenced, digitised, modified, printed out and put inside an empty cell to produce the first man-made organism. The scientists – we should be frightened of them – produced 'Mycoplasma mycoides JCVI-syn1.0' cells which obeyed their command to be fruitful and multiply. Synthetic biology was born and gave humanity the ability to design and create life. God did cling on, because the synthetic genome was transplanted into the empty cell of a related bacterium which was already 'alive'. But the competition between man and God had escalated beyond all measure since God banished Adam and Eve from the Garden of Eden – and he was denied the power of immortality. 'See the man has become like one of us, knowing good and evil; and now, he might reach out his hand and take also from the tree of life, and eat, and live for ever' (Genesis 3.22). Yes!

The Book of Genesis is full of instances of man being punished for his attempts to become like God. For billions of years life had been created out of the sea, and then in a primal swamp. A life form developed from mixing and rearranging existing natural genes from different species, and through selection and adaptation we became nearer and nearer to a God-like form. And then BANG. After billions of years, and only for the second time, life was created; this time synthetically. There have been several mass extinctions in human history, but this is only the second Creation, and it happened not in the Garden of Eden but in a Californian laboratory.

God in his infinite wisdom had seen the threat to his divine pre-eminence. Before, in Genesis 11.3, he once again saw humanity trespassing on his prerogative when he built the Tower of Babel and reached into heaven. His answer was a clever one: he divided humans into uncomprehending groups who could not understand each others language.

But now God faces the ultimate challenge. Life is now reducible to chemistry. There is one language – the single language of science. No soul, no afterlife, just an equation. Man has become the creator of life, and also its destroyer. He is God. Or is he?

6

Oiks

I have noticed in the past fifty years or so that people are different; habits, languages, cultural behaviour and preferences have had a seismic shift, all during my lifetime. Darwin would be amazed at the sheer pace of adaptation – technology, in particular, has dictated an acceleration of natural selection in the young – so my next move is to consult 'the Social Affairs Unit' about what sort of people that I need to take with me on this trip – I want examples of the younger generation. I have therefore headed this chapter 'Oiks'.

I approach the Social Affairs Unit for guidance. I know that it is regarded as a counter-revolutionary conspiracy by the liberal intelligentsia who read the *Guardian* and work in the BBC. In 2004 a senior member wrote a pamphlet entitled 'We're All Oiks Now', which describes the surrender of Middle England to the yob culture of today. Yob culture is about the collapse of what used to be defined as middle-class attitudes and behaviour with its moralistic disdain for the habits and language of the lower orders; a disdain held on contrary terms by would-be intellectuals and young aristocrats for what they see as the moralistic attitudes of the provincial petit-bourgeoisie.

Chambers' Dictionary describes an 'oik' as a cad, an ignorant, a chap, a bloke, a mate. 'How's you this morning, mate? On the tiles last night, eh, mate? Ha! Ha! Did you get a shag? Ha! Ha!'

The Social Affairs Unit published this pamphlet which said that Middle England has capitulated in one of three ways. It has simply given up on old-fashioned traditional values and behaviour; or it is too frightened to declare them in public places for fear of abuse. Worst of all, the largest part of Middle England has deserted to the enemy, aping the accents, dress and behaviour of the lower orders. Members from the best schools and Oxford University speak with regional accents or in estuary English so that they can merge seamlessly with the working classes.

Middle England no longer moralises about the behaviour of the so-called lower orders while chatting in small shops, leaning against the bar in the village pub or preaching against modern Britain in the guise of a church warden or a magistrate. The modern Anglican rarely talks about right and wrong. He favours prizes for all, and talks about 'moving forward'. She mutters approvingly as she reads Melanie Phillips in the *Daily Mail*.

This fashion can be seen most vividly in politics. In the old days there was an admirable but rather dotty institution called the Labour Party, or 'old' Labour. It actually believed in a whole set of barmy ideas which were more important to it than winning elections. Then a new generation of deserters from Middle England infiltrated it and sophisticated, public school-educated oiks like Tony Blair said, never mind what you believe in, it's all about winning elections, without power you cannot achieve anything, or nothing as the case may be.

Now the Conservative Party wants to win elections. It says that it must de-contaminate its traditional brand. In fact, it has failed to detoxify the Tory brand; it has simply made it unrecognisable, even to Tories. We are told it must 'connect' with modern Britain. For example, if it is embarrassing or boring to 'bang on' about the iniquities of the European Union, its power-hungry elite, its endemic corruption, the European gravy-train, better to say nothing and not 'bang on' about it because modern Britain is only interested in an education system where nobody fails exams and in a healthy Britain where nobody dies; we want to drive around in a chauffeur-driven Mondeo from the government car pool.

An unknown man called Richard Law, albeit that he was the son of a Prime Minister, wrote the following while he worked in the Conservative Research Department in the 1950s.

> The floating vote lives up to its name. It floats with the tide and whoever most influences it, must first influence the tide. You attract it, not by angling for it, and changing your fly from pool to pool, but by convincing it that you yourself are convinced.

No politician believes this any more: they read focus group reports so that they can 'connect' with modern Britain. Are they 'convinced' about anything?

These thoughts occurred to me while I was pondering what kind of people I wanted to take with me if I decide to set up my survival community in the Southern Hemisphere. Do I want to establish a community which values orderliness, punctuality, independence, self-reliance, prudence, modesty, reticence, saving, one which deplores intellectuals and smart alecs, *all* journalists, London, exhibitionism, foreign food, trades unions, taxes, sex, foreigners and perverts? Or would I feel more comfortable in a community like modern Britain with unlimited self-indulgence, abundant credit, wastefulness, debt, frivolity, ill discipline verging on personal anarchy, exhibitionism, football, sex, second-hand cars and Jeremy Clarkson?

After reading the pamphlet by the Social Affairs Unit I become more familiar with the sort of behaviour that one can see in the late-night streets of modern Britain. But what about the so-called upper classes at play? Do they behave differently?

In a spirit of enquiry I attended (as an observer) the Bullingdon Club Reunion Dinner held at White's Club in St James's. This is a group of self-appointed representatives of the upper classes drawn from Oxford University. On this occasion it was hosted by an aspiring politician, whom we shall call 'Charlie', and I noticed that a school called Eton was heavily represented by the politicians present. Champagne and Pernod cocktails were consumed to generate a Bullingdon atmosphere after which 'Charlie' called the reunion to order. 'Remember,' as Theresa May told us, when she was the Chairman of the Conservative Party, the **old** Conservatives are 'unchanged, unrepentant, just plain unattractive.'

'The purpose of this dinner,' Charlie said, 'is to invent new liberal policies, but first please remove your ties to show that we are "connected' with the plebs outside.' Charlie then reported that he had just attended a black school in the East End. 'Good old Charlie.' Hooray, Hooray, *Floreat Etona*. 'De-bag the Provost', shouted the approving Bullingdonians and their guests. The evening was progressing to form.

'Up your Nottinghill' shouted one guest. 'Peter Sellers for Headmaster,' shouted another, Frank Bruno for Music Master etc., etc.. Ha, ha, hooray, hooray!

Buns were thrown, a jug of water was emptied over the chief policy adviser, Oliver Leftwing, an Etonian, of course; champagne was sprayed at the pictures of war heroes who fell at the bottom of the stairs. Ha! Ha! Hooray, hooray, *Floreat Etona*, Boating Song.

Charlie called for order. 'The evening has just begun,' he said. 'We are here to invent more "policies" to put to our party and the country.' Much laughter. 'I have called my "mates" together to discuss more "silly things",' Hooray, hooray. 'Tomorrow I go to the Wetlands Centre in Barnes to meet an old Eton friend of mine, Jonathan Porritt of Greenpeace.' Hooray, hooray, *Floreat Etona*. 'I am planning to save our party and the country by connecting with our focus groups.' Hooray, hooray. 'Let's raise our glasses to more Mondeos for the government car pool. Higher taxes. It's all about "style". We can show Mandelson and Campbell how to spin it.'

Hooray, hooray, *Floreat Etona*. Cheers, cheers.

'I have put up my friend Ken to reinvent our policies. Good old Ken. Grammar school boy. College scarf. Europhile, Green issues. Windmills. Treadmills. Wave power. Donkeys. Darkness. Hypothermia.' Ha! Ha! Hooray, hooray.

Charlie then gathered up half his guests – the other half were under the tables.

'Each of us must contribute £5,000 to defray the damage to furniture, pictures, plates and glasses at this, my first, research group meeting. I assess the damage at £50,000 – rather less than at our usual dinners. Please join me on a visit to an 'establishment' where we can connect with the lads, our mates – and join with the girls who we will invite to form the 'A' list of candidates.'

Hear! Hear! Hooray, hooray, *Floreat Etona*. What a **modern** lot we are. Connect, connect.

The sun was shining on the sea,
Shining with all his might:
He did his very best to make
The billows smooth and bright,
You could not see a cloud, because
No cloud was in the sky:
'O, Oysters, come and walk with us!'
A figure did beseech.
'A pleasant walk, a pleasant talk,
Along the briny beach'

The wisest Oyster [me!] looked at him.
But never a word he said:
The wisest Oyster winked his eye,
And shook his heavy head.

But four young Tory oysters hurried up,
All eager for the treat:

Tory Oysters followed them,
And yet another four;
And thick and fast they came at last,
And more, and more, and more.

'The time has come,' a Tory Oyster said,
To talk of silly things:
Of shoes – and ships – and sealing-wax –
Of cabbages – and kings –
And why the sea is boiling hot –
And whether pigs have wings.'

'It seems a shame,' I did retort,
To play them such a trick,
After we've brought them out so far,
And made them trot so quick!'

'O, Oysters,' said the politician
You've had a pleasant run!
Shall we be trotting home again?'
But answer came there none –
And this was scarcely odd, because
Ambition had eaten every single one of them.

7

The Interview I

The doorbell rings and I descend three flights of stairs to answer it. 'Hello,' she says. 'How are you, darling? It's great to see you again. You look younger than ever, darling. I am so happy to be back here.'

'Excuse me, madam,' I say, drawing myself up to my full five foot ten inches (it was six foot a few years ago), 'and who might you be?'

'John,' she says, 'I am mortified. You don't recognise me, I can't believe it. I'm Crystal, but call me Chris, I used to spell it with a "K". I was here to interview you for a focus group several years ago and Mr Philip Gould, latterly Lord Gould, my dear, was so delighted with your answers that his successors have sent me round again to see how you're getting on.'

'I really don't remember it,' I say. 'They are always telephoning me with their wretched surveys. What was so special about yours? But come inside, it is cold standing on the doorstep.'

'We are now conducting,' Chris continues as she strides ahead of me into my own drawing room, 'focus group surveys for the Prime Minister, Dave, as we call him. We feed our results directly into No. 10 and our findings lead to all sorts of policy adjustments, reversals, upheavals, decisions and sometimes indecisions, particularly when the answers are ambiguous (as is normally the case). I am here, John, because I have been asked to obtain your views on politics.

'Your last interview on politics was of great importance. Not only did it lead to my promotion – I am now a Gold Star interviewer – but your replies had a great impact on the General Election. Mr Gould, sorry, the former Lord Gould, thought you were typical of the voters whom, at that time, we were trying to attract to New Labour.'

No more – we have now changed sides, as I will explain.

'As a professional,' says Chris, 'the key to my original enquiry was to place you in one of the social categories used in all government surveys, particularly in the National Census: if you remember I asked whether you were an "A" (higher managerial or professional – Chief Constable, barrister, etc.), a "B" (intermediate managerial – air traffic controller, parson, squadron leader in the RAF, etc.), a "C1" (supervisory – bank cashier, RSPCA inspector etc.), a "C2" (skilled manual worker – barber, bus driver, etc.), a "D" (semi-skilled manual worker – window cleaner, fork-lift truck driver, minicab driver etc.), or "E" (state pensioner, unemployed for more than six months, widow etc.). You claimed that you fell, as a state pensioner, into Category E and your answers certainly indicated that your views coincided with this class of person.'

Slowly recollection returns to my befuddled brain. Yes, I had given an interview to a focus group before the last election, but I regarded the whole process as being so utterly ridiculous that I had invented all my answers as it had always been an ambition of mine to fuck-up a focus group. She is correct.

'Well, now,' says Chris, 'you were surprised to hear that our agency is no longer working for New Labour. Mr Gould, sorry, the late Lord Gould, was approached by Dave Cameroon the day after the leadership election to ask if he would conduct political interviews for the New Conservative Party instead of New Labour. My agency jumped at the opportunity. The agency likes being on the winning side – and the focus group reports which we were sending to Tony Blair and then to Gordon Brown were so depressing and insulting to the then Prime Minister – the questions we were required to ask so authoritarian and bellicose – so twisted to engage favourable replies to the Iraq War, ASBOs, arrest without trial, torture, speed cameras and the rest that Lord Gould could not, given the high ethical code of our profession, any more tailor his reports to accord with the prejudices of his client. Lord Gould saw immediately that Dave Cameroon revelled in PR stunts, spin and the Centrist ideas that had once motivated Mr Blair – so he decided his liberal conscience would rest better with the New Conservatives.

'Anyhow, Lord Gould was a neighbour of Dave and his reactionary sidekick George Osborne in Notting Hill and had a high opinion of the trendy attitudes among the middle-, sorry, upper-class, liberal activists, BBC managers and restaurant aficionados that inhabit that bleak location. You told us, John, that you are entirely non-political – should I say apolitical? – so you are likely to "connect" with the lifestyle which the New Conservatives so admire and are seeking to attract to their cause.

'The successors of Lord Gould knew that you would welcome an opportunity to contribute your opinions to a new political focus group, even though its content will now be tailored for submission to the New Conservatives. After all, John, although you did not know it at the time, you helped to design the policies that lost the election for New Labour. You are a beacon with your opinionated views – sorry, with your ideas – when it comes to suggesting a winning formula for elections. We have prepared a list of questions for you which, after refinement, will go to the policy supremo, Mr Oliver Leftwing, on its way to the Great Leader, I mean Dave.'

Great, I think; although I am a Tory by instinct this will give me the same opportunity to foul up the liberals in the New Conservative elite as I succeeded in doing with New Labour. In my time in government we called them the 'Wets'. They were nearly all Etonians! It was the smugness of these Etonians that was hard to take. I am not a Conservative or a Whig, or a Liberal, but a radical Tory, a believer in a small state, low taxes, personal responsibility, but I recognise these concepts are out of fashion; there are very few radical Tories left these days – they were dismissed by the burqa-hugging Theresa May as members of the 'Nasty Party', you see.

'The first question,' says Chris, 'may surprise you, but it is cleverly designed to probe into your inner Freudian psychosis. You are, after all, an "E" in our social category, a state pensioner, and it may be assumed that you harbour certain racist and cultural prejudices.

Question One: 'Would you feel more comfortable sharing a bedroom with a public schoolgirl from Notting Hill or a beautiful African virgin from the Congo?'

'Definitely with the African virgin,' I reply.

'How interesting,' says Chris, 'that is not the reply I would have expected from an eighty-year-old Conservative. Your reply could be of interest to the Metropolitan Police.'

Question Two: 'Are you in favour of free contraceptive advice to all children in secondary schools?'

'Of course,' I say.

'Wow,' says Chris, 'you are an odd pensioner.'

Question Three: 'Are you in favour of a free National Health Service for everyone regardless of cost and higher taxes, or a system where people contribute directly through insurance to the cost of their own health?'

'I am old,' I reply, 'I am opposed to death. I therefore favour more money being pumped into the Health Service regardless of cost.'

*The Home Secretary (Theresa May) and other 'Modernisers' escaping from the '**Nasty Party**'.*

Question Four: 'Are you in favour of diverting more of your pension into the Swiss bank accounts of Mr Mugabe and other African dictators – or do you support the Make Poverty History Campaign?'

'I am in favour of supporting all African dictators out of my diminishing pension assets as I trust them implicitly to act in the interests of their people.'

'In that case,' says Chris, 'you are presumably a supporter of Bob Geldorff?'

'Of course,' I reply, 'I think Sir Geldorff is wonderful, such a well-spoken, well-mannered and well-dressed young man. Together with the equally hirsute Sir Virgin Branscombe, he is a true hero of modern times. It was a triumph when Dave persuaded Sir Geldorff to spend ten minutes a year helping us to save the world.'

Question Five: 'Were you in favour of the invasion of Iraq?'

'Of course,' I reply. 'Saddam Hussein was fiercely opposed to all liberals. He had to be eliminated with other reactionary elements in our own society.'

'So you are in favour, then,' says Chris, 'of eliminating or at least dismissing every subscribing member of the Conservative Party over the age of forty?'

'Most certainly,' I say. 'I call them swivel-eyed loons. They have been a major drag on the Conservative Party for many years. We are a young modernising party. We need to keep our elderly supporters out of sight, particularly at our conference; we put them at the back of the hall so that the front seats are taken up by young ethnic supporters of the Party.'

'I think I get the drift,' says Chris. 'You are in favour of appointing young ministers, sometimes in their twenties, rather than persons of experience in the outside world.'

'Yes, of course. We don't want senior ministers confused and polluted by outside experience, it might cloud their judgement.

Ideally any government should comprise persons who have come straight from school into research and public relations. Politicians should be trained in politics, not in other skills.'

'I have the impression that your traditional supporters are restless about the country being run from Brussels, and not from Westminster; they seem to be abandoning you for UKIP. Is Dave planning to grasp the problem by urgently restoring democratic government to Westminster?'

'Well,' I say, 'it is a problem. We are planning to placate them by undertaking a ten-year programme of negotiation with our European partners. For Dave to get what he wants in Europe, he must know what he wants. I am not sure that he does. I think the solution is to kick the whole ugly problem into the long grass; certainly this is the advice of Sir Humphrey Appleby and our Liberal partners. Meanwhile, the Deputy Prime Minister and Dave will attend weekly European summits with their accompanying photo-opportunities; in this way people can see that the New Conservatives are responding to public opinion. There cannot be a simple Yes or No answer to complex issues, so we must prevaricate.

'I think,' says Chris, 'given your contempt for local democracy, that I can guess your attitude to women-only shortlists, or an "A" list; presumably you are in favour of keeping talented young men out of Parliament in order to get attractive totty into marginal seats where they can flash their tits at the electorate?'

'That is an utterly sexist question,' I reply, 'it is beneath me to answer such a loaded question.'

'What is your opinion of Mrs Thatcher, John?'

'I do not follow politics and I had not heard of her until recently. I understand that she was a well-known housewife in the 1980s.'

'Have you heard of Carol Thatcher, John?'

'Of course, she is famous for winning a celebrity contest in Australia. She represents, with the contestants in television shows like *Big Brother* – as you know I was a television executive myself – just the sort of person we want to attract to the Conservatives. Celebrities are an important target for us. We should admire their ability to capture the headlines.'

'What is your opinion of the Mayor of London, John?'

'We do not discuss Boris Johnson in polite circles, I'm afraid.'

'John – what is your feeling about fossil fuels? Would you not agree that they have been responsible for an enormous increase in the world's prosperity?'

'No,' I say, 'I prefer solar, hydro, windmills, wave power, treadmills, camels, donkeys and watermills to coal-fired power stations, natural gas and nuclear fusion. Given the choice, like all liberals I would be happy to suffer darkness and hypothermia for the sake of a better world.'

'Your heart is in the right place,' says Chris. 'Are you sure that you are not a New Conservative – or are you just sucking up to Dave?

'You said at the outset of the interview that you are not a Conservative. Is Dave Cameroon a Conservative?'

'I think he describes himself as a liberal Conservative, whatever that may mean. He is a personable, kindly and intelligent man but most traditional Conservatives do not share his politics'.

A Note from the Editor

Richard: John, I accept that your dialogue with Chris is a satirical summary of current politics, but would it not be more constructive if you wish to avoid another bout of socialist mismanagement following the next General Election, to give a more serious criticism of Conservative strategy?

John: Yes, Richard, I will do just that: David Cameron made one fatal political misjudgement at the outset which a more experienced politician would certainly have avoided. He should have soldiered on with a minority government and challenged the opposition parties to bring him down. It would have been a risky strategy but even had he lost the second General Election the Conservative Party would have remained a viable force for government; instead the Liberal coalition has greatly damaged the integrity of the Conservative Party and its future. The fixed term parliament is an abomination.

So far as my satirical dialogue is concerned, I would say as follows: the problem is politics does not differ much from the dilemma faced by a business, especially in retailing where the sole arbiter is the consumer. Business experience is invaluable for politicians. From my own experience, and I spent more time in business than in politics, I know that there is the ever-present temptation to abandon the old-time conservative customer in favour of the more trendy younger fashion-conscious punter. How is it possible to capture a whole raft of younger customers without losing, or antagonising, the more conservative customers upon which the former prosperity of the business was founded?

This dilemma is similar to the issues confronting political

policymakers. Naturally there will always be an element of subjective choice when designing policies that appeal to the electorate – the ultimate political consumer. How to produce and maintain, on given policy lines, an evolving constellation of political constituencies, deciding whose support to maintain, whose to win over and who to discard.

It helps to have an overall sense of direction and avoid being diverted continuously by 'focus groups' which change their attitudes from day to day and are not much interested in traditional values. It requires sustaining the loyalty of 'the home base' of more ideological supporters while simultaneously appealing to the other audience, most of whom will interpret political rhetoric foremost in relation to their own self-interest, as opposed to identifying with a political agenda. Success or failure will depend on how far a party can get this diverse audience to subscribe to the political narrative.

I have no criticism of this government; as a government it is undertaking an agenda of quite brave but necessary reforms in welfare, education and economic policy. Theresa May has been a good Home Secretary in very difficult circumstances. The hero of the government has been Duncan Smith who has persisted with his reforms against normal Treasury obstruction. The Prime Minister should be applauded for holding on to an unpopular course for the longer-term objective of greater social and economic stability.

The criticism is that, in doing so, he has ignored the prejudices of the Conservative Party's ideological supporters. Many have been terminally alienated. Older voters tend to be politically sophisticated; they realise that the financial deficit has to be closed. But, as a recent McKinsey study estimated, older savers have lost out on nearly £400 billion of savings interest in the Western economies as a result of quantitative easing and loose monetary policies, while governments have gained over £1,000 billion from these policies. On urging by the Liberals, a pledge to raise the Estate Duty threshold has been abandoned, annuity rates have been forced down, and pension accumulation has been attacked under the Coalition. Subliminally, older voters understand these things and have become alienated from former party loyalties, partly as a result of the massive diversion of their savings into the coffers of governments.

The Conservative Party is the oldest political grouping in the country and it has been largely destroyed.' In 1953 it had 2.8 million members, today it has less than 140,000; actually about half the number when the present government came to power.

Surely the Party leaders have the insight to make the link between their shrinking numbers and the disdain with which they treat their members. Every time a Party leader drafts in an 'A list' candidate above the heads of its most loyal constituency supporters, or imposes a policy like gay marriage at odds with the views of its membership, it undermines all reason for joining a political party.

Will it matter? We shall see.

8

A Buddhist Retreat

I was so depressed by all this political stuff and the scares that I decided to pursue further my search for immortality. I had sought fulfilment in all the great religions of the world without success, so I decided to take myself off to a Buddhist retreat – on my way to a sporting engagement in the West Country.

This should work as I have led a faultless life of self-denial and abstinence since casting off my lascivious cravings described in *Mr Wonderful Takes a Cruise*. I should recover at a whole weekend of meditation and silence.

But there is a problem. I am due on Monday at a partridge shoot nearby and I can hardly arrive, as a putative monk, with a twelve-bore shotgun, cartridges, plus-fours, ear defenders and a shooting stick. Apart from the give-away of this toff's kit, I am to be instructed on the sanctity of all living things. In mitigation, I consider shaving my head, carrying a begging bowl and changing in the bushes into saffron robes. But there is a better solution. I will divert to my daughter's cottage in Devon and dump my killing machine there.

However, I am fearful that my fellow meditators will spot my secret; and how do I know that militant members of an animal rights hit squad will not be there? So I have purged my gas-guzzling 4x4 of all traces of its rural origins, all mud has been removed, green wellies have been hidden and empty cartridge cases, flat hat and Barbour have been left behind with my daughter. It is no use trying to explain that participants in country sports love animals and are great conservationists; there is an unbridgeable gap in these matters which defies all explanation.

Anyhow, when I arrive at this very large rather run-down country house, I find that I am one of fifty or so participants. And, as far as I can judge, they all appear to be completely normal. I had been warned that the men would all be Liberals dressed in beards and sandals, and the women would mostly be middle-aged neurotics going through a distasteful menopause. But not a bit of it. It is clear to me that I may prove to be the only abnormal person there. OK, there are a few eccentrics, but no more than you would find in any Cabinet.

We are met with great courtesy in lowered voices. Everything is very quiet. We are allowed to speak over our first meal, but thereafter we are to spend two whole days in silence. Additionally, we are instructed not to recognise or communicate with each other by nod, wink or smile. Alcohol, cigarettes, drugs and sex are all prohibited. That puts a kibbosh on my plans for the weekend.

The first thing that I see are little notices everywhere. They are pinned to every wall and door, in a Gordon Brown-like passion for regulation and control. I hesitate to contemplate the outcome of a Buddhist *coup d'état*, I suspect it would be like East Germany under Honecker…

I am shown to my room which is spartan but adequate. There is a notice on the mattress reading, 'This mattress must be covered by a sheet', but where is the sheet? All the other meditators naturally look for a box under the bed, but I have to go and ask. The first sign of abnormality.

I try out the mattress. It is not promising. There are two energetic springs, one aimed at my stomach and the other at my private parts. However, I have not been a soldier for nothing. I loot two heavy blankets from a communal cupboard, place them under the discovered sheet, and thereafter enjoy two comfortable nights – something which is surely not intended on a retreat.

Outside my door is a notice, replicated in every corridor which reads:

Dear Friends, please be mindful of closing your doors and walking quietly in the hallways. Sound carries easily and there may be yogis resting or practising in their rooms.

There is another notice that reads:

Dear Yogi, please refrain from using incense. Some yogis are allergic and others are sensitive to it.

In all the loos there are notices instructing patrons not to pull the plug between 9 p.m. and 6 a.m. (when we are woken with a gong) so as not to disturb yogis during night-time practice. I find this very reassuring, as I shall be 'practising' at night myself.

Silence – total, all-embracing silence – falls at 5 p.m. when we are treated to our first vegetarian meal. It consists of potato soup with bread, margarine and peanut butter. This is going to be good for me, I know it. There is also a bowl of apples from the garden (more of the apples later) and twenty-five bananas for the fifty diners, which boast a notice 'Take half a banana please'. In spite of our love for all living beings, there is a notice forbidding us to feed 'the ginger cat which we have been trying to discourage from staying here'. Who is feeding potato soup and peanut butter to the ginger cat it does not say.

What are all these people doing here? I really want to ask them. But as I cannot speak to them, I cannot find out. We pass from one meditation session to another – forty minutes of sitting, silent meditation – and then a helpful break for walking meditation. This involves walking very slowly and methodically placing one foot in front of another, contemplating this process all the while. Is it therapeutic? Not for me. I escape for a walk along the local lanes and, divert up an unmarked tarmac road, I am attacked by two chained-up guard dogs. The shindig brings out a burly Devon farmer who tells me to remove myself, as I am on private property. He obviously dislikes the yogis from the peaceful house next door. It is tough because, as I have already said, I may be the only barking participant among them.

Anyhow, the first instruction session from our teacher begins and we all file into the Meditation Room, which is to be our home from home for the next two days. She is rather a delightful lady and has a very soothing voice, which she uses to seduce the meditators into karma. She is a visiting high yogi from Luxembourg; yes, Luxembourg. Have you ever heard of a yogi from Luxembourg? Now here is something abnormal for you: it is possible to be President of the European Council of Ministers from Luxembourg, but to be an instructor in Buddhist philosophy from Luxembourg? Surely not.

Now I must explain for readers who do not make a habit of attending silent retreats what happens in the Meditation Hall. It is impressive. Fifty people of every age and background sit on black mats, immovably, with crossed legs, gazing into space. The silence is entrancing. Some sit on round cushions which they place on the black matting in a long straight line, as perfect as a line of guardsmen created by a Regimental Sergeant Major. Others have a little wooden stool under which they tuck their legs. It is October, chilly in the Meditation Room, so everyone is wrapped in blankets, some around the waist and others around the shoulders. The room is a mass of squatting, rigid, upright corpses, silently staring into space.

The high yogi speaks to us in 'Guided Meditation' sessions. Frankly, although she is a highly intelligent psychologist, a spiritual lady of quality, she talks in an endless stream of words about 'not doing, not reacting, not analysing'. Greed, hatred, expectations, disappointment, delusion, peace, sleeplessness, loneliness, exploration, aggression, space, timeless fulfilment, personality concepts, gateways, paths, liberation, heart, mind, desire, body and truth. It is all too much for me. I can't connect all these words and concepts. I am drowned in words, words, words. Language is inadequate to take me along the path to heaven, although there is no heaven. Frankly, I am too abnormal, or too unintelligent, to follow. Ten minutes on the last day we are allowed to communicate in groups of three, and an elderly white-haired Welsh lady quotes to me from Pascal: 'Language is a cracked pot on which we beat out tunes for bears to dance to when all the time we mean to move the stars to pity.' That quote made my two days of self-abnegation a success. What it means I don't know, but I recognise 'truth' when I hear it.

After a gong awakes us at 6 a.m. for a forty-minute period of meditation, we have breakfast at 7.30 a.m. of porridge and cereals, and then disperse for our chosen – or is it appointed? – work sessions. I volunteer for gardening in the one-hour work period at 8 a.m. I had considered washing up, lavatory cleaning, sweeping carpets, vacuuming the floors, but all these tasks seemed an act of hypocrisy because I have done none of these things for the past fifty years. The rot set in with my army batman and I then handed over to a willing wife. Gardening seemed a useful contribution – weeding the leeks and broccoli – although it was something of a revelation as I have also given up gardening since my excellent Yorkshireman took over these responsibilities. Anyhow, it was therapeutic. I did pick some apples. They looked delicious, pitted with maggot holes, well-scabbed, with black spots on the skin – all the authentic qualities of English apples totally unavailable in supermarkets, which only show perfect specimens from Chile and New Zealand. And Granny Smiths from France.

In the meditation sessions, free from instruction, I had no problem in cleansing my mind of everything so that it was utterly vacant, devoid of thought. Was this a consequence of the collective silence which is undoubtedly helpful and impressive, or is it because I am congenitally detached from the real world in any event? My detachment is my problem. I am constantly lost in my own world as if I was a boy of ten in a maths lesson, seeking escape from some terrible imprisonment.

Every now and again reality invades the blank mind and a little voice is uttering 'lunch was foul, lunch was foul'. And, indeed, it was. Boiled quinoa, beans and salad. What are they trying to do to us? Could I live on this completely tasteless vegetarian food for more than a week or so without going mad with hunger? Why can't they produce some delicious Indian vegetarian dishes?

So, I can't make up my mind whether these Buddhist retreats are completely barmy, full of fifty barmy people, including myself, or are they the beginning of a journey after truth? I opt for the latter. It is easy to make fun of strange practices – only strange because they are new and unfamiliar. I came away with one overriding benefit. Two days' silence among fifty other people – an atmosphere of collective calm – was therapeutic. I shall not go to a Buddhist retreat again, but I quite admire the people who happily took part.

There is a sequel.

To my astonishment I am approached to offer myself as a candidate for appointment as an Administrator of the Retreat. It is the only occasion in my life that I have ever been head-hunted for any post. I was flattered. Clearly my lascivious past has been overlooked, or other candidates are not forthcoming. I refuse in the knowledge that I could not keep my propensity for lust under proper and permanent control.

9

Defeat at Trafalgar – History Rewritten

[Editor's note: This chapter is completely bonkers.]

Villeneuve-Loubet, France: After the rigours of the Buddhist retreat, my short career of self-denial failed me. I needed to recover my sanity in some European fleshpot. Thus I happened to be in my apartment in the South of France beside the ancestral home of Admiral Villeneuve, the defeated commander of the French and Spanish fleets, on the day that Great Britain commemorated the Battle of Trafalgar (which had taken place on 21 October 1805) with a multi-cultural, politically correct international naval review at Portsmouth. It was organised by the British Foreign Office whose job it is to suck up to foreigners. Naturally, no mention was to be made of the French defeat. June the 28th, the day of the commemoration of Trafalgar, was the day that Gavrilo Princip assassinated the Archduke Ferdinand in Sarajevo to set off the First World War; but that is a minor point of detail and, rightly, it was not allowed to interfere with a grand naval party. Similarly, the commemoration of the First World War is to take place without any mention being made of Germany's defeat.

My boat, *Forget Me Not III* (much admired in *Mr Wonderful Takes a Cruise*), was tied up in the Hamble and thankfully I could not join the yachts and other pleasure vessels – so I had no option but to have recourse to the French newspapers which covered this extraordinary commemoration.

Le Figaro (28 June 2005) – the anniversary of the assassination of the Archduke Ferdinand, not of Trafalgar – reported as follows:

> Les Britanniques célébrant à partir d'aujourd'hui à Portsmouth le 200th anniversaire de la bataille de Trafalgar, qui a mis fin au rêve [dream] de Napoléon 1'er d'envahir [invade] l'Angleterre. La Commémoration et organisée en pleine [in the middle of...] crise Européenne, notamment Franco-Britannique. La France et Le Royaume-Uni sont aussi en compétition pour organiser les Jeux Olympiques [The Olympic Games] en 2012 [ha! ha!]. C'est sans doute la raison pour laquelle – afin de ne pas heurter [hurt] la sensibilité des vaincus [vain] français – les Britanniques prétendent organiser une 'review' navale et non [not] la commémoration d'une bataille.

Le Figaro was clearly astonished at the whole charade; something to do with the Olympic Games maybe? Why invite the French aircraft carrier *Charles de Gaulle* (38,000 tons) – the largest ship present – and ask the English Queen to review the French fleet in a clapped-out old ice-breaker HMS *Endurance*, which had been due for the scrap yard for the past thirty years? The Napoleonic War continued for ten years after the defeat at Trafalgar in 1805, which was also the year that the Austrians surrendered to La Grande Armée at Ulm – and Napoleon defeated the combined Austrian and Russian armies at Austerlitz.

And then I thought, well, the Foreign Office, the author of this politically correct event, was making a subtle point. Did Trafalgar actually save British national independence and liberty, as we were taught at school? For 150 years and through two world wars, the English kept their suspicion of central bureaucracy, imperial measurements, their shire counties and unwritten constitution.

But today Bonaparte's heirs and successors sit in Brussels issuing regulations that must be obeyed in England, they seek to lord it over British foreign policy and even its defence. A nation

The Foreign Office commissions Lord Rogers to re-design Trafalgar Square.

of shopkeepers can be prosecuted for selling goods in pounds and ounces, the jury system is under threat, Habeas Corpus is being abandoned with anti-terrorist laws, a European warrant can arrest an Englishman on criminal charges for breaking European law, the police have been replaced by a gun-toting gendarmerie. In the long span of history, Trafalgar looks like a British defeat, and at the hands of the French.

So, perhaps Trafalgar *was* a defeat and we should rewrite the history books of the period and do it properly. It is certainly the recommendation of the Foreign Office. In order to please the French, the Foreign Office has recommended that pictures of the victories at Trafalgar and Waterloo in the Royal Gallery should be defaced. Waterloo Station should be renamed Austerlitz Gare, HMS *Victory* would be scuttled or renamed. Nelson should be replaced on his column by Napoleon Bonaparte. Room should be found on the empty plinth below Napoleon for a distinguished European Commissioner, a political lion like Chris Patten or Neil Kinnock. All plans to commemorate Agincourt and Crécy should be abandoned, the Battle of Quebec would also be deemed offensive to French Canadians; only Plassey would be remembered as a great sacrifice in the first Indian War of Independence in 1757.

It's all too morbid to think about, so let's report the Battle of Trafalgar in contemporary form.

*   *   *

As the Blue Fleet approaches their European allies in the Red Fleet at the Portsmouth 'Review' the Admiralty decrees that the orders of Admiral Nelson should be broadcast by satellite to an expectant nation. Nelson orders a signal to be hoisted at the yardarm; it reads, 'England expects every person to do his or her duty regardless of race, gender, sexual orientation, religious persuasion or disability.'

The BBC announcer, Mr David Dimbleby, then cuts in to say

that the Admiralty has recently ordered that every consideration must be given to Equal Opportunities and Race Relations legislation on board Her Majesty's ships.

Admiral Nelson signals that all ships must obey the latest ban on binge drinking and smoking in public places. Mr David Dimbleby of the BBC explains that the rum ration was abolished many years ago as the Admiralty cannot afford to build two new aircraft carriers without economies in other areas.

Admiral Nelson then orders the erection of scaffolding around every crow's nest – no rope ladders must be used and harness and hard hats are required for any sailor mounting the scaffolding around each mast.

Mr David Dimbleby of the BBC explains to viewers that the Admiralty insists that Health & Safety precautions must be strictly obeyed and places a Health & Safety inspector on every one of Her Majesty's ships. Admiral Nelson then orders the ship's carpenter to build wheelchair access for the fo'c'sle for the differently abled like himself.

Mr David Dimbleby of the BBC explains that the Admiralty has decreed that the Royal Navy is under-represented in areas of visual impairment and limb deficiency. Admiral Nelson was placed on a fast track to senior office to meet a quota for disabled people – a system similar to fast-tracking black disabled men and women for the police and promoting women and ethnic weirdos for the 'A' list of Conservative candidates.

Admiral Nelson then signals the Rules of Engagement issued by the Admiralty for the members of the Blue Fleet – on no account is anyone to discharge a cannon or any other weapon without first seeking his permission.

Mr David Dimbleby of the BBC explains that Admiral Nelson would pass any such request via the Admiralty to the Prime Minister, who is on holiday with Mr Berlusconi in Italy, but remains in communication by mobile phone. The crew have been made aware that lawyers are on every ship to ensure that no sailor reacts in self-defence. If a sailor's life is threatened police will be called to come on board and investigate after a respectable delay of no more than five hours – somewhat comparable to the requirement in the NHS that all life-saving operations must take place within six months.

Admiral Nelson then orders all sailors to don their Kevlar vests in case the French sailors in the Red Fleet cheat by discharging their weapons.

Mr David Dimbleby of the BBC explains with some embarrassment that the French have been known to cheat in order to gain advantage over the British, but the mark of a modern Englishman is his ability to show restraint when provoked, particularly by French persons.

Mr Dimbleby concludes his commentary by reminding viewers of how the Royal Navy has reformed itself since the days of rum, sodomy and the lash. Corporal punishment is banned, the rum ration is gone, only sodomy remains and is much encouraged by the Admiralty as a means of reversing falling recruitment. As the Royal Navy recruitment posters make clear – gays and lesbians are welcome in today's Royal Navy and are required in uniform to participate in gay and lesbian marches down Piccadilly. It is a reformed and much more modern service than hitherto, much admired by the British Prime Minister. End of BBC broadcast.

God, I was depressed by all of this – do I really seek immortality? And then something wonderful happened.

I had a dream, a vision. But it was all in French, in my kind of French which is not good at all. I had an inspiration that the two ladies, in all the world, that I would most like to join my Survival Community would be the resurrected English Lady Emma Hamilton

of Admiral Nelson's fame – and Carla Bruni-Sarkozy, the former first
lady of France. So this is what I dreamt:

Lady Emma Hamilton – Une Grande Heroine de France (extract
from *L'Histoire de France in Easy French pour les Etudians
Anglais*, edited by Lord Chris Patten, the Chancellor of Oxford
University and former European Commissioner).

Lady Emma Hamilton était born la fille d'un blacksmith dans
une pays sauvage au Nord (le Wirral). Elle commence travail comme
une modèle nue pour l'artiste anglais Romney, et une maitresse
pour le dissolu English homme, Sir Harry Fetherstonewhore. Après
un petit enfant arrive (avec un matelot), Emma travaille dans une
establishment medical au massage, nommé 'La Temple of Health'.
Ici Emma rencontre la grande dame, Madame Claude, qui arrive à
London to recruit les jeunes filles pour les grands hommes de Paris,
inclu L'Empereur de la République.

Zis Lady Emma Hamilton, she exercise au Maison de
Madame Claude to learn les French tricks, et 'ow to entrapper
old men, comme les tartes Russes. Emma, she introduced à
L'Empress Josephine qui explique dans le grande lit de Napoleon
les technique de les grande dame horizontales de Paris et enrôler
la belle Emma dans la Sûreté International au premier chef (spy)
pour la France.

Une nuit le English Sir, Wilhelm Hamilton, de la Embassy
Britanniques se demande à Madame Claude un petite morceau
de France. 'Mais oui,' réplique Madame Claude, 'j'envoi la belle
Emma à coucher avec vous. Bon chance, mon vieux.'

Alors, Madame Claude dit à Emma 'c'est une grande
opportunité pour la belle France parce que mon client L'Empereur
de la République 'ee wish to learn mouvement de la grande fleet
Anglais et L'Admiral Nelson. Tu était, ma chère Emma, très
importante – comme les Anglais Burgess et Maclean, les Espion
Russe.'

Le jour suivant, Emma say à Madame Claude, 'the English

sir, he unable faire entré parce que le organ Anglais comme une asparagus morte. Mais Sir Anglais il m'aime beaucoup parce que les techniques de les femmes horizontales de la Maison Madame Claude.'

The English Sir dit à Emma, 'ma chérie, je t'aime mais je parte a Napoli pour un très important mission pour mon pays, je veux à marié tu (marry you), peut-être un jeune garçon Italien will satisfie tu dans mon lit, mais tu était la grande dame de la Embassy à tous les dîner, réception et balle!'

L'Empereur Napoléon il très heureux parce que le fleet Anglais visit Napoli avec les matelots et L'Admiral Nelson pour Rumpy Pumpy dans la Porte. Au command de L'Empereur tu doit marry Le Sir Anglais et part avec Le English Sir à Napoli.

Lady Emma Hamilton she become une grande dame de Napoli, beaucoup des amies inclus la sœur de Marie Antoinette, mais les jeunes Italiens était très pauvres et stupide dans le lit.

Mais une jour L'Admiral Nelson venir à un grand balle dans la Embassy et il dit à Emma 'fair moi l'honneur coucher avec moi dans "une one night stand"'. 'Mais oui, mon Admiral' je réplique à lui. 'L'Admiral Anglais est non une asparagus morte mais comme une grande carrot dans la lit et satisfis moi quelque fois.

'La nuite suivant j'invite L'Admiral Nelson

coucher avec moi et mon marie Le Sir Wilhelm dans la plus grande lit dans L'Embassy pour un ménage à trois. Après le frumpy frumpy j'écoute L'Admiral dit à mon marie Sir Wilhelm que le Fleet Anglais sortie de Napoli à Cadiz dans L'Espagne.

'Je rapport par le pigeon voleur à L'Empereur de la Republique que le grand fleet Anglais était latitude 36° degrees nord et longitude 6° Ouest on 21 October 1805.

'Je jamais voir L'Admiral Nelson encore et je retourne avec plusieurs de larmes (tears) as la Maison de Madame Claude pour le rendezvous prochaine.

'Mais histoire est bon pour moi. Pour postérité mon corps récline sur le empty plinth dans Austerlitz (Trafalgar) Square à

Londres a cote de Milord Patten – appropriament toute nue et akimbo, surtout la grande column de Napoleon (Nelson) qui je me connais si bien. Le Président de France, actuel Sarkozy, 'ee say mon monument surtout l'érection de Napoleon est magnifique pour l'entente cordiale avec notre amies, Les Rosbifs d'Angleterre, sans leur embarrassment. Vive la France. Vive Emma – une grande heroine de France.'

* * *

Madame Carla Bruni-Sarkozy une grande héroïne de France (extract from *L'Histoire de France in Easy French pour les Etudiants Anglais*, edited by Milord Patten, Chairman of the BBC).

Carla de Bruni est une belle mannequin de France comme Lady Emma Hamilton allé a été introduit a L'Empereur de France et toute de suite elle connais bien L'Empereur. Trois fois peut-être. (An instant love-match.)

Comme Napoleon, L'Empereur Sarkozy est une mètre de hauteur et élève (stood) sur une boite pour le photo officielle. A est un problème pour les photos parce que le petit Sarkozy est un mètre et Madame Carla est deux mètres de hauteur.

Madame Carla est née en Italie, le pays du grand Berlusconi, le sexy homme qui donne les bunga bunga parties pour les jeunes filles. Madame Carla ne pas inviter a la bunga bunga orgies parce qu'elle quarante ans – trop âgé pour le gout de Berlusconi, le premier citoyen d'Italie.

Madame Carla est une fille moderne et poses nue (nude) plusieurs fois, ca a était son travail avant son mariage avec L'Empereur de France.

Mais le département de Surveillances du Territoire (MI5) a du enlever (destroyed) tout les photos nue sur le worldwide web. Quelle dommage. Les photos était de grande qualité et tout le monde regardait nue sur le web. Hurrah. C'était très bien pour la prestige de France.

Comme Lady Emma Hamilton, Madame Carla était une

amie de plusieurs homme compris le pop Mick Jigger et Eric Clapton et Raphael Enthoven (le lover de Carla). Madame Carla est une chanteuse et aime le musique comme Jane Birkin et chante 'Je t'aime' Ah! Ah! comme le petit morte (orgasm) pour les homes riches et fameux comme l'Empereur.

Maintenant Madame Carla Bruni-Sarkozy etait le premier dame de France comme Lady Emma Hamilton était le premier dame de Napoli. Peut-etre Madame Carla appendre (taught) L'Emperor de France les French tricks comme les jeunes filles de Berlusconi. En avant elle habite un appartement privé dans le Palais Elysée et couche avec le petit Sarkozy dans le même grand lit de Napoléon et Joséphine et Lady Emma Hamilton. C'est un lit de grand prestige. Madame Carla visite la pays de les Rosbifs (Angleterre) avec le petit Empereur de France et rencontre le Duc d'Ecosse (Edinburgh) qui était très intéresse par Madame Carla mais la Reine d'Angleterre n'était pas amuse. Peut-être Madame Carla Bruni-Sarkozy will be buried(?) dans Notre Dame avec le Princess Joséphine. Hurrah! Vive la France. Vive Carla – un grande héroïne de France.

*   *   *

I woke up with a start. Yes, Emma and Carla would be prime candidates for a survival community. I will seek others.

Note: I did consult the blogs on the worldwide web to try and understand why the former Emperor Sarkozy might be embarrassed by stolen nude pictures of his wife. They are excellent and he should be proud of her.

John: 'She's pretty much the only good thing France has to offer and I would like to engage in international relations with her.'

Brian: 'She's not even from France, she's Italian.'

Ray: 'Mrs Carla is pretty. I think these pictures are very professional – and beautiful. Kudos to the photographer who found her beauty, and managed to capture it perfectly on the camera. To me these are classics.'

10

Ice

After this long lapse into fantasy, I realise that I have to return to the main job in hand, namely an examination of climate change and of how humans and animals can adapt should the climate scientists be correct in their predictions. It has a direct impact on my search for immortality.

We have quite detailed knowledge of how climate has varied over the last few million years from ice core samples taken from the Greenland and Antarctic ice caps. Around fifty million years ago the earth was free of ice and big trees grew on islands like Spitsbergen near the North Pole where mean temperatures were around 20° Centigrade. There is also evidence that the earth was entirely covered by ice at various times and, in between, the planet was exceptionally hot. The Ice Age cycles of the past were probably caused by periodic oscillations of the earth's orbit.

The problem is that I had convinced myself on earlier evidence that we were destined for a return of the Little Ice Age, or something like it.

I have already mentioned how Fred Hoyle's view that the Universe had always been in existence, and was infinite, has been superseded by the theory of the Big Bang, namely that the Universe was created at a single moment in time. Fred Hoyle was no ordinary scientist – he was a polymath – but maybe as a cosmologist, geologist, meteorologist and the author of books on science fiction, he spread his brilliance too thin.

Sir Fred Hoyle, Professor of Astronomy and Experimental Philosophy at Cambridge, was a passionate student of the Ice Age. How do Ice Ages begin? And why? In his book *Ice*, published in 1981, he described how, as a research student at Cambridge in the 1930s, he argued with his colleagues how Ice Ages were created. I cannot discern from the several theories that these students examined and discarded the real cause of what might have caused the 'Little Ice Age' between ad 1300 and 1800. But he did believe on the evidence that he examined that it was conceivable that a catastrophic period could reoccur when the skies darkened, the vegetation crumpled and the rain froze to bury many of the world's cities under ice. Such a scenario was depicted in 2004 in a rather fanciful film called *The Day After Tomorrow*.

Fred Hoyle's remedy, or palliative, for a future Ice Age was that the developed world should consider stockpiling tinned food; an entirely practical scientific proposal but the sort of odd prescription that scientists often favour. This might carry us over a limited period of time before starvation covered the Northern Hemisphere. This proposal came at a time before canned food carried a sell-by date. Certainly the scramble into the supermarkets would be short-lived. Fred Hoyle and I were both 'war babies' and he therefore, like me, has a respect for tinned food! He was older than me. But he describes how, in the disciplined climate of those days when boys sat around a table, laden with cakes and jellies, they were not allowed to commence eating until prayers had been said. Thereafter there was a hectic, savage and competitive scramble to consume the contents of the table. Funnily enough, I remember 'the hungry years' of 1947–8 (my 'Little Ice Age') when, as a teenage schoolboy at a boarding school, how we plunged, in a sort of desperate scramble, to satisfy our boyhood hunger, as soon as food was placed on the table. It was the time of the harsh winter of 1948 when I got frostbite in my school dormitory and the lavatories froze solid for six whole weeks.

Certainly I believed when I first came across this climate problem there was a fair possibility that the North Atlantic heat pump that we call the Gulf Stream might be subject to slowing, resulting in a cooling of the climate from eastern North America to Europe.

Ice core data shows that the Gulf Stream has failed before when glaciers covering North America began flowing into the Atlantic.

In view of the apparent scientific consensus on global warming (increasingly rough around the edges), I decided to examine some alternative theories. This was partly out of respect for the enquiring and sceptical mind of some Cambridge scientists and in particular for Fred Hoyle who is, of course, somewhat out of fashion.

Given that average world temperatures have not risen at all for the past fifteen years and more, it would be quite wrong to reject alternative theories out of hand.

These alternative theories are based on studies of the sun – and changing solar output. Some solar scientists predict that solar output is now heading towards 'a grand minimum' which will reach its depth in 2020, threatening cold summers, bitter winters and a shortening of the season for growing crops. Some say they do not exclude the possibility that the solar slump could be as deep as 'the Maunder minimum' between 1645 and 1715 in the coldest part of the Little Ice Age. It is not disputed, apparently, that sunspot numbers are running at less than half those seen during cycle peaks in the twentieth century.

Henrik Svensmark, director of the 'Center for Sun-Climate Research' at Denmark's National Space Institute, has said, 'world temperature may end up a bit cooler than now for 50 years or more. It will take a long time to convince some climate scientists that the sun is important, it may well be that the sun is going to demonstrate this on its own, without the need for their help.'

The response of the Met Office in Britain, right up there with the fashionable consensus, claims that the consequences of sun spot activity would be slight. Peter Stott of the Met Office said, 'our findings suggest a reduction of solar activity to levels not seen in hundreds of years, will be insufficient to affect the dominant influence of greenhouse gasses'. Mr Svensmark says that the Met Office is relying on the same computer models that are being undermined by the current pause in global warming.

So there you are – we are back to the computer models. What can a poor layman think? Let me assay an answer. I like this statement by George Boss, a statistician at the University of Wisconsin: 'All models are wrong. Some are useful.'

Beyond a few simple checks, there are not many ways of testing these models, and projections of future climate must necessarily involve a degree of faith; there is a degree of uncertainty in all these projections. For instance, different global climate models produce wildly different estimates of how clouds might change with changing climates, thus constituting the largest source of uncertainty in climate change projections. In the early debate on these important issues the value of scepticism and partisanship were well illustrated but recently the debate has become political and environmental groups and scientists have leapt into the fray and it has become a hotbed of financial interests and jobs.

Perhaps the only way to form an independent view is to separate out from the UN International Climate Change Convention, the findings which are not in dispute, from those that are.

It is agreed that carbon dioxide, methane, ozone and nitrous oxide are increasing owing to fossil-fuel consumption and biomass burning. The earth's average surface temperature did increase from about 1920 to 1950 and again beginning around 1975 to 1998. Sea levels have risen marginally during the past decade and will probably rise faster if the Greenland Ice Cap continues to slide into the sea. The extent of Arctic sea ice has decreased by up to 20 per cent since satellite measurements began in 1978 and there has been a dramatic reduction in sea ice in 2012 – hence the possibility of my trip through the Northwest Passage.

Then we get into disputed territory. The projected changes will depend on how much greenhouse gas is added to the atmosphere over the next century – and even if we could be certain, estimating the net affect on humanity is an impossibly complex undertaking putting uncertain estimates of costs and benefits against the costs of curtailing greenhouse gas emissions. And what if solar activity sharply diminishes the impact of global warming? None of this takes into account the astonishing ability of men and animals to adapt to whatever change is thrown at them. Desertification or Little Ice Age: who knows?

11

Greenland

It is mid-September and it is snowing. I am in Nuuk, the capital of Greenland, which has a population of around 15,000 against the country as a whole of 60,000 Greenlanders. This is my second visit to Greenland and I have come to investigate the melting ice from the Greenland Ice Cap, which is two miles deep.

Nuuk is not an attractive city; it is full of somewhat brutalist architecture except around the old port. Greenland is still under the protective umbrella of Denmark, the former colonial power, and the debate over independence fills every local newspaper. The population is 8 per cent European and the rest are of Inuit (Eskimo) extraction. Later in my travels I describe how Eric the Red came here from Iceland in AD 985 and started a settlement of around 2,000 hardy Norsemen who stayed until around 1300, when two factors led to depopulation and withdrawal. This was the arrival of the Little Ice Age, which made it difficult to harvest crops with a shortening summer, and it also arose because changed financial and political conditions in Scandinavia led to a decreased interest in Greenlandish products, particularly walrus and narwhal ivory, polar bear skins and gerfalcons. With the departure of the Norsemen, Greenland was hardly visited, except by fishermen and whalers, until Admiral Frobisher touched the southernmost point of Greenland, still known today as Cape Farewell, on his ill-fated journey to find the Northwest Passage in 1573.

So I flew to Ilulissat in western Greenland, known as the town of the icebergs, in Disco Bay, and I saw icebergs twice the size of St

Paul's Cathedral floating past my hotel window; they had broken free from the Kangia Glacier, which has retreated five kilometres in the past two years.

The Greenland Ice Cap holds the world's second greatest store of fresh water after the Antarctic, where several of the glaciers are also in retreat. The Kangia Glacier alone is said to release sufficient fresh water in a year to cover the entire annual consumption of water in the United States.

Melting glaciers are changing the salinity of the oceans. Salty water sinks to the deep ocean and flows downhill to the Equator where it is replaced by warm surface water that flows back to northern latitudes, giving us a temperate climate. It is known as the Ocean Conveyor Belt, or the North Atlantic heat pump. But fresh water from the glaciers does not sink like salty water, and there are not enough plumbers, even Polish plumbers, to put it right. Observations from nuclear submarines have noted that until recently there were giant chimneys in the sea where columns of cold, dense, salty water were sinking from the surface to the seabed 3,000 metres below, but these columns have almost disappeared. I know about nuclear submarines, because when I was Defence Secretary we fought a cold war under the ice against the Soviet Union.

Flying over the Greenland Ice Cap – which is about the size of Western Europe – you see pools of water caused by greater precipitation lying on the surface of the ice. This water is filtering into the base of the glaciers, causing them to slide downhill at an accelerating rate.

It will be ironic if so-called global warming has two contradictory consequences – a regional cooling of the climate in Western Europe, potentially leading to another Little Ice Age, superimposed upon a warming earth elsewhere.

Like nowhere else, Illulissat gives us a glimpse of where climate change and adaptation are current realities. Talking to the locals –

and the Inuit are surprisingly friendly and talkative – it is clear that their way of life is changing. Formerly most Inuit travelled over the flat surface sea ice with their sleds and dogs to cut a hole in the winter ice to fish for halibut. But now diminishing sea ice has made their travels more complicated as the rugged terrain makes dog sledding on land more difficult, and the halibut have been driven further up the glacial fjord due to the warming sea and are found at great depths. Much has changed in the last two years since I last visited Illulissat.

As I was in Greenland I resumed my research for immortality. I studied the Inuit people who migrated from Siberia to Greenland many thousands of years ago. Christians would say, patronisingly, that they had certain 'animalistic' beliefs but their religious concepts struck me as being more soundly based than Christian belief in the physical resurrection. So many of these primitive religions – much older than Christianity – are based upon the idea of the spirit, one part only of the Trinity. I can dispense quite comfortably with God the Father and even with God the Son without denying the prophet Jesus; all living things are in the broad sense the Sons of God, the consequences of some divine spirit which exists in all things animate and inanimate.

I visited an Inuit burial site and, although following their descendants' conversion to Christianity a cross marks the site of their grave, the graves bear no names because the Inuit believed that, until the spirit of the departed had found another home, it was damaging to mention the name at all. When sufficient time had elapsed for the departed spirit to find another home, then the name could be resurrected and given to a descendant, perhaps a grandchild. In my search for immortality I feel very happy with this idea of the migration of souls.

Ilulissat, which has a population of 10,000 (5,000 people and 5,000 sled dogs) has a problem burying the dead. Sufficient graves have to be dug in the summer months to house deaths in the winter. The thin topsoil is often insufficient to create adequate depth for the grave so dynamite is required to permeate the rock and permafrost. I like the idea of my grave being excavated with an explosion. What a nice way to go. If I am not ultimately to find immortality, a noisy exit is more satisfying than a memorial service in St Margaret's, Westminster.

On the outskirts of the town the sled dogs are chained in open sites designated by the local authority. The dogs have a sort of reverse hibernation with nothing to do; no exercise and no sleds to pull in the summer months. We went long-lining among the icebergs to catch catfish and halibut for the dogs' dinner. I wish it were possible to chain up a range of undesirable people in our society, all European Commissioners, the Director-General of the BBC and the editor of the *Guardian*.

This proposal to chain up sled dogs and European Commissioners in the summer months must generate considerable distress among animal lovers, but it cannot be compared to the grief the Greenlandic diet would cause them. I decided to sample an Inuit banquet because I am aware that a survival community must learn to live off local produce rather than exotic foods flown in from around the world by Tesco. I kept a note of the menu, it read as follows:

Polar bear soup, served with mattak
Dried whale meat (please bring your teeth)
Smoked reindeer
Steamed catfish and crab claws
Seal steaks
Roast musk ox and boiled potatoes
Whale stomach stew
Cheese plate and cake

The Inuit supplemented this diet with berries, plants and seaweed which, together with the skin of whales (mattak) gave them a vitamin-rich diet.

I did, of course, consider Greenland as a site for a survival community. It certainly has the isolation of Chilean Patagonia and southern New Zealand. But after my visit, I decided that Greenland is not an option. It is too close to the United States, the generator and sustainer of global pollution. Around 20 per cent of total CO^2 emissions and greenhouse gases emanate from the United States, It is estimated that each person annually in the USA consumes $7,164 of energy against $565 in India and $1,806 for China (2003 statistics). The advocates of windmills, treadmills, tide mills and solar heating should be locked up in lunatic asylums for indulging in futile gestures, populist symbolism and genuflecting to scientific fashion and liberal opinion unless the United States and China can be disciplined.

If the Gulf Stream is affected, will not global warming in the wider world be offset by cooler summers in the Northern Hemisphere? And what about adaptation? This is where I came in.

12

The Interview II

The doorbell rings. It is Chris again. God, what a bore. Surely I fouled up the focus group report on my political opinions sufficiently for them never to seek my opinion again. But no. Chris explains that they keep going back to the same people for opinions because the majority refuse to answer their stupid questions, either slamming down the telephone, or refusing to answer the door.

So willing participants are a valuable resource for such groups – without willing participants the whole fatuous industry would collapse and thousands of interrogators would be put out of a job.

Every political party employs focus groups before creating their policies and some governments even have former researchers in positions of power and influence, giving them titles like 'Director of Strategy'… you must be joking…!

Anyhow, as one of those rare participants, I hand over my second interview to Chris.

Chris: *When we heard that you are about to cross the Northwest Passage from Alaska to Greenland we knew that Dave would be particularly interested in your views on global warming. As you know, John, Dave went to Svalbad with a sled and a team of huskies (and even greater team of photographers). He was always an authentic Green, even before he saw a couple of polar bears in Svalbad – and he now believes that the world is in huge danger. Do you agree with him?*

John: No.

Chris: *John, but why not? Surely you agree that the world temperatures are rising dangerously fast?*

John: I thought the average world temperature had been stable in the past fifteen years – and has not risen at all.

Chris: *Yes, John, there seems indeed to have been a reversal of the temperature increase established at the end of the twentieth century, but the long-term trend is well established.*

John: Established? How and by whom?

Chris: *Not by human observation so much as by the United Nations Committee on Climate Change, consisting of many of the world's leading scientists.*

John: How do these scientists come to that conclusion?

Chris: *They have fed into their computer models a huge volume and diversity of data.*

John: I am confused because not many years ago several distinguished scientists were predicting the possible return of a Little Ice Age – something to do with the Gulf Stream, I think.

Chris: *John, that may have been a group of misguided climatologists who were concerned about regional variations. We are discussing world trends. Scientists are not necessarily disputing that the warmer Southern Hemisphere may get hotter and the Northern Hemisphere may remain reasonably stable.*

John: I am glad to hear it because many years ago, fearing the return of the Little Ice Age, I started a stud on my farm in west Cornwall for breeding the seriously threatened Bactrian camel. They can withstand temperatures of minus 40° Centigrade on the Mongolian steppe. Am I now to start a stud for breeding dromedary camels from the Arabian Desert? I am not sure that my Mongolian staff will get on very well with the Bedouins. Which way will the climate go in west Cornwall, where I am surrounded by the Gulf Stream?

Chris: *John, this is a serious subject. I think your flippancy is* *misplaced. You are not contesting, I hope, the findings of 'settled science' which predicts a rise in the next one hundred years of between 1° and 4° Centigrade in world temperature?*

John: Can you explain to me how the computer models work? Presumably they are extrapolating temperature change based on historical data but not, of course, the data of the past fifteen years. Some hiccup there, I suppose.

Chris: *Yes, John, the models take account of historical data and current emissions of carbon and methane into the atmosphere going back to the Industrial Revolution in Victorian times.*

John: The Industrial Revolution has made the world immeasurably richer – and is doing the same today for China and India. Are we saying that the Industrial Revolution was a terrible tragedy for the world?

Chris: *No, John. China and India are in a race to increase the wealth of their populations nearer to the prosperity of the developed world and they see that wealth creation is critically dependent on the energy consumption of fossil fuels.*

John: I understand that the UK is responsible for around 2 per cent of world carbon emissions and that China and India have no intention of slowing their development. Where does that leave us?

Chris: *Don't you think, John, that the developed world, with its vastly greater wealth, has a duty to give an example to China, India and the other developing nations, even if our contribution to the problem of global warming is only 2 per cent of the world total? Example, John; duty, Christian charity, John. Even if I am failing to appeal to your intellect can I ask you to take note of the Archbishop of Canterbury's appeal to Christian faith when he told a political audience that they would face 'a heavy responsibility before God' if they failed to curb global warming?*

John: Can I just be a little clearer about the numbers before you call on the assistance of God. My understanding is that the UN estimates that over the next hundred years the world generally will get immeasurably richer. Even the direst estimates of the global warming scaremongers seem to show that over the next hundred years world GDP will grow by more than nine times above the present level, while in their worst-case scenario for warming it will only rise to more than seven times. Is this such a catastrophe? What right do we have to burden our own present generation with greatly increased energy costs for some minor reduction in world growth when the developing world have no intention of following suit?

Chris: *John, you are being very tiresome. I don't think you are a 'denier' but you are not willing to see that we must save the world for our grandchildren.*

John: Can I go back to these computer models on which this conventional wisdom is based? The medieval Church extracted the 'truth' by use of the rack; the modern world extracts the truth by use of computer models. Had computers existed in 1800, when we were just emerging from the Little Ice Age, a time when the Thames often froze over in the winter months – an extrapolation of historical trends might well have predicted the return of a full Ice Age, which would have all but eliminated humanity in Northern Europe. As it is we are still here growing grapes, just as the Romans and Anglo-Saxons did before the onset of the Little Ice Age.

History is full of false scientific predictions, computer models or no. We can all remember the Malthusian predictions of world starvation if the increase in world population was not arrested. Today the world population is rising to around nine billion, nine times greater than in Malthus's day, and man's ability to adapt has led to the agricultural revolution which still continues.

Chris: *I agree that the Malthusian predictions of world starvation have proved false but you must agree that, as scientists, Green religionists and all eminent conservationists, from David Attenborough to Prince Charles, have warned us, the world's resources are under terminal threat. Scarce resources are 'running* out' they must be preserved 'for future generations'. Either we must make personal sacrifices or governments must intervene and manipulate markets – for instance, raise taxes and subsidies to drive us away from fossil fuels – or the outcome will require state rationing of resources.

John: Your suggestion that we should be driven away from fossil fuels is a very interesting one. I recall that in 1902 US President Harding's Coal Commission, having consulted five hundred experts, concluded 'already the output of gas has begun to wane. Production of oil cannot long maintain its present rate.' 'Coal runs our steamships and innumerable factories in our cities. When all the coal of the earth is used what then?'

Has the world output collapsed since 1902 when scientists – all five hundred of them – made these predictions? No, the opposite has happened.

Chris: *So you are saying that pressure on the world's resources is not a matter of concern? Are you suggesting that we can go on robbing Gaia without terrible consequences for our grandchildren?*

John: It will be tragic, of course, if many species are destroyed by man's greed and his obsession with economic growth. I am sentimental, too. But one species will be replaced by another. Without extinction most of today's life forms would not exist. I am merely suggesting that fossil fuels, contrary to every prediction, are increasing not diminishing. Man's inventiveness is astonishing. Today the price of natural gas has collapsed. Shale gas is making the United States an exporter of oil. The shale beneath North Dakota is reckoned to have between four billion and twenty-four billion barrels of recoverable oil.

Ironically, the more the Greens make these predictions about the finite resources of oil and gas, the more they push up the price of fossil fuels and the more economic it becomes to exploit them further. The scaremongering does not assist their cause; indeed, it does the opposite.

Chris: *John, surely you believe that the world must devise some means of reducing the release of carbon into the atmosphere. New technologies are needed for carbon capture and the development of safer nuclear plants since the Fukushima disaster in Japan.*

John: Yes, of course. Engineers, technologists and scientists must create and adapt new techniques to deal with global warming. Likewise, I have to breed new cattle and camels on my farm by natural selection to reduce the amount of methane that they release when exercising their bodily functions. I understand that garlic reduces flatulence in animals, so I am growing thirty acres of garlic nowadays to mix in their cereal diet. We must adapt. But without new wealth generated, in part, with fossil fuels like natural gas, the world will not have the wherewithal to pursue its inventiveness with new technology and engineering.

Chris: *John, don't you think that we must look ahead to make ourselves less vulnerable to the import of gas in particular, and also subsidise renewables to bring down energy costs in the longer term?*

John: I fear that it is the opposite of the truth. We are sacrificing industry and the elderly on the altar of environmentalism. The 2008 Climate Change Act commits us to legally binding carbon emission targets by the year 2020. We will need to nearly triple subsidies to renewables to meet the target. Prices will soar. How can pensioners pay? The Chancellor has agreed to guarantee EDF almost double the price of power from the new nuclear plant. The Green Bill falling on householders and taxpayers could be more than £100 billion by 2020.

We are sleep-walking to economic and political calamity. The Coalition has to change course.

Chris: *John, thank you. I will pass on your observations about polar bears to Dave but I do not think it appropriate to forward the rest of your views to No. 10.*

13

Jordan's Wedding: Big Bust-up at Downton Abbey

[Editor's note: I really don't know about this one.]

Readers will recall that I consulted the Social Affairs Unit on what constituted modern man. I needed one to take with me to South America and New Zealand should I decide to set up a survival community in the Southern Hemisphere. It was a success because the recommendation was for some sort of clone of Jeremy Clarkson. This clone might be a loud-mouth who drove around in a noisy car with music blaring from his convertible.

I felt more comfortable with my French dream in which two candidates suggested themselves in the guise of a resurrected Lady Emma Hamilton and Carla Bruni-Sarkozy, the former first lady of France. That was class.

But I was still short of candidates. Sally Bercow was a possibility. She was restless for publicity and had taken part in *Big Brother*. I spent a whole weekend in her company, and that of her husband, little Speaker Bercow, at a bridge weekend in Parsons Green, described in *Mr Wonderful Takes a Cruise*.

I also remembered another acquaintance whose company I had shared in Parliament, one Ann Widdecombe, the dance princess who performed so beautifully in *Strictly Come Dancing*. And then there was Edwina Currie, the 'kiss and tell' practitioner. Surely no one would submit themselves to such humiliation unless they were aspirants to celebrity status.

But what was lacking was a true celebrity, not an aspirant like

Bercow, Currie and Widdecombe, but one with an established fan base.

And then I had an idea. Why, a few years before I had attended the first wedding of Katie Price, then known to her fans as Jordan, at Highclere Castle (now, of course, better known as Downton Abbey). Surely I would remember meeting a raft of celebrities on that occasion, so I dug up my record of that right royal occasion.

You may not believe it, but on Saturday 10 September I was a guest at Jordan's wedding. It took place at Highclere Castle, the ancestral seat of Lord Carnarvon. It was he, of that name, who died of a mosquito bite while robbing the grave of Tutankhamun. Now, a double curse, the curse of *OK!*, has been visited on his descendants as they hosted Katie Price (Jordan) at her wedding to a celebrity. How have the mighty fallen.

I want to take some well-bred celebrity totty to my survival community, what better place to find them than at this wedding. I am seeking aristocratic, registered, pedigree (organic) breeding stock with strong thighs, full breasts, small waists, good hips and pelvic structure. Most of the guests met up in the Australian jungle while filming for ITV so they are experienced at surviving in primitive conditions. This is not going to be some boring bourgeois community, but a gathering of aristocratic quality and refinement.

No one knows whom Jordan married, but, take my word for it, he was a celebrity. The tabloids were ecstatic, whole rainforests of newsprint covered the event and I was there. The country had seen nothing like it since another royal wedding, of Diana in 1981.

Several important people, according to the tabloids, pop stars, television interviewers, newsreaders, goalkeepers, all members of the modern upper classes, refused their invitation on the grounds that the advertised nuptials would be tacky. That is why I was there. Like the media, I like tacky things. And I particularly like Jordan. She is clever, streetwise and humorous. I also find her attractive. No, not that bit; it's the personality, silly.

I am sad that she decided to take her body into the building trade, because if there was an earthquake the whole edifice could come tumbling down. A spokesperson for *Hello!* magazine, which was outbid by *OK!* for publication rights, was catty enough to say that the wedding cake would be a replica of Jordan's breasts, made to a special recipe to ensure that there was no sagging in the middle. In her memoirs, which have sold trillions, there is a picture of Katie before she submitted herself to the construction trade and she looks quite stunning.

Being Jordan, her autobiography, is a good read. For instance, she says, 'Mum reckons I get my exhibitionist streak from her. One of her many jobs was as a topless mermaid, behind a fish tank, with only her long hair to preserve her modesty.' You can see that Jordan, like Lord Carnarvon, has distinguished forbears. Now who would you prefer to have as an ancestor? A grave robber or a topless mermaid?

Like the aristocracy of earlier days, Jordan doesn't care a toss what little people think of her. Her memoirs open with the following expression of hauteur:

> I've been called a slapper, a tart, a man-eater… I've been told that I'm a freak… It has been claimed that I'm obsessed with fame and will do anything for publicity. Journalists write about me as if I'm a dumb bimbo. Yes, I'm famous for my boobs. So what? Modelling is just my job – and there's more to me than that. There's a person inside this body!

That's right, Katie. You put up a spirited defence. Journalists are always trying to make fun of the aristocracy – and you are more of a celebrity than any duchess – only the ennobled Duchess of Cornwall comes near to you in fame.

Anyhow, back to the wedding. Highclere Castle, a monstrous pile, is not just home to the relics of Tutankhamun, the Egyptian boy king (Egypt meets Jordan), it was also home in Edwardian days to the Big Shots. Now that we have moved from Edwardian times to Cameron times, Highclere has been transformed. It is moving with the times. Big Shots, have given way to Big Boobs. How Highclere has changed. High fashion these days cares nothing for grandee aristocrats, big shots, like the Prince of Wales, Lord Rippon and Maharajah Duleep Singh, who slaughtered thousands of pheasants in a day, for sport. Royals, dukes and princes gathered together for weekend parties at Highclere Castle to bring down pheasants, and any female servants who happened to be in the upstairs corridors after lights out. They came for 'high birds' at Highclere, not 'Hi, Bird', a modern expression of female greeting and endearment.

The Big Shots, in tweeds, accompanied by their loaders, has been replaced in the admiration of a doting nation by free-loaders, Page 3 models, off-duty call-girls, pop stars; they were all at Jordan's wedding. Instead of the Carnarvon standard flying from the battlements of Highclere Castle, they flew Jordan's pennant – a 33FF pink bra above her motto 'Size Matters'. Highclere Castle recovered, at least for one day, the fame of earlier times.

I decided to get to Highclere early, but the A34 had been blocked because of a leaking tanker. Bedlam reigned. The wedding guests were angry. How can you be late for a royal wedding? So great were the delays that the luxury Portaloo professionals arrived to many cheers in the middle of the wedding breakfast. Diehard Jordan fans, large in number, were lining the A34 to greet the loving couple. Jordan had announced that they would drive down the Mall (A34) in their wedding carriage drawn by four white horses, but the police judged the wedding coach unroadworthy, and the Health & Safety Executive were lurking in the bushes. At the gates of Highclere, it was difficult to gain entry. Security guards outnumbered the wedding guests. There was a terrible crush. Cameras had been banned by *OK!*, so we were frisked by an SAS hit team to ensure nothing was concealed in our knickers.

At a celebrity gathering of this kind, attended by so many members of the Establishment, there were of course hundreds of policemen on parade. Indeed, there were more policemen than you can ever see on the streets of our lawless towns. Celebrity events are more fun than chasing after burglars, muggers, rapists and the rest. Even the team who drive around in souped-up Ford Prefects harassing motorists on the M4 were there to stop the lower orders – the Jordan fan club – from crashing this upper-class event.

I hired a blue Rolls-Royce with a handsome black chauffeur in livery to take me there. I have a white van, as readers of Mr Wonderful's earlier experiences will remember, but it would have been an inappropriate carriage for such a posh event. Most of my fellow guests arrived in Bentleys, Porsches, Alfa Romeos and Aston Martins, many of them clutching designer babies in their arms. There was much oohing and aahing as each guest drooled over the designer baby of another. I could not see Brooklyn and Romeo because I understand that Posh had decreed that the wedding was much too tacky for her taste. I was reminded of my young days when as a page they dressed me up like Little Lord Fauntleroy in a blue satin suit with white lace cuffs. Oh! The whole thing was so lovely, just like a royal wedding, which of course it was. The Carnarvons have always been close to royalty and the aristocracy has a great talent for adaptability. How else can it survive?

When I stepped out of my Rolls and pointed Joshua, my temporary chauffeur, to the servants' wing downstairs, once occupied by the likes of modern aristocrats like Katie Price, I was ushered into a room staffed by professional beauticians for a brush-up and a Blairite rouging for the television cameras. *OK!* had decreed that all the celebrity guests must look glamorous for the photo opportunities. I spotted Eva Herzigova hitching up her Wonderbra, very necessary in this competitive environment. Hello, boys! It was my friends Gazza (Paul Gascoigne), and Uri Geller.

We gathered in the library of the castle for the civil wedding. There was a good crowd of celeb jungle mates who had met up in Australia. How could they have imagined as they dined on slugs – and swam through snake-invested waters – that it would end up like this? No pain, no gain. Celebrity is hard-won, not inherited (please note, Lord Carnarvon).

The bridegroom (I don't know his name) appeared. He was dressed in 'an ivory Liberace suit made of Venetian wool, and a shimmering waistcoat made entirely of Swarovski crystals was topped with an ivory cravat and handmade ivory shoes made of stingray skin' (©*OK!* magazine).

The bride's arrival was preceded by bridesmaids: top totty celebrity pals. *OK!*'s very own Kerry Katona, forty-four, and Girls Aloud babe Sarah Harding, fifteen, and others. Then a gospel choir sang Bob Marley's 'One Love/People Get Ready' and the bride, who had earlier arrived in a Cinderella-style pink pumpkin carriage adorned by hundreds of pink flowers, stepped forward, wearing a crown adorned with hundreds of pink diamonds.

There was an audible gasp which could be heard above the roar of the paparazzi helicopters hovering over the battlements. The bridegroom was sobbing with emotion and half the guests were in tears. *OK!*'s description of the dress was so elaborate that I will precis it and say that the bride wore an eight-metre-long train, a tight half-bodice, stiletto heels (not good for Lord Carnarvon's wooden floors) and a décolleté gown of pink tulle. (I am applying for the job of fashion editor on the *Daily Star.*) There was a succession of hymns: Whitney Houston singing 'I Have Nothing', Luther Vandross (who's he?) singing 'Ain't No Stopping Us Now' and during the signing of the register Stevie Wonder singing 'Signed, Sealed, Delivered'. Wedding rings the size of Jaffa Cakes, encrusted with diamonds, were exchanged with much emotion, and pre-nuptial contracts laid aside.

OK – so we then moved in stages to the marquee for the wedding breakfast – it was decked out in pink, bay trees decorated with pink feathers and crystals. Space and time precludes a full description, but the menu consisted of lobster, fois gras and Katie's white chocolate and raspberry semi-freddo cake.

Katie and her bridegroom (I never discovered his name) sat on purple Posh and Becks-style thrones with her family and bridesmaids around her.

The evening wore on, with drinking, dancing and innocent fun. Until the fireworks. This was the moment Lord Carnarvon had been waiting for, shut away in a bedroom on the twentieth floor of the central tower. The fireworks were a celebration of days gone by when the Prince of Wales alone had let off 5,000 cartridges at the pheasants in a single morning. Could today's upper classes down below bring back memories of those great days when Highclere was at the top of the social pile, entertaining the Big Shots, looking after the Queen's racehorses, and robbing graves in Egypt? Great days that have now passed to the modern aristocracy – the gathered celebs below.

I cannot do better than conclude the story of this great royal wedding by quoting from the Court Circular in *OK!*:

The marriage took place at Highclere Castle on 10 September of Miss Katie Price, model and socialite, and a popular singer (whose name we cannot remember). The bride was wearing etc. (already mentioned) and arrived in a glass-domed coach drawn by four clapped-out white nags loaned (for a fee) by Lord Carnarvon from Her Majesty The Queen's (Porchey's own) racing stable. Guests included Mr Paul Gascoigne and Sir John Nott. The honeymoon will be spent as guests of Mr Richard Desmond, the owner of *OK!*, in a secret location, actually No. 4 Belgrave Square, so that the paparazzi can respect the privacy of the happy couple.

There is only one very emotional and private matter left to report. According to Mr Desmond's *Daily Star*, the bridegroom's wedding present to his bride was a waxing. He visited a unisex establishment and had his whole body depilated, waxed; his back, his chest and his wedding tackle – a process evidently known as 'back, sack and crack'.

Jordan, when she heard of it, said, 'It was a thrilling present, a thrilling way to end a thrilling day'. She had always wanted her boyfriend waxed; she was delirious in anticipation of the wedding night.

How can anyone say that Jordan's wedding was tacky? It was summed up by a fellow guest of mine who said that 'the most subtle thing at the wedding were the bride's 33FF knockers'. What class. Was it all a dream?

14

São Paulo

At last – I am off to South America to investigate a site for my survival community.

Descending into the smog that hangs like a poisonous cloud over São Paulo, a city of over twenty million, I have a sense of anticipation, perhaps even expectation. On my way to Santiago, the capital of Chile, a trip that will end in Punta Arenas, the southernmost town in Patagonia, I decide to explore the night life of Brazil.

São Paulo is an industrial city that somehow accommodates a daily influx of 6,000 new immigrants a day; they come, without jobs or qualifications, from northern Brazil, Bolivia and Peru seeking work, and hope. Few find either. Many of the young join the homeless street children, sent out by their parents each day to beg or steal enough cash to feed the family back in the favelas, the shacks around the city. If the children do not return with the cash they are thrown back on the streets, which, strangely, give them some short-lived dignity, comradeship and independence. No one knows exactly how many children live this destitute life on the streets of the city, but most people have read of the vigilante gangs who murder these children in the cause of ridding the streets of São Paulo and Rio of these young thieving vermin.

In contrast, walking down the fashionable streets and sitting in the cafés you become aware of an unspoken caste system based on race – a system which to an outsider seems to dominate Brazil's social structure. It is not the same as the Hindu religious hierarchy headed by the Brahmin caste. But the blond, fair-haired blue-eyed descendants of European stock, with their riches, seem to sit on the top of the pile, with a middle class of car-crazy professionals and businessmen that keeps the wheels of the consumer society turning. At the bottom are the poverty-stricken inhabitants of the favelas, largely people of Indian descent. What, on a first visit, is surprising, although I have been to Rio on a previous occasion, is the lack of good-looking women in the fashionable centre; even on Oscar Friere, the most exclusive street lined by fashion houses and cafés, you see only one attractive well-dressed girl when you would see ten in the King's Road, Chelsea. In this melting pot of many races and cultures, Portuguese, Spanish, German, Japanese, Indian, Croatian and half-caste mulattos, you might expect to see a plethora of dusky, proud, self-confident women like the famous Brazilian model Gisele Bündchen, but it seems that they hide away in the heat of the day.

Sitting across the dining room was an Italian gentleman who was accompanied by a young Brazilian girl. She was very pretty and appeared to be about half his age. I noticed her first because all her clothes, while attractively sparse and revealing, seemed to have come straight out of an expensive boutique – and a fashion label was firmly attached to her jeans which fitted very snugly across her pert and uplifted bottom. She was wolfing down her food as if there was no tomorrow.

That evening the Italian gentleman was sitting in the bar and my wife, who cannot resist exercising her excellent Italian, enquired of him what he was about.

'I come to São Paulo once a year on business,' he said. 'In the motor business this town is really the Mecca for all automobile transactions in South America. I find São Paulo a hot and ugly town, with the largest population in South America. I get so frustrated and lonely in this dreadful place that a few years ago I decided to find some female company. The concierge at my luxury hotel recommended an agency which rented out pretty girls from the favelas. So, nowadays, when I come here I rent a Carioca girl from a favela. She stays with me for the whole week – and no one seems to raise an eyebrow. The rent is remarkably low given the good humour and attractiveness of all these young Brazilian girls, but the cost is quite stupendous.' 'I am sorry,' I interrupted. 'I thought you said the rent was low – there seems to be some contradiction with the cost, as you describe it.'

'Oh, the explanation is very simple,' he replied. 'First, as I am staying with her in a five-star luxury hotel, I have to kit her out in new clothes. She arrives full of smiles, friendliness and bonhomie, in a tattered t-shirt and a really tattered pair of jeans. I am not embarrassed or ashamed at being seen by the tourists with a young girl, although I can tell by their whispered conversations that they suspect me of being accompanied by a hostess. But I know no one in the hotel – and the likelihood of anyone that I know reporting back to Italy is remote. So I take her down fashionable Oscar Freire and she plunges into one fashion house after another – Valentino, Chanel, they are all here. I want to be generous, and, to be more honest about it, I want the sly looks of the other hotel guests to be astonished at the beauty and fashion consciousness of my weekly partner. This all sets me back at least two thousand dollars. But that is just the beginning of it.

'Each year my Carioca girl from the favela – and they are all the same – consumes vast quantities of food. She never stops eating; she wolfs down simply vast quantities of luxury food. Worst of all, of an evening when I am engaged in entertaining, my tenant for the week gets on to her mobile, apparently the only item in her possession, and calls up another friend from the favela so that they can entertain me in the bedroom with their own particular version of Rio Carioca. I quite enjoy the dancing, and the giggles which accompany the dancing, but the neighbours in the adjoining bedroom call up the management to complain about the noise. But that is not the worst of it. As soon as the two girls get together, they head straight for room service and order up a whole mountain of luxury food. They never stop eating. Between the dances, they return to the food and wolf down what would be a whole day of food for me.

'I try to persuade my girl to come out on the town with me and share a triple cheeseburger at McDonald's, but she looks at me with such appealing eyes that I have to accede to her wishes which are wholly directed at my luxury bedroom. She simply loves being in the hotel, ordering room service several times a day – and lying around on the sheets – showering frequently and dressing up in the bathroom dressing gown. Because she is always eating – indeed, because her mouth is always stuffed with food, I hardly have to talk to her. I know that we can just about converse in Italian or Portuguese but the weeks pass by with very little communication.

'Unfortunately, I have to go out for a business interview occasionally, leaving her in the hotel bedroom. When I return there is always an empty food trolley, a Champagne bottle, an ice bucket and empty plates all around the room; like all Brazilian girls she has a very attractive and rather large backside which she displays on every possible occasion and when she is entertaining me with carioca, it performs the most exquisite gyrations.

'But all this food apparently does no damage to her figure, which is remarkably slim and agile. I assume that girls from the favelas who live hand to mouth and are utterly dependent on whatever criminal drug dealer adopts them as his dancer, have a sort of camel-like capacity to store starch, protein, vitamins, minerals in some obscure part of their anatomy until some other punter comes along, and she can refuel by wolfing down the absolute maximum of luxury food.

'When I leave at the end of the week, and I become very fond of my Carioca girl, the hotel bill is absolutely nothing beside the "extras" which are listed in room service. Last time my account for room service came to eight thousand dollars.'

Brazil is an explosive BRICS – the term used for five high-growth developing countries – but it is better known for its football. You can see its players in any European city. What you cannot see and feel without coming here is the revolution in dance which has captured the imagination of the disenfranchised young.

In 2010, the city that gave the world the samba and the bossa nova, a new craze in the 1970s and 1980s captured the young women from the city slums – and it then took hold in São Paulo. It is known as funk or funky carioca – a mixture of uninhibited dance and sexual innuendo which celebrates casual sex and ghetto life.

I was met by Leonard, who spoke some English, and his girlfriend Eveline, a biology student who worked in a snake farm extracting venom from rattlesnakes. She was short, good-looking and scantily clad, but actually in relative terms rather overdressed, as I was to discover.

Eveline explained that funk was for the poor girls from the favelas – a protest about the hardship of life, an escape from the squalor of the favelas; and underlying it was the violent gang life that dominated their environment. The rhythm had come from the United States, but the overtly sexual movements and lyrics were authentically Rio-born. Precocious girls as young as twelve or thirteen escaped from their mothers under the protection of local drug dealers, the aristocracy of the favelas. The leading thugs adopted several girls, paid them, attended the dance and cheered them on. Their mothers protested but there was nothing that they could do. The girls wore minis and no underwear. The dancers performed back to back, and used their bottoms in a way that only Brazilian dance aficionados could appreciate; the female backside being worshipped in South America in the same way that breasts are the source of similar lascivious interest in North American culture.

I was not able to understand the lyrics, but there was a heavy concentration on *barraqueira*, fighting and shagging, to use a vulgar English expression. In the poorer dance venues the singer expressed herself to be *cachorra*, or 'I am a bitch'; bad language was the inspiration of the lyrics, vulgarity the key, or so Leonard and Eveline informed me.

When we set out to explore the scene, I asked whether we were going to the outskirts of the city where the favelas had taken hold. 'Certainly not,' said Leonard, 'it is far too dangerous and it would be madness for an outsider to enter that world.'

However, he would take me to two or three dance locations starting at the Freedom Club; quite low, if not at the bottom end. Certainly as we drove downtown there were crowds of young people on the street, strong evidence of police pressure with several alleys blocked off by the flashing lights of police cars. 'Must have been a fight,' said Leonard. What was in evidence were plenty of very tall, rather beautiful hookers; at last I had seen some genuinely good-looking Brazilian girls quite up to the quality of patrolling English public school girls on their half-term manhunt along the King's Road.

The sight of the hookers led to an exchange of information about sexual health in São Paulo. The killer, according to Leonard, was hepatitis B – not Aids, which was mainly concentrated in Brazilian ports. He said there had been a satisfactory growth of safe sex and contraception in the favelas – condoms were issued free by the government against the opposition of the powerful Catholic Church; the average size of families had halved in recent years. Religion carried little weight, but Catholic superstition was still strong.

It is impossible to describe each dance location individually, but in the largest one made up, it seemed, of hundreds of middle-class São Paulans, the music was quite deafening. The singer was a famous funk singer called Tati Quebra Barraco, the crush breathtaking and the uniform quite conformist. It consisted of a thin halter top for the girls with the maximum breast exposure; jeans slung low enough just to cover the essentials, but not the tattoos, which peeped out the front and the cleft of the posterior cheeks behind. The atmosphere was happy and electric, the music deafening, the dancing frenzied and it was all about sex, sex, sex. Maybe it was no different from the discos at any large British provincial city. Would I want to be young again – no. But it was a real tonic to see young people happy and enjoying themselves. I left at 3 a.m. The last train, which took the dancers home, left from the local terminus at 5.30 a.m.

The night was a short one for me as first call was at 5.30 a.m. for the flight to Santiago. What a contrast! After the Third World so evident in São Paulo, with its polluted industrial infrastructure, belching lorries, pitted roads and relative chaos at the airport, the Varig flight to Santiago was something of a haven. We stopped at Porto Allegra, an attractive looking town in the far south of Brazil, and then on to Chile in a half-empty aircraft. After a night at the funky clubs, I stretched out and slept. I awoke as we crossed the Andes and descended into civilisation at Santiago airport. Everything was clean, fast and efficient. The girl at the Immigration waved me through as if to say: 'You English, we like them here.' Santiago is a modern city oozing wealth, the girls good-looking and full of charm. I spent a night at the Ritz Carlton, a modern luxury tourist haven, and the next morning was up and away for the flight to Patagonia, several thousand miles to the south.

15

Punta Arenas

I did stop over on the long journey to Patagonia, the last place in the Americas, if not on earth. In fact, Punta Arenas, with a population of some 130,000, where I was heading, is not the southernmost settlement in Chile; this is a small port called Puerto Williams. The Welsh are everywhere in this extremity of the earth as you can guess by its name: Puerto Williams. It is just opposite the southernmost port in Argentina, Ushuaia, which is the departure point of virtually every Antarctic cruise. And thereby hangs a tale. Actually, I am in Chile because of the British Foreign Secretary, as I will explain.

I had booked a cruise to Antarctica and in my fevered dreams I had planned a reconnaissance of South Georgia on route. Elsewhere in this book I have mentioned my crazy scheme to start a survival community in the Southern Hemisphere, and the old whaling station at Grutviken on South Georgia seemed far enough off the beaten track, as it were, to hold some promise. As the island is normally uninhabited I had contemplated taking a lease of it from the British government. The rent would not be high as the only other permanent inhabitants are the penguins. South Georgia is about the size of England.

However, my proposed visit to Antarctica via South Georgia somehow became known to the Foreign Office. One day I was in my kitchen in Cornwall, the telephone rang and the following conversation took place...

Wife: You are wanted on the telephone.

Me: Oh, I can't be bothered with it, just say I am away.

Wife: I think you ought to take the call.

Me: Why – who is it?

Wife: I don't know – he says he is called Jack Straw.

Me: I don't know anyone called Jack Straw.

Wife: I think you do – he is the Foreign Secretary.

Me: Hello, Jack, how are you [although I had never met him]? Are you well? Can I help you?

Jack Straw: John, I am happy that I have tracked you down... my people tell me that you have booked a trip to Antarctica.

Me: How do you know that, Jack?

Jack Straw: Oh, we have means of knowing these things, John. I am advised that you ought to pause before going through Argentine immigration in Ushuaia. Of course, it is entirely up to you, but in view of your role as Defence Secretary during the Falklands War, I am not sure that you should take the risk. We have our disagreements with the Argentines about the future of the Falklands and it is an emotive business. We could never guarantee that an immigration officer might not notice your name, and report it to some aggrieved individual.

Me: Oh dear, I have already booked and paid for my trip, but I will see what I can do. As you know we were always seeking a negotiated solution. I must say that I do not relish being detained in Argentina in the same way we detained Pinochet in England, but thank you, Jack, for calling me I am flattered that you took the trouble to call an old political opponent – best wishes.

*   *   *

I called the shipping company and explained my dilemma, pointing out that Puerto Williams in Chile was directly opposite the Beagle Channel from Ushuaia; it would be entirely possible for them to put a boat ashore in Chile and take me on board, but, no, the bureaucracy ruled against it. However, they did refund my payment. I could not

'We are doing everything to reach a negotiated solution.'

Thatcher, Pym and me at sea.

get a refund on my air ticket to Chile, hence my exploratory survival visit. I worked my way south by plane and unmade roads, stopping three times at various rivers to fish.

Going south I decided that this was a marvellous country – endless lakes, glaciers, snow-clad volcanoes, fertile valleys. I fished in the Baker River, the largest in Patagonia. It is a strong, mighty river as wide as the Thames, but the waters are crystal-clear. The glaciers which can be seen at the head of the river feed into a vast land-locked lake so that the silt is buried in the lake rather than flowing down the river. It is full of rainbow trout. I was guided by a delightful but rather dour Chilean with obvious Spanish ancestry. He had the dark looks you see all over the Arab world, Arabs to Spain, Spain to South America, with a little Mestizo blood, to make him an authentic Chilean.

I joined my wife in the Torres del Paine National Park, at the famous Explora Hotel. I took a solo flight to get there because there is only one unmade road through parts of Patagonia before it peters out altogether. I was taken to a so-called airstrip which was a bumpy gravel track on which many one-foot bushes had taken hold. Even my Chilean guide expressed his surprise that any aeroplane could land in such a spot. For the first time I saw a smile spread across his face. But land it did and in a great whirlwind of gravel, sticks and undergrowth. I climbed aboard the tiny aircraft and with a roar we cleared the last line of bushes by a few feet, up and over a brilliant lake and snow-clad mountains. I had only once before travelled in such a tiny flying machine and that was over the glaciers and high mountains of Mount Cook from Queenstown in the South Island of New Zealand, another hazardous journey. All to catch a fish!

In earliest times Patagonia was inhabited by several Indian tribes that lived there as nomads and hunters. The Ona lived in the forests on the Argentine side of Terra del Fuego and the Fuegian Indians on the Chilean side. Further north were the Tehuelche

Indians. Magellan, the Portuguese explorer, financed by Charles I of Spain, took thirty-eight days to sail the Strait in 1520; it bears his name. The Spanish tried to keep the Strait a closely guarded secret. However, Francis Drake sailed it in the *Golden Hind* in 1578 on his way to raid the Chilean and Peruvian coasts.

It is hard to describe the landscape of Tierra del Fuego because it was a vast canvas, an empty desert, stretching into infinity. Why I found it so absorbing I do not know, but I shall never forget that barren desert of stunted, yellowing grasses, with those foot-high thorny bushes and undergrowth. It had no end.

I think Charles Darwin, writing in *The Voyage of the Beagle*, caught the spirit of the place better than I could ever do:

In calling up the images of the past I find that the plains of Patagonia frequently cross before my eyes; yet these plains are pronounced by all wretched and useless. They can be described only by negative characters; without habitations, without water, without mountains, they support merely a few dwarf plants. Why then, and the case is not peculiar to myself, have these arid wastes taken so firm a hold on my memory? I can scarcely analyse these feelings; but it must be partly owing to the free scope given to the imagination.

Is it any coincidence that Tierra del Fuego and Patagonia would seem to be the origin, not just of Darwin's Theory of Evolution, but Dante's Hell, Shakespeare's Caliban, Coleridge's Ancient Mariner, Swift's Brobdingnagions and Conan Doyle's Lost World? And maybe John Nott's survival community.

Captain Fitzroy had been sent in HMS *Beagle* by the Admiralty to make a further study of the Southern Ocean and especially to chart the intricate, little-known coasts of southern South America. The Beagle Channel lay some way south, parallel to the Strait of Magellan, named after Magellan's visit in 1520. It is more than possible that these passages from the Pacific to the Atlantic had been discovered by the Chinese in 1423, but no certain proof exists of this.

Anyhow, Captain Fitzroy became anxious when the Fuegian Indians surrounded the *Beagle* in their canoes – and a whaling boat had disappeared – he decided to take four Indians as hostages. He called them 'Boat Memory', 'York Minster', 'Fuegia Basket' and 'Jemmy Button', whose name expresses his purchase money.

Nine months after their arrival back in England with Captain Fitzroy, after the Fuegians had been sent to school, three of them (the fourth, Boat Memory, had died of smallpox) were summoned to appear before King William IV at St James's Palace. It was reported that Queen Adelaide was much taken with Fuegia Basket and placed her own lace cap upon her head. This caused surprise because the rumour had spread that these children belonged to a race of cannibals and moved around naked in their bark canoes, eating seal, birds and fish when they were not eating each other. Charles Darwin did nothing for their reputation and said that not only civilisation but also natural selection had passed them by!

I quote two extracts from Charles Darwin's diary of the *Voyage*:

December 17th 1832
I will describe our first arrival in Tierra del Fuego...in the afternoon we anchored in the Bay of Good Success. While entering we were saluted in a manner becoming the inhabitants of this savage land... The savages followed the ship and just before dark we saw their fire, and again heard their wild cry. When we were onshore...it was without exception the most curious and interesting spectacle I have ever beheld. I could not have believed how wide was the difference between savage and civilised man; it is greater than between a wild and domesticated animal.

December 25th 1832
While going one day on shore, we pulled alongside a canoe of

six Fuegians. They were the most abject and miserable creatures I ever beheld. These Fuegians...were quite naked, and even one full-grown woman was absolutely so. Not far distant a woman who was suckling a new born child, came alongside whilst the sleet fell and thawed on her naked bosom, and on the skin of her naked baby... At night, five or six human beings, naked and scarcely protected from the wind and rain of this tempestuous climate, sleep on the wet ground, coiled up like animals.

...I heard Mr Low, a sealing master, intimately acquainted with the natives of this country give a curious account, and also that of Jemmy Button that when pressed in winter by hunger, they kill and devour their old women before they kill their dogs. 'Doggies catch otters, old women no'... he described the manner in which they are killed by being held over smoke and thus choked... and described the parts of their bodies which are considered best to eat.

In England two years later the three Fuegian hostages, after their audience with the King and Queen, had been given tools, utensils, books, provisions and garden seeds and returned in the *Beagle* with Charles Darwin to their home onshore. Also on board the *Beagle* was a young catechist, Mr Richard Matthews, sent by the Church Missionary Society to instruct the three Fuegians on the voyage from England, which took a whole year.

When the *Beagle* anchored, Fitzroy, Darwin and Matthews set off to the shore laden with goods from England. Land was dug and sown for a vegetable garden and three huts were built, one for Matthews who was to stay with the Indians, one for Jemmy Button and the third for York Minster and Fuegia Basket, who then married. Hundreds of the local Indians arrived in their canoes and watched with astonishment. Fitzroy and the others had been expecting an interesting meeting between the natives and the three hostages from England, but the local Indians showed complete indifference and retired, showing no pleasure or surprise. Later, Matthews was discovered in a dreadful naked state; the Indians had driven him crazy and it was decided to take him away before he was eaten by the savages. So ended the first attempt to convert the Indians to the ways of our Lord.

Darwin described the farewell to Jemmy Button:

> Every soul on board was heartily sorry to shake hands with him for the last time... Everyone must sincerely hope that Captain Fitzroy's noble hope may be rewarded for the many generous sacrifices which he has made for these Fuegians, by some shipwrecked sailor being protected by the descendants of Jemmy Button and his tribe! When Jemmy reached the shore, he lighted a signal fire bidding us a last and long farewell.

Fifteen months later, Fitzroy, before leaving back for England, returned to find the place deserted, but that evening canoes arrived crowded with Indians. One wild-looking savage, naked except for a small loincloth with long unkempt hair, gave them a military salute. It was Jemmy Button. York Minster had built a large canoe and assisted by the faithful Fuegia Basket had loaded it with the combined possessions of all three, and left Jemmy Button on his own.

What Fitzroy saw convinced him that it was no use to attempt to civilise these people, but each visitor to the Beagle Channel thereafter sought out Jemmy Button, who had became famous when his appearance and actions as a primitive Indian were reported back in England.

It all ended badly when, twenty-five years later, Jemmy Button, the guest of King William IV, instigated the massacre of a group of unarmed missionaries engaged in their Sunday service in this same spot. Enough of Jemmy Button – such is fame.

Lucas Bridges, a landowner, missionary and author of the best book written about the area, spent his whole life with the Fuegian

Indians, and was most upset that Charles Darwin, 'the seeker after truth', should have believed this story about cannibalism.

> We who later passed many years of our lives in daily contact with these people can find only one explanation of this shocking mistake. We suppose that when questioned, York Minster or Jemmy Button, would not trouble in the least to answer truthfully, but would merely give the reply that he felt was expected or desired.
>
> 'Did you kill and eat men?'
>
> No answer.
>
> 'Do you eat bad people?'
>
> 'Yes.'
>
> 'When there are no bad people what then?'
>
> No answer.
>
> 'Do you eat old women?'
>
> 'Yes.'
>
> This delectable fiction, once firmly established, any subsequent attempt at denial would not have been believed, but would have been attributed to a growing unwillingness to confess the horrors in which they had formerly indulged.

Similarly today, a lie told by the British press has to be perpetuated because denial would not be believed.

Back to Punta Arenas – the southernmost town in the world. By 1842 the original convict settlement there – a group of log huts in a high wooden stockade – had attained a population of over six hundred souls, after at least one serious uprising of the convicts. Following a long interval without any visit from the north, a new governor arrived to find the place reduced to ashes and skeletons, without a living soul to be discovered there. It had looked as if a horde of vandals had destroyed it and the Tehuelche Indians had finished it off.

A new settlement was formed in 1848 and the population

increased to about a thousand persons, most of them convicts, and their soldier guards.

Then, in 1877, there has been a third rising, in which the guards had joined. There had been much bloodshed and the mutineers and convicts, fearing reprisals, had scattered into Patagonia; they were undesirable immigrants and a bad influence on the Tehuelche Indians. Many of them were captured later, ordered to dig their own graves and shot, and others killed each other off.

Punta Arenas had survived its third blow and within four years developed into a little town with a population of nearly 2,000, a church, a small fort, a score of houses and the prison. The change was due to the fact that every month at least four Peninsular Steam Navigation Company (P&O) liners either west or eastbound through the Magellan Strait, touched at this port. It was also the only place in the whole of Patagonia where the Teluelche Indians could dispose of their pelts and feathers. And at about this time someone whispered *gold*.

Before the end of the nineteenth century, Punta Arenas had become a thriving city and the opera house, the big mansions of the farmers and the town square had all been extended and embellished. Even today it is possible to imagine its activity and prosperity in its great days before the opening of the Panama Canal in 1914. The most impressive sight of all is the Municipal Cemetery, which must surely be one of the grandest cemeteries in all the world. I have never before seen anything so rich, emotive and well kept. It is deservedly famous.

Punta Arenas became the entry point – and sometime place of settlement – for Serbs, Croats and Slovenes seeking to avoid conscription into the Austro-Hungarian army before the First World War; also Afrikaners, the Welsh, Scots, English gentlemen farmers, missionaries and just Europeans seeking work. The Welsh, refugees from cramped mining villages, had come from the middle of the nineteenth century to found a New Wales, and to find open spaces uncontaminated by Englishmen. They had been part of a Welsh independence movement, stimulated by the British parliament ban on Welsh schools. Punta Arenas became a vital hub for the Chilean guano trade and then a transit for the hysteria in the Californian (and local) gold rush when the great clipper ships used it as a haven before travelling up the Pacific Coast. And, sheep, the 'white gold' of Patagonia, became the foundation of great farming estates and enormous prosperity.

16

Camels

I hurried back from Terra del Fuego when I heard that fighting had broken out on my farm in Cornwall. I referred briefly to the fact in an earlier chapter, 'A Nervous Breakdown', that I had bought a breeding herd of Bactrian camels from Mongolia when I had read that Fred Hoyle and other climate scientists had suggested that an interruption of the North Atlantic heat pump – the Gulf Stream – was a possibility and that the change could be quite sudden – I referred earlier to Fred Hoyle's book entitled *Ice*.

My interest in camels was first stimulated by watching the King of Saudi Arabia's dromedaries copulating in an enclosure of his palace. This was the King's stud – don't misunderstand me – I am not referring to the King's personal stud or harem, but to this breeding enterprise for the royal camels.

As a guest of the King I was taken to visit the stud, but found myself in the presence of a whole team of giggling teenage princesses dressed in black chadors who seemed much interested in the copulating camels. I found them more attractive and interesting than the camels, but these girls stimulated my desire to learn more about this interesting animal – in this case the dromedary, the Arabian camel.

My great-grandfather had been a sepoy general of the Indian Army commanding the 1st Division of the Army of the Indus which set off from Bengal to march the thousand or so miles to Kabul in

1838; this march had preceded the 1st Afghan War. My grandfather was a camel expert, as all marching soldiers in the nineteenth century had to be.

The camel in those days was a cross between a Hercules aircraft and a Chinook helicopter. It had to carry all the baggage, the heavy guns and all the key supplies for the army in the field.

My grandfather was stuck in Kandahar and couldn't march on Kabul because he lacked transport in the form of camels. It was the practice for the soldiers to march on foot, followed by their camels, followed by the camp followers driving cattle as they went and, lastly, by the rearguard. This retinue numbering 10,000 soldiers, 30,000 camels and 40,000 camp followers comprised the Army of the Indus which was to join up with the Bombay Army at the River Indus before marching on Kabul. Several of his despatches from the march read as follows:

> The march lay through extensive sandy deserts and dry jungles; the water was muddy, brackish, stagnant, poisonous; forage was obtained with great difficulty; the camels died by fifties and hundreds; the Baluchi mountaineers plundered at every opportunity, assassinating stragglers and bearing off their burdens... The 4th Brigade alone has lost during the last four days 244 camels – by death – namely starved.

Now this is the background to my first interest in the camel. It all took place in preparation for the creation of my own camel stud on my farm in west Cornwall. In the far west, the Gulf Stream passes north and south around Land's End within a mile or two of my farm. And the reason for this enterprise was the hysteria which surrounded the likely return of the Little Ice Age. I actually came to believe that, at some point of time, the Bactrian camel would become again the necessary and chosen means of transport in the twenty-first century. No doubt an EU directive would designate them a compulsory form of transport if climate change happened in a surprising direction.

I had a problem finding accommodation for the Mongolian camel keepers who normally live in yurts. I could not trust our local builders to erect yurts in expectation of the arrival of the Mongolians. Our builders are expert at blocking drains, letting water in through the roof, fusing electrical installations and generally causing distress to their customers, but yurt building, no. As a result I brought in a team of Polish builders to do the job; my farm coolers, normally used for taking the heat out of the vegetables, were switched to ice production. It all worked well – although I had problems with the planners, the Border Agency, the Race Relations Board, the Health & Safety inspector, English Heritage, Natural England and the PAYE Inspectorate. When I explained that the yurts were not permanent structures, they passed them as moveable erections. I then shipped in the Mongolians in closed lorries marked 'Ice for St Ives hoteliers'; thus we evaded border controls. And the Mongolians were happily settled for a time, making friends with all the Poles, Ukrainians, Bulgarians, Romanians and Latvians who work on the farm vegetables.

I must explain that it is very difficult to make money in agriculture. We are always advised by urban experts working in the Ministry of Agriculture, whose experience of the countryside is embraced by walking their dogs in Highbury Fields, that diversification is essential. Invention and diversification: this cry from the experts in the ministry has led to all sorts of experiments. You can find farms which specialise in breeding ostriches for their plumage, meat and eggs. But more usual are the alpaca farms which breed these animals from the wide spaces of Patagonia and the foothills of the Andes. They are said to be valuable for their wool.

Encouraged by the Ministry of Agriculture, I therefore decided to create a stud farm breeding the Bactrian camel, based on the best information that I could garner from Fred Hoyle and oceanologists that the North Atlantic Current was subject to disruption from the melting ice cap in Greenland. In an environment where my cattle were likely to perish from the cold, and where tight controls had been placed on the extraction of fossil fuels, it was clear that the future of motor transport was very questionable, particularly if Mr John Gumbug, the environmental supremo, got involved.

At this point politics intervened; the Greens were improving their position quite sharply in Europe – they even had a member in the British Parliament. There was a move by the Liberal Party in Britain to ban nuclear power although it was, of course, the most secure means of reducing carbon into the atmosphere. When this anti-nuclear lobby was successful in Germany, and Angela Merkel suspended all nuclear development following the Japanese nuclear disaster at Fukushima, it gave substantial authority for a similar move in Britain. The advocates like Mr John Gumbug – the environmental expert – and all good Greens and Liberals got real wind in their sails.

The Greens and Liberals believed that any move, however futile, by Europeans was to be applauded. If Europe could ban nuclear power we could show 'leadership' in Europe by doing likewise and go much further by banning the motorcar – a major cause of carbon release, albeit much less so than the methane (itself twenty-three times more lethal than Co^2) released by farm animals who, it was said, were responsible for 16 per cent of greenhouse gas emissions worldwide, animals being responsible for more greenhouse gases than all motor transport put together. Being patriotic, I considered slaughtering all my farm animals but, instead, followed EU advice to grow garlic. I mentioned this in an earlier chapter but did not elaborate on the fact that garlic is a well-known antidote to flatulence (burping and farting) in animals (and Frenchmen).

The EU had already advised all member states to seek alternative means of transport to the motorcar and alternative means of generating electricity without fossil fuels. The Bactrian camel might

*We are a Green Party seeking every **un**economic means of generating alternative energy.*

again become the chosen and necessary form of transport if the Little Ice Age returned to Britain.

It was the continuing desire of 'Europeans' in Britain to find means of showing 'leadership' in Europe hence the recommendation of Mr John Gumbug's research group, backed up by all 'Europeans' like Lords Heseltine, Howe, Clarke, Brittan, etc., to support the generation of power by windmills, wave power, treadmills and donkeys – and transport by camels.

Seeing an entrepreneurial opportunity I set up this breeding herd of Bactrian camels to provide a new means of transport that would be suitable if there were to be a serious decline of temperature trending towards another Little Ice Age. I knew that my Bactrian camels could withstand temperatures of minus 50° centigrade in Mongolia and that they could go for great distances without water (to be rationed under a new EU directive). It was a brilliant entrepreneurial move and satisfied the EU directive to diversify away from GM crops to growing garlic. It was a double-whammy for the Greens and the climate change lobby as it diverted arable agriculture away from GM crops to garlic as well as reducing the release of methane into the atmosphere.

Indeed, so excited were the EU authorities in Brussels that they required subsidies to farmers in the United Kingdom under the Single Farm Payment – to be restricted to farmers growing a specific percentage of garlic on their farms. This directive was strongly supported by the Liberal members of the British government – and was not opposed by the Green members in the Conservative administration.

Well, all of this was fine – and my new breeding policy proceeded – and was widely applauded in the British press and by the Chairman of the European Union. Then, of course, disaster struck. The scientists changed their mind. No longer were we in danger of another Little Ice Age for which I had prepared myself in accordance with EU policy. A complete reversal by the world scientific experts in the UN Committee on Climate Change now concluded that the world was in danger of terminal collapse if average world temperatures rose by 3 per cent in the next one hundred years.

I nearly sent my Bactrian camels for slaughter and even considered the repatriation of their Mongolian keepers, while at the same time importing a breeding herd of dromedaries. EU agricultural policy changed – and so did political, scientific, religious and media opinion. Farmers were to prepare themselves, under EU agricultural policy, for the desertification of much of southern England. We were not to anticipate a Little Ice Age after all, but a rapid advance of the Sahara Desert into Europe, known as global warming. Global warming had replaced global cooling.

What did I do as an entrepreneur, as always subject to the whims of governments and experts? I went out to the Yemen, engaged a team of Bedouin camel drivers and bought a herd of dromedary camels –and had them shipped in sealed lorries labelled 'Sand for St Ives Beach'. The lorries managed to evade our extensive border controls, although the Bedouin keepers were rather breathless when they emerged from the lorries. I then led the camels myself down the Cornish lanes from St Ives to my farm. People lined the streets and lanes and cheered me as I rode the leading camel shouting, 'Good on you, John, for being such a great British patriot'. An EU delegation of scientific experts (part of the EU gravy train) met me and welcomed me to my farm, assuring me that the garlic (now growing on thirty acres) was as an equally effective counter-flatulence measure for dromedary as for Bactrian camels (and Frenchmen).

Now all this happened before I had left for South America, with my wife looking at the guanaco, the third member of the camel family. I had learnt that the South American Indians covered their loins in guanaco skins and it followed that they were used by well-known fashion designers in Paris and Milan for the same purpose.

Here was a third entrepreneurial opportunity if I imported some guanaco camels to the farm.

I mentioned that I hurried back to England because a fight had broken out on my farm. In my absence, the Mongolian keepers had got drunk on kumis (a strong, fermented mare's milk) and had made some slighting remarks about the Prophet. The Muslim herdsmen had been outraged at this sacrilege and had persuaded the Imam at the Penzance Mosque to issue a fatwa against my employees. Violence threatened. The whole situation was fraught with danger, so I referred it to the Race Relations Board and am still waiting their recommendations. Life is not easy as a farmer.

*   *   *

Perhaps I should conclude by explaining how I came to visit Outer Mongolia and develop my interest in the Bactrian camel.

The wild Bactrian camel now only lives in China and the south-western area of the Mongolian Gobi Desert, which I visited in 1971. These camels are believed to be the last remnants of the herds which crossed from the Arizona desert over the land bridge into Asia many millions of years ago. Camels were domesticated 4,000 years ago but the Bactrian wild camel somehow avoided it. They have adapted beautifully to my project in Cornwall as they seem to have survived radiation from over forty atmospheric nuclear tests by the Chinese, and in the absence of fresh water seem to have adapted to drinking salt water, of which we have plenty around Land's End. As I have said, they can survive extremes of temperature ranging from minus 40° degrees Centigrade to plus 30° degrees Centigrade. Now there is adaption and survival for you. Do we really have to bang on about the dangers of climate change?

The London Zoological Society has an active research project in Mongolia to preserve the wild camel, which has been utterly decimated by hunting over centuries of time. Sven Hedin, the intrepid explorer, has wonderful descriptions of the prolific and shy wild camels in their natural environment which he saw at the end of the nineteenth century, but they are now reduced to small herds in isolated areas. The wild camel is threatened by illegal mining, competition from introduced livestock by disease transmission and hybridisation with domestic camels.

How did I come to visit Mongolia in 1971 and write a report on it which I have consulted? It happened when I was part of a parliamentary delegation in that year. At this time a very cold war was being fought out between the Chinese and Russian communists for influence in Outer Mongolia, a quasi-independent buffer state. The Russians had covered their border with nuclear missiles in anticipation of an attack by the Maoist communists and the Chinese had stationed several divisions of the Red Army on their border in case of an assault on China by the Soviets. OK – this seems far-fetched today and a long time ago but it is part of my final mission in life to remind my readers of various historical facets of the Cold War.

The Mongolian Peoples' Republic decided, as part of this dispute between their neighbours, to invite the first British delegation to their country, presumably in a rather hopeless attempt at bolstering support for their independence. The United Kingdom was not such a feeble influence in the world in 1971 as it has become today, a mere foreign policy appendage to the United States.

I remember the visit vividly for having to share a large double bed with a large baronet, one Sir Clive Bossom (the son of a famous political diarist) in the state guest house, the only accommodation provided. We had two meals a day which never varied – caviar and sardines washed down by Hungarian communist wine. Another member of the delegation was a delightful poet with long straggly hair, the former Lord Moyne, by far the richest member of the Guinness family and the Chairman of the Guinness Book of Records which he carried everywhere in Mongolia in an old army satchel around his neck. I note it because in company with the Mongolian pilot of our plane, I caught a twenty-three pound trout which Lord Moyne wanted to put in *The Guinness Book of Records*. It was a taimen!

Perhaps I should conclude the story of our visit with Bactrian camels which we encountered in a large collective farm that covered over 100,000 acres of the Mongolian steppe, a copy of Salisbury Plain, by describing our trip from Moscow.

We left Brezhnev's Moscow, a place then of miserable demeanour and gloomy, downtrodden subjects in an Aeroflot Ilyushin aircraft bound for Ulan Bator via Irkutsk in Siberia; this dreadful aeroplane shuddered through the night. Rosa Klebb and her twin sister, vast air hostesses, marched in their prison-guard uniform up and down the corridor eyeing their captive travellers with utter disdain. No water, no food, no relief was offered until 04:00 hours in the morning when Rosa Klebb slammed down a large cardboard box of caviar in front of us. No doubt Lord Moyne broke his nightly fast each morning with a large helping of caviar and a huge smile spread across his face, as did mine. Between us sat a very pretty twelve-year-old pioneer presumably on a camping trip to Siberia; she pushed away her caviar in disgust. At 05:00 hours, I saw Lord Moyne's grizzled hand reach out and grab the young pioneer's breakfast. Students of human behaviour and of the survival of the species would understand that travelling in an Aeroflot aircraft has a levelling and survival imperative.

On arrival we were flown around the country – a vast area of the Gobi Desert and rolling grassland. We visited Genghis Khan's capital of Kharakorum, which was a ruin, maybe in retribution and memory of the ruins with which his Mongolian horde devastated half the civilised world. But it was at a horse breeding cooperative, where we were plied with kumis, that gave me the idea of importing Bactrian camels to Cornwall and locating their handlers in ghers or yurts. Everything has a history!

17

Agriculture

When the majority of the world's scientists and their scientific bodies are joined by God's representatives on earth, in the persons of David Attenborough and the Archbishop of Canterbury, we should sit up and take notice. Unfortunately the historic record of 'settled science' hardly gives us confidence. Thinking people suspect near unanimity in anything. Most of the world's advances in science have challenged unanimity. Galileo, Newton and Darwin were hardly followers of prevailing fashion; they set themselves against the orthodoxies of their day. And global warming is an orthodoxy.

We cannot know whether the world climate of today is the best for us in all possible worlds, until it changes. Warming may well turn out to be for the benefit of mankind. And the change predicted by most computer models is hardly comparable with the large swings in climate of the past.

There is a problem with the world's temperature – it may be changing gradually. If a rise of 3° Centigrade, on average, in world temperature in the next one hundred years were to come about there would be winners as well as losers. Some species would become extinct; others would replace them. Tokyo and New York might disappear under water. The Thames Barrier would have to be strengthened and heightened.

But a warmer world in general should improve agricultural yields in all temperate climates – and added carbon with its fertilisation effect should help agricultural crops. Greater precipitation should increase cloud cover and therefore rain in many parts of the world. It is quite likely that warming will help us to feed the extra two billion people expected in the world, particularly if we stop turning 5 per cent of the world's grain crop into motor fuel. The consequence of warming in the late Anglo-Saxon period from AD 900 until the Norman Conquest helped England to become one of the most prosperous farming societies in the European world. Then the Little Ice Age hit us.

Farming hardly figures in the exaggerated scare stories that we read about in the media today. It is more telling to blame warming on Jeremy Clarkson and his noisy, stinking cars and young families holidaymaking with Ryanair than on the humble cow. Who can blame the cow for flatulence? It is forced to eat more than three times what is necessary for its own maintenance in order to give us milk. In the greatest act of human cruelty against animals its new-born calf is taken from its mother shortly after birth. That we treat animals in this way is a prime example of human selfishness. But, whether we are vegans or carnivores, we have to accept that farming is one of the greatest polluters of them all. With fossil fuels we have a simple choice: warmer and richer or cooler and poorer. With agriculture the starkest choice is between meat-eating and vegetarianism.

If the United Nations' own estimates are to be believed world GDP should see a multiple increase in the next one hundred years – around nine times greater than today seems to be the consensus figure, even among the doomsters. If this were to be the case it is hard to see why today's consumers should be loaded with the large extra costs of alternative energy when their grandchildren will be immeasurably richer than themselves. What justification is there for poor old granny to subsidise her much richer grandchild? Of course, her grandchild will only be richer if the world continues to burn fossil fuels since there is no conceivable possibility of the world being able to finance a total replacement of fossil fuels by nuclear energy –

currently the only economic alternative to gas and coal.

The Chinese, who have doubled the number of coal-fired power stations in the last ten years – and continue to accelerate their consumption of fossil fuels, must think it very odd that Great Britain, responsible for only 2 per cent of world pollution, should place constraints and extra costs upon its population and its industry while they refuse to follow suit. And why should they, when the Chinese people have an average annual income per head of $9,223 against $33,527 for the European Union and $49,965 for the United States? Fossil fuel consumption is the only ready economic means for them to catch us up.

Let us look at the figures for world agriculture, although, of course, they vary. The Food and Agriculture Organisation (FAO) of the United Nations seems the most reliable source. A man called Henning Steinfeld, an official of the FAO, said:

> The environmental costs per unit of livestock production must be cut by one half just to avoid the level of damage worsening beyond its present level.

With emissions from land use included, the livestock sector accounts for 9 per cent of CO^2 deriving from human-related activities, but it produces a much larger share of even more harmful greenhouse gases like methane. It accounts for 37 per cent of all human-induced methane (twenty-three times as warming as CO^2), which is partly produced by the digestive system of ruminants.

With increased prosperity people are consuming more meat and dairy products every year. Global meat production is projected to more than double between 2000 and 2050. Overall, livestock production is responsible for more greenhouse gas emissions worldwide than all the planes, trains and automobiles on the planet.

Scientists are trying to develop new varieties of feed grasses that are more energy efficient and have targeted breeding to produce a less gassy strain of cattle. My reference to garlic in the last chapter is an attempt to produce a feed mix that will contribute to less flatulence. One scientific paper suggested that feeding dairy cows sunflower oil decreased their methane emissions by 20 per cent. More sunflower oil – less forests, of course. It is give and take.

Dr James Hansen, who has been described as the 'Grandfather of the Global Warming Theory', is the Director of NASA's Goddard Institute for Space Studies. He complains of the focus solely on CO^2, while methane is responsible for nearly as much global warming as all other non-CO^2 greenhouse gases put together. It is claimed that atmospheric concentrations of CO^2 have risen by about 31 per cent since pre-industrial times, while methane concentrations have risen more than 100 per cent. Methane is produced from coal mining and landfills, but the number one source is worldwide animal agriculture. Scientists dismiss methane as it disperses quite quickly in the atmosphere, while CO^2 gases can last for a century or more.

So what are the experts' recommendations? Frankly, they are even more ridiculous than trying to suspend world growth by banning or sharply reducing the use of fossil fuels.

It is proposed that government policy should encourage vegetarianism, preferably vegan diets. Consideration should be given to an environmental tax on meat, similar to the environmental tax on gasoline. There needs to be a shift from farm subsidies to encourage plant agriculture rather than animal agriculture – and emphasis on vegetarian diets in schools.

This is the best that the climate scaremongers can offer when the world population's craving for meat and dairy products is set to double. Can you believe that we will be able to persuade 1½ billion Chinese to become vegans – or Prince Charles, a leading doomster, to sell his cows and insist on vegetarian meals at all royal palaces?

Research for greater adaptation in agriculture can yield results, so long as the madness of Greenpeace can be resisted. We should ask what opportunities are presented for longer growing seasons; what could be the impact of warmer soil on seed germination; what will be the change required by less or more water availability; can there be a need for fewer fertilisers and how can we develop crops better suited to a future climate than current crops? The scientists in companies like Monsanto are making a huge contribution to climate change, but they are resisted by so-called conservationists in every quarter. Here is where greater wealth can help humanity adapt to change; I can grow rich on growing garlic!

18

The Arctic

I have explained how I went to Greenland to find out how the Inuit respected their dead, and preserved their bodies for immortality by burying them deep in the permafrost, after an explosive farewell.

I realised that if we still discovered the woolly mammoth lying in Arctic glaciers and then reassembled their bodies for show in museums, it was a form of physical resurrection – and hence immortality of a kind. Admittedly it fell short of having one's semen frozen and stored in the Millennium Seed Bank at Wakehurst Place, but immortality takes many forms.

But I realised that, apart from a short visit to Greenland, I had not properly researched the Arctic as a survival location, and I needed to familiarise myself with the farthest north, just as I had done in the farthest south in Patagonia; not least because I was due to visit Iceland on my way to Alaska, where I was to join my Ark – *The World*.

The farthest north was the island of Spitsbergen, the nearest inhabited place to the North Pole which boasted a resident population (as of 2009 anyway) of some 2,753 souls. There had been controversy about whether Spitsbergen had been discovered by the Vikings in the tenth century, or by the Pomor people from the Arctic Russia in the fifteenth or, as mythology claims, by William Barents when he stumbled, by chance, on Spitsbergen as he sought the Northeast Passage across northern Siberia to China and the East.

Anyhow, I decided to visit Spitsbergen, partly because as

a passionate fisherman I had been obsessed with the history of whaling in Spitsbergen, the location of a long cold war between the Dutch and the English in the sixteenth century for domination of the hugely rich trade in whale oil that lit the candles and lamps of medieval Europe.

As I said earlier, I was very familiar with Murmansk in Arctic Russia as a result of my time as Defence Secretary during the Cold War, when we fought a bloodless submarine war in the Greenland, Iceland and Norwegian gap. At least once a week I was shown satellite images of the Soviet Northern Fleet, which was based in Murmansk and the Kola Peninsula. We followed it by satellite and sonar as it moved in and out of the Atlantic and the Arctic seas.

I confess that I wanted to visit Murmansk and Arctic Russia to fish for salmon in the rivers of the Kola Peninsula – and also to see what had happened to this northern region of the world in the intervening thirty years since I retired as Defence Secretary.

I had also been told by scientists about the slow melting of the permafrost in Siberia, which had the ability to release vast quantities of methane that could dwarf even the methane emitted by farting cows, Frenchmen and other ruminants.

The readers of my chapters on Spitsbergen, Murmansk and Arctic Russia must therefore be patient with my nostalgia for the cold wars fought over whaling in the sixteenth century – and the more recent Cold War with the Soviets in these Arctic regions.

19

Murmansk – Arctic Russia

I also wanted to visit Arctic Russia because it is a prime example of man's destructiveness; a principle cause of pollution which is poisoning our seas; and, as I have said already, the potential source of a massive escape of methane as the permafrost slowly thaws in the Siberian wilderness. The former is more directly man-made as a result of the near collapse of the Russian nuclear fleet – and the irresponsibility of the Soviet leadership; the latter is an example of the impossibility of mitigating climate change if the Northern Hemisphere continues to show some warming over future years. How can I study mortality without observing the threat to humanity by nuclear pollution, a far greater catastrophe than a modest change in climate over the next one hundred years? The one threat, pollution by the dumping of nuclear waste and rotting nuclear submarines; the other, a natural consequence of thawing permafrost.

I cannot consider Arctic Russia as a survival location while Putin is around. I may, however, approach the girls of Pussy Riot when they are all finally released from Putin's gulag because I am attracted to their anarchist beliefs; they would do well in Punta Arenas or on Stewart Island.

On an earlier visit to Russia, I had spent a few days at Irkutsk on Lake Baikal in eastern Siberia. I was on my way to Mongolia by Aeroflot. There I gazed at one of God's wonders, a lake that still holds one-fifth of the world's surface fresh water. It is the world's deepest, clearest and oldest lake, and is home to around 2,000 species of plants and animals.

In spite of this unique place, a large pulp and paper mill opened in the Brezhnev era is polluting the lake with chlorine; it was closed but was reopened recently by Putin. This example of Soviet era destructiveness is relevant in that it stands beside the horrors of the Aral Sea, formerly one of the four largest lakes in the world covering an area of 26,000 square miles. By 2007 it had shrunk to 10 per cent of its original size as a result of extraction for the cotton industry. The surrounding eco-systems have been destroyed through weapons testing, industrial projects, pesticides and fertiliser run-offs. And the Murmansk region could go the same way, as nuclear residues become even more apparent in future years.

As we flew into Murmansk I realised that this was the destination of the Arctic convoys in the Second World War. I was conscious of the terrible conditions suffered by the merchant ships and their naval escorts in that dreadful war. Between 1941 and 1945, of 811 loaded merchant ships, 104 were sunk with the loss of over 3,000 men. A man only lasted a few minutes in the water before he froze to death. But the contribution to victory before Stalingrad was immense: over 7,000 aircraft and 5,000 tanks were delivered to the Russians to fight in the fiercest and most ruthless battles of the war. The Russians were hugely suspicious of the British and remembered how we had helped the White Russians in Archangel in 1918 and they deeply resented our quality of life beside their own.

Murmansk airport was a derelict world of pitted concrete and cold, grisly neglected buildings. Yet it was the aviation link of the largest Russian town in the Arctic Circle. There was one Finnair aircraft on the apron and discarded scraps of metal everywhere, including rusting, collapsed boarding steps.

The airport building was virtually deserted, apart from a small army of Russian military personnel – and strange looking ladies in clogs, with red hennaed hair and skimpy mini-skirts. The décor was neglected military, fading and peeling, painted kerbstones, flowerbeds which had hardly been treated since the collapse of Communism.

After our flight there was widespread demand for a visit to the public conveniences, but that required fifteen roubles – and no one had any roubles. There were two options: either the trees on the airport approach, which had not been cleared since a visit by the Comintern in 1955, or to await the arrival of our guide, Victor, bearing a plastic bag of roubles for those in need. Then came the 'visit'.

She sat on a sort of throne – for her authority over the public conveniences was absolute. She ruled over her empire by the Divine Right of Queens. It is true that she had a double who presided in her absence – but the double was a blonde while the Queen had red hennaed hair piled high about her crown. Her authority was not paternal; it was stern, unbending and fearful. She ruled over the conveniences with a sense of superiority and menace. The cubicle from which she surveyed her clients, as they hurried to do their business, was perched high above the entrance so that she could gaze down at them, humiliating them as members of the lower orders. When she demanded tributes from her throne, she gazed unblinking and severe at the humble mortals as they passed her turnstile. All around were green tiles, cold, uninviting, as if to say 'all ye who enter here do so by authority of the state. The state decides, levies fifteen roubles.'

Eventually we were gathered together and, after our bags had been screened for the umpteenth time, we were bussed on to a large Russian naval helicopter with our suitcases piled high in the middle of the aircraft. With a great shuddering roar the leviathan took to the air. Without ear defenders, which hung on a wire cable around the roof, we would have been deaf for days on end. Up and over one hundred miles or so of empty tundra, bogs and lakes, which made me think of permafrost and escaping methane. We were landed at our fishing camp; there we met our team of Russian guides, tough, well-mannered, considerate beings, rather silent and introspective but generally admirable men, eager to do their job to the very best of their ability. William, my grandson, and I had a guide from Murmansk called Jemka. I could not praise him enough. On one occasion William twisted his ankle and he carried this heavy boy on his back up a steep cliff to the waiting helicopter as we were taken out and back to the river each day by Russian helicopter pilots.

I took a helicopter that had won its spurs in Afghanistan on an excursion from the fishing camp. We travelled along the River Rynda, which curled along, often between deep gorges, through pine and birch forests. Sometimes it was flat water, often tumbling white water where the river flowed along a shallow bed. Below us the bog varied from one colour to another, often with good berry ground and lichen, the sustenance of the reindeer herds.

It was a magnificent scene – no man, no tracks or dwelling to be seen, just bogs and taiga. When we reached the mouth of the river as it emptied into the Barents Sea, there was a deserted Pomor fishing village, derelict wooden houses which could have accommodated several families before they were forcibly evicted and collectivised by Stalin. Along the coast there was a mass of timber and here and there vast tree trunks which had been swept down the Siberian rivers further north and east, along the Northeast Passage first explored by the English explorers Willoughby and Chancellor. Some of this timber would find its way with the sea currents around the North Cape of Norway – to be washed up on the barren shores of Spitzbergen in the Svalbard archipelago.

Murmansk had its best days during the 1960s and 1970s when hundreds of thousands of Soviet citizens came north for work, and the much coveted Arctic premium which earned them up to 100 per cent above the normal wage. The population rose to well over one million by 1989. For those who slaved away in Stalin's collectives it enabled them an escape with prospects, a place to raise a family and accumulate a small fortune before moving south again. For young women, too, the town was swarming with young eligible naval men from the Northern Fleet. A huge fishing industry was there and also the supply fleet which provided fuel and food along the northern coast of Siberia – the Northeast Passage. At its peak the fishing fleet was large. As well as the thousands of small trawlers fishing in the White Sea and the Barents Sea, there were usually two hundred or more large fishing ships based at Murmansk, which stayed at sea for years working the Atlantic and Pacific oceans, processing millions of tons of fish. The scale of this effort is hard to measure, but it is believed that the exports were valued at up to $2,000 million.

And then, with the demise of the Soviet Union, the whole industry collapsed. Investment in new ships and port facilities ceased. Fish quotas were introduced. New businessmen bought up sections of the industry for nothing – and the fishing industry moved to modern facilities in Norway. Political bosses made a killing. Murmansk, with its large multi-ethnic immigrant population, had a problem. Huge multi-storey apartment blocks, in the Soviet brutalist style of architecture, had been erected to meet the influx. It is not a pretty town. But the people are sound – pioneers by spirit.

Which brings me to the Russian Northern Fleet, one of the great navies of the world during its heyday in the Cold War. It had top priority for investment and naval families shut away in closed towns like Severomorsk prospered and lived a life of pride and dignity.

Although the whole area was a military zone – and still is – it was not closed to me. As I have said, as Britain's Defence Secretary during the Cold War I was briefed continuously by our defence intelligence staff on developments in the whole of the Kola Peninsula – and that included the comings and goings of the Russian nuclear fleet. Satellite imagery enabled us to observe the smallest movement in these closed zones. I could watch people and vehicles moving about their business, even when under heavy cloud. The intelligence community were excited when they discovered the building of a new aircraft carrier, or submarine. They did their best to excite me, but I realised that much of their briefing was an indirect way of persuading me that our defence expenditure was inadequate. The Chiefs of Staff were always irresponsible and profligate when it came to money. But thankfully the Cold War remained cold when it could so easily have become a hot war in this region. The contest to build the fastest, quietest and best armed nuclear submarine was constant. Whenever we despatched our nuclear submariners to this area, I realised the hazardous nature of their mission. We had to spy on the Russian Northern Fleet and, in particular, the sonar capability of their submarines. This submarine war, often under the ice around Greenland, Iceland and Spitsbergen, was constant and intense. It could so easily have exploded into a crisis, leading from a violent accident between our respective submarines. Fortunately, our submarines were much more silent than their Russian counterparts and only minor accidents occurred when it was in the interests of both parties to say nothing.

Today the Russian navy is a shadow of its former Soviet days. All along the Kola Peninsula are discarded, rotting nuclear facilities and submarines. Together with the nickel-smelting plants, the whole area is a pollution nightmare; neglected, derelict, suspicious, pessimistic, it is a ticking time bomb for the world. The Russian defence industries bankrupted the Russian state. The collapse of Russia's Northern Fleet must be one of the greatest setbacks ever suffered by the military. In 1989 the Soviet navy had some 120 nuclear submarines in active operation; today there are probably around twenty.

It was not until the 1994 report entitled 'Sources of Radioactive Contamination in Murmansk and Archangel' was published by the Bellona Foundation that the world realised the startling facts and dangers resulting from years of neglect and incompetence by the Northern Fleet. This Foundation, started by a Norwegian conservationist in 1986, became a hugely active and important player in the international atomic energy firmament. It was clear that the Russians had been dumping nuclear waste into the sea along the northern coast of Siberia and in the Barents and Kara seas, where they had held many of their nuclear tests.

The area has become the world's largest repository of spent nuclear fuel and radioactive waste. There are up to one hundred rotting nuclear submarines in the Barents and Kara seas, and this in spite of American, German and Norwegian help; Russian paranoia and suspicion of the West means it is an uphill struggle to mitigate this nightmare for posterity.

What can be done about Mr Putin's state? Maybe the punks of Pussy Riot had cause for their 'unacceptable' behaviour in an Orthodox cathedral. Certainly Russia is not a place where one would hanker after immortality. The population is falling, and life expectancy, partly as a result of alcoholism, is much shorter than elsewhere in Europe. The economy is held together only by the price of gas. Huge swaths of Siberia suffer from terminal decline and grinding poverty.

Yet thanks to the disintegration of the state with the collapse of Communism, members of the former nomenclatures grabbed state assets at a knockdown price. Many of these modern pirates, subject only to their mafia supporters and fear of Mr Putin's legal hegemony, have escaped to London where they go by the description of oligarchy and are distinguished not by their plundered wealth but by the vulgarity of their behaviour.

How sad it is that the wonderful Russian people of great attractiveness and huge talent are still being exploited by their leadership, as indeed has been the case throughout history. Perhaps we can be content that more civilised European nations have benefited from Russian literature and music without the pain that brought them about.

So, perhaps I might contemplate immortality if I lived in Sydney or Vancouver, but I might pray for an early release in Putin's Moscow or St Petersburg.

20

The Punta Arenas Survival Project

On my return to Cornwall from South America I went some way to mollify the Bedouin camel drivers and explain to them that the Mongolians were simple peasant descendants of the peace-loving Genghis Khan. I explained that they had meant no harm and had just got plastered on fermented mare's milk, which was not classified as alcohol in the Koran. In any event, I doubted that they would stand much truck from expatriate Muslim towel-heads from the Yemen. Their ancestors on horseback had slaughtered a great raft of the Muslim world in the fifteenth century and we did not want such violence to reoccur again around St Ives; the Mongolians had got on well with the multi-cultural community who picked vegetables on the local farms and the Muslims should try harder to integrate. How tiresome that men were always causing trouble. We still awaited the enquiry by the Race Relations Board.

So I gave consideration as to whether my reconnaissance of Punta Arenas as a location for a survival community made any sense. It had several advantages. It had an enviable infrastructure, including an airfield and a port of sorts. There was a good public square, many fine mansions, a local beach by the sea, many penguin settlements and an Anglican church. The cemetery was a particular advantage because, as they say, we establish immortality by living on the memory of our descendants and the cemetery was full of fine memorials to the dead. The place, moreover, had an interesting political tradition; the socialist Señor Salvador Allende was its

Deputy before he became President of Chile and was eliminated by General Pinochet. I thought Sally Bercow would feel comfortable in this political environment.

I have always had a 'close relationship' with the celebrity class, as evidenced by my attendance at Jordan's wedding. Going back to my time as a sidekick of Margaret Thatcher, I have had a particular affinity with political celebrity and its problems (self-absorption, publicity craving, general physiological distress, etc.). Of course, our current political celebrity, the Prime Minister, does not suffer from any of these problems; he is perfectly normal in every way. He gets his frustration with the press, his Cabinet colleagues, his back benchers, the 'swivel-eyed loons' in his party and his hopeless civil servants out of his system by drip-feeding the media with some PR stunt on a daily basis; this satisfies his natural inclination and talent for PR while also feeding the insatiable appetite for news, however trivial, of the twenty-four-hour media circus.

But my task, as I see it, going right back to Lady Emma Hamilton and in more recent times to Carla Bruni-Sarkozy, is to help out the leading political figures of the day with their problems, often considerable ones.

The mention of Señor Allende reminded me that Mr Speaker Bercow, the parliamentary tyro, might find the antics of his wife, Sally, quite difficult to handle. He holds a position of great distinction and discretion but, as is quite usual in marital relationships, he seems unable to control his wife. I feel some sympathy with him because, as I had illustrated in the first *Mr Wonderful*, he and I had attended bridge lessons together at the Julian Dobson Bridge Club in Parsons Green. At that time I had been much taken with the intelligence and good looks of his wife. Sally Bercow was an obvious candidate for my survival community in Punta Arenas and I knew that Speaker Bercow would welcome an opportunity of getting her off his hands.

I knew, however, that if it was going to work I had to find

congenial company for Sally, now that Senor Allende had been eliminated by President Pinochet. I had noticed the fading popularity of Monsieur Hollande, the President of France, who was having a similar problem with his women. In a spirit of goodwill, entente cordiale and all that, I contacted the President about the two women in his life who had been the cause of his poor showing in the polls. The ravishing Ségolène Royal, who had been his partner for many years and the mother of his four children, was being traduced by the President's new squeeze, Valérie Trierweiler, known in the French press as 'the Rottweiler'.

Valérie Trierweiler is a victim of her own uncertain status. She and Hollande remain unmarried and he is on record as saying he believes marriage is a 'bourgeois' institution. He intended to behave normally. Then Valérie had been the First Lady of France. She seemed incapable of giving her man a simpering kiss in public and performing the often humiliating antics expected of a politician's wife. I wondered whether I could find another attractive lady from this stable, the Elysée, as I had done with Carla.

Monsieur Hollande was delighted when I offered to take one of his women off his hands. He offered me the Croix de Guerre. Anything that could be done to end the spat between his two partners and the ridicule that it caused in the French press would be for the 'Glory of France' and, more important, a recovery of his popularity in the polls.

I chose the ravishing Ségolène Royal, a prominent socialist like Sally, instead of Madame Trierweiler, as she had already held high political office as a presidential candidate in France; she clearly had plenty of spirit and had proved her breeding credentials when she was the President's partner. I also thought that Ségolène would cause less trouble than 'the Rottweiler' in Punta Arenas.

Then all hell broke loose. My friend, the President of France was caught on the back of a scooter with his bodyguard after an assignment with a new lover, a youngish actress called Julie Gayet. Did she have ambitions to be the First Lady of France or was she captivated by the sexual allure of the ageing Monsieur Hollande? Hard to tell. I was not allowed by my wife to express my complete understanding of the President's behaviour. To escape the flummery that surrounded him in the Elysée Palace for the company of a younger squeeze than 'the Rottweiler', seemed entirely 'normal' and 'masculine' behaviour.

The French Press is expressing its horror at the behaviour of the President but if I know any thing of the French electorate, I suspect it will boost Monsieur Hollande's rating in the polls as Mr Berlusconi's bunga bunga parties did for him. At the time of writing this drama of Shakesperian proportions has still to be played out.

The problem with Puntas Arenas was employment; I had to keep the community occupied, otherwise they would be restless and disappear somewhere in Terra del Fuego and revert to savagery like Jemmy Button and Fuegia Basket. I try not to think of Ann Widdecome as Fuegia Basket or Clarkson as Jemmy Button. I visited several dance halls and could set up Ann Widdecombe as the proprietor of a dance studio; this might attract candidates from the South American favelas, where Ann was known to be an international expert, to brush up on the bossa nova, tango and funk carioco.

Carla Bruni-Sarkozy could establish a model agency with Jordan and train up some dusky Chilean maidens as glamour models for employment in New York and other urban centres. She would also be able to record songs with the equally famous Tati Quebra Barraco from Rio de Janeiro. Clarkson could drive noisily up and down the main street and maybe establish a test site on the unmade roads of Patagonia for the Land Rover subsidiary in São Paulo.

Sir Elton was a problem because he had a baby in tow. He assured me, however, that Lady John was good at changing nappies, and he offered to accompany Carla on the piano in the Widdecombe Dance Emporium. Admittedly, Sir Elton and Lady John were unable to breed but they could establish an adoption agency for the abandoned street children from the favelas.

Edwina Currie caused me the greatest difficulty. Carla Bruni-Sarkozy and Lady Emma Hamilton did not want her around. They did not trust her. She had the reputation of selling 'kiss and tell' stories for publicity, and cash. The publicity they understood, but why should she publish books about her former lover, a totally charming and insignificant man who never did any harm to anyone?

Carla had suffered from endless false stories about her private life, and Emma had died in poverty as a result of vile gossip about her platonic relationship with an admiral.

I decided that the best means of occupying Edwina was to promote her as an egg chef in the Punta Arenas synagogue – that should keep her out of trouble.

Lady Emma Hamilton might open a 'Temple of Health' in association with Madame Chuka, as famous in Punta Arenas as Madame Claude had been in Paris. I anticipated recruiting some candidates for the Temple of Health when I passed through Bangkok, on my way to New Zealand.

But somehow the project lacked credibility – and I did not really want to end my life in Punta Arenas on the odd chance that one of Martin Rees's calamities might hit the Northern Hemisphere. Better to look elsewhere.

21

Spitsbergen 80° North

I had recently returned from Punta Arenas, the southernmost town in the world, and I was not impressed. Surely the Northern Hemisphere can do better.

So here I am sitting in the airport lounge in Oslo – ready to catch my flight to Spitsbergen in the Svalbard archipelago; except for a few scientific locations, it is the northernmost inhabited island in the world.

I decided on this voyage of exploration partly to acclimatise myself to the region before I set off for the Northwest Passage. In fact, although we will be cruising along the top of the world from northern Alaska to Greenland, the passage is still very many miles south of Spitsbergen, which is perilously close to the North Pole.

Of course I will fall in love with Stewart Island off the southern tip of New Zealand when I get there, but I still think that the Northern Hemisphere has more to offer than the far south.

I would much prefer to establish my survival community in Spitsbergen rather than Punta Arenas, but my chosen people would never settle down in a place that is in total darkness for half the year, and where hungry polar bears roam the countryside seeking out human flesh; that is when seals are hard to come by.

I am told that on my visit I will always be accompanied by a guide with a rifle, as a defence against hungry polar bears. I arrive at my final destination, a disused radio station some two hours' boating in calm water across the Arctic Sea in a polar Zodiac from

Longyearbyan. The radio station claims to be the world's remotest camp and can only be approached over two days or so in winter by dog sled or snowmobile. No one is allowed out of the door without a rifle. Everyone takes the danger from polar bears very seriously. Earlier in the month a bear had come right into the camp and had gone for the huskies in their cage. It tore down the surrounding wire fence but was driven off by clashing saucepan lids before it wreaked too much damage.

There are believed to be some 3,000 bears in the Svalbard archipelago and they are thriving now that hunting has been banned; but it is clear that they are a continuing and ever present danger. The technique with a charging bear – and they can move much faster than a human being – is to hit the creature in the body and, when it stops and characteristically tries to paw the wound, fell it with a shot to the head. Sounds quite bloodthirsty but a hungry, charging polar bear is not to be trifled with.

Anyhow, I went to chat with one of the Norwegian girls who look after the camp. This was her second season, which lasts from March, when the temperature averages minus 15° Centigrade, to September. The wind chill can take it down to minus 30° Centigrade. Until May the ground is snowbound, and there is a growing activity in winter sports in Spitsbergen including a two-day husky sled safari led by these amazing Norwegian girls over the snow and ice from Longyearbyan to the radio station.

My Norwegian girl is twenty-nine years old and a qualified veterinary nurse, but she says that it is difficult to get a job because her profession is overcrowded. She comes from the south of Oslo, and she is a keen hunter; she does a lot of deer hunting back in southern Norway.

'Do you go out of the door to the adjoining hut?' I ask. 'Never,' she says; 'you can never tell whether a hungry bear is hiding behind a shed and they move extremely fast. I am good with a rifle.

I went everywhere on my visit in a polar Kirkel Zodiac and always in a Hansen immersion suit in case of accident. The suit is said to prolong survival in the polar seas by at least one hour. The Zodiac cruised at thirty-five knots, normally in a calm, oily sea, but when the swell got up it was something of an uncomfortable ride as we banged our way over the waves.

As we set off to see the bird life on the massive cliffs that rose 600 metres straight out of the sea, we passed a pod of beluga whales, which are the only species left the locals can hunt on licence. The bird life was astonishing in its numbers and variety. The guillemot colony was departing south, but the kittiwakes seemed to be perched on the cliffs in their thousands. We saw little auks, puffins aplenty and Arctic skuas, which attacked the kittiwakes as they swerved and dipped to avoid this Arctic predator. When we arrived at a fjord headed by a massive glacier for a picnic lunch, we were mobbed by huge numbers of Arctic tern that dive-bombed us in their characteristic fashion.

The glacier was huge and beautiful. Apart from the glaciers in Greenland, it was much more impressive than anything in southern Chile. Unlike some of the Greenland glaciers, this one was hardly retreating at all. Why? My guide did not explain why the glaciers on the Svalbard archipelago, which covers 60 per cent of the entire area, seem to be reasonably stable. The whole archipelago is about the size of Belgium and Holland put together.

At the foot of the glacier, only one of several we visited, there was quite a community of ring-necked seals lying with their pups on the ice floes that had broken off from the glacier. But no sign of polar bears, which normally hunt seals on the ice edge, not on open land or sea. Sandpipers were feeding all along the sea edge as the tide ebbed and flowed.

Spitsbergen has a fascinating history. As I have mentioned, it may have been discovered by the Vikings, travelling probably from Iceland, but they never settled it in the same way as they settled

Greenland for a few hundred years – that is until the Little Ice Age drove them away. There are stories in the sagas of Norsemen visiting islands in the far north, but there have been no Viking discoveries in the islands. The first acknowledged discovery was made by the Dutchman Willem Barents in 1596. The Russians claim that Pomor hunters from Arctic Russia hunted and partially settled here in the summer months in an earlier century, but again there is no real evidence of the dates.

Willem Barents discovered Spitsbergen as a result of faulty navigation in his attempt to find a northern passage to Asia across the top of Russia. His visit was part of the general attempt by the Dutch and the English to find a northern passage to China and India.

Whatever the arguments about who were the earliest discoverers, the fact remains that even in earlier medieval times large parts of Europe were familiar with products from walrus hunting, blubber oil, walrus tusks and leather, so much so that the walrus community was reduced to near extinction.

By the seventeenth and eighteenth centuries whaling in Spitsbergen waters had become a major industry; thousands of men from hundreds of ships were engaged in the catching, processing, sale and shipping of the product in Europe, and many of them are buried on remote islands in the archipelago. By 1610 the English were conducting the trade in blubber oil through the Muscovy Company, founded in 1553 to trade in northern areas and especially with Russia. In 1612 Henry Hudson, the great navigator of Arctic waters, found Dutch and Spanish whalers in Svalbard and turned them away, claiming exclusive rights for the English for their hunting grounds. Reports indicate that every bay in Spitsbergen was teeming with Greenland whales. The Dutch appointed the famous jurist Hugo Grotius, really the founder of the international law of the sea as we know it today, to pronounce on entitlement, and he, hardly surprisingly, said that whaling should be free to anyone who wanted to trade. The English despatched a naval task force to police the trade, but eventually a sort of tenuous truce was arrived at – and over the years it led to the internationalisation of the trade, leading right up to 1920 when Norwegian authority of the Svalbard archipelago was agreed by treaty but granting all neighbouring nations, Russia in particular, the right to exploit its resources.

Here I must tell of the experience of William Scoresby, a rather great Englishman. His father was born near the booming whaling port of Whitby, Yorkshire, and made a fortune in the Arctic whale fishery. Scoresby made his first voyage to the Arctic at the age of eleven. After leaving school he joined his father's whaler, *Resolution*, as Chief Officer, and in 1806 succeeded in reaching 81° North, the northern tip of Greenland, the highest northern latitude attained for several years to come. The next year he began his study of meteorology and wrote a book, *An Account of the Arctic Regions and the Northern Whale Fishery*, which as a classic of English literature can stand proud with Macaulay and Gibbon. He made several whaling expeditions to Spitsbergen and wrote about its history. He was shipwrecked in the ice in his ship, the *Esk*, but was rescued and was able to complete his last voyage in 1822, surveying the east coast of Greenland.

He then went to Cambridge, took his degree, became a Doctor of Divinity and joined the Church. He continued with his scientific works, which included studies of the magnetic North Pole, and became a fellow of the Royal Society.

Why, when the cod fishermen of Newfoundland and the whalers from Hull and Whitby knew these Arctic waters like their own, did the Admiralty never ask them to explore the Northwest Passage?

The only surviving industry in Spitsbergen is mining for coal. Before the coal industry took off in the 1920s the only activity, apart from the whaling, which was largely exhausted by 1800, was hunting and trapping for fur.

Before polar bear hunting was banned in 1976, the Russians in particular wintered in Svalbard to hunt polar bears, Arctic foxes and seals. However, the work of a trapper no longer pays well, primarily because of the low prices on the fur of the polar fox. The other animal that was hunted ruthlessly is the Svalbard reindeer. There are still a good number of wild reindeer, but hunting reduced them, until it was banned, except on licence.

The sedimentary rocks in several areas of Svalbard are rich in fossils. They provide evidence about conditions in earlier geological epochs. It is clear from fossil finds that vegetation was far more luxuriant than might be expected at such a northerly latitude, but it supports the theory of the so-called continental drift which indicates that Svalbard moved northwards from the Equator some 350 million years ago, and it explains the prolific coal seams which are thought to have been laid down 150 million years ago from organic material somewhere off the coast of Western Europe. There should be oil, but none has been discovered; interest now focuses on the continental shelf forming the bottom of the adjacent shallow-ocean Arctic areas. The coal industry has had its ups and downs. There are only two mines still working, one by the Norwegians near Longyearbyan and another by a Russian mining community of some 350 persons. But everywhere you see the derelict consequences of earlier mining. It is thought that the cost of shipping the coal has made the mining uneconomic.

I met a group of permafrost scientists in our camp who were just starting their annual research into the state of the ground in the immediate area. The head of the team, a rather fierce looking lady from the university in Longyearbyan, said that the permafrost layer was the 'warmest' in the northern latitude. The top layer of about half a metre thaws and re-freezes every winter, but the lower layer, which has existed for millions of years, is diminishing very slowly. I had a brief exchange with one of the team, a Scottish engineer, who said that we were in an inter-glacial period of climate change and the issue was whether the climate could flip over quite quickly either way, and whether the speed of change would enable the world to adapt in time. Had the change already gone too far to enable modern technology and engineering to deal with the carbon explosion, I asked? He thought not. The problem would certainly be greatly increased if the permafrost in Arctic Russia, which was highly organic in Siberia, reduced at a rate whereby it could release large quantities of methane into the atmosphere. This would have a serious reinforcing influence and would be hard to check.

We discussed recent research that indicated that the sulphates released by the Chinese coal-fired power stations, whose numbers had doubled in the past ten years, were thrusting the warm air back into the stratosphere and masking average global temperatures, which have not increased in the past fifteen years or more. It has the same impact on world climate as the super-volcanoes of the past. The problem was that these released sulphates were a temporary protection while the carbon had long-term adverse effects on world climate.

The more I travel in the far north, whether it is in Iceland, Norway or Spitsbergen, the more I ask myself this question: wouldn't it be better to breed with a Viking girl to produce a clean, blond, outdoor-loving set of descendants, rather than with a raddled group of celebrities? What is this stupid notion of mine to take a group of ego-driven, publicity-seeking, poxy celebs from the old world to the far corners of the earth? Better to die among my own Viking cousins from Martin Rees's menu of disasters than live miserably in Punta Arenas, or have a long and slow decline from utter boredom in a southern outpost of New Zealand. After all, although I love New Zealand and its rugged people, the place is always closed. On my several visits I have come away convinced the New Zealanders live in a place which has no opening hours. It is permanently closed – or that's the feeling anyway.

But back to these Norwegian women – Martha, Linda, Camilla – they were all so quiet, well-mannered, self-contained, open, fresh and genuine that I cannot imagine why lonely men seek the company of women from the Philippines and Thailand. Of course a Norwegian girl, well-educated and full of initiative, is hardly likely to be an obedient slave to any man. Perhaps I am deluded by always meeting frontier types in Iceland and Norway. There must be something in the character of a girl who seeks out the rigours and harshness of a frontier town.

Look at Martha. She collected me in a disastrously derelict van and drove me five miles or so outside Longyearbyan to her kennels. There, with another Norwegian girl, she looked after ninety huskies, big, strong dogs that can travel on the ice for ten hours a day with only short stops for water. When guiding travellers on winter safaris, Martha and her friend can spend days away in the harshest conditions and remain cheerful and generous throughout. We only took a team of six huskies on a short trip, but to see the excitement of the dogs and the strength needed by Martha to harness these animals, thrilled at the thought of exercise, was quite an education. It was a fitting final morning before I took a flight via Tromsø and Oslo back to London.

22

Bangkok

Oh gentleman, Sir, Miss Pretty Girl welcomes you Sultan Turkish Bath, gentle, polite, massage, put you in dreamland with perfume soap. Latest gramophone music. Oh, such service. You come now! Miss Pretty Girl want you, massage you from tippy-toe to head-top, nice, clean, to enter Gates of Heaven.

Somerset Maugham, 'The Gentleman in the Parlour', London, 1930

I am on my way to Stewart Island, off the southern coast of New Zealand. Apart from the odd weather station in the Campbell and Auckland islands, this is the closest I can get to Antarctica.

Long ago, I learnt one lesson. If you have to pass through Bangkok on the way to some other destination, there is only one 'must'. You arrive stressed out after a twelve-hour flight from Heathrow on BA Business Class. Escape from modern travel, airports, fellow passengers, tourists, and particularly white perspiring businessmen, is an urgent necessity.

I had a young high-net-worth, upwardly mobile City banker in the adjoining bunk, but we did not exchange a civil word. He scowled at me, a geriatric grey-haired pensioner, not worth a networking minute, and I scowled at him, an overpaid, arrogant puppy lacking any civilised qualities except the squalid urge to earn his City bonus. I later learnt that his name was Dave.

However I felt a minor twinge of conscience as we organised

ourselves for disembarkation. Noblesse oblige etc., should not the former chairman of a City bank show some interest, offer some courtesy, to my uninvited sleeping partner from the adjoining bunk? So I asked him where he was headed. 'I am staying at the Oriental Hotel,' he said. 'So am I,' I replied, 'you are welcome to share the hotel limousine that I have ordered.' It was a serious mistake. It was ten o'clock London time. Markets had just opened.

The excerpt at the head of the chapter comes from a story written by Somerset Maugham in 1930, when he was accosted on emerging from the said hotel. Evocative English doesn't get much better than Somerset Maugham's description; nor does Thai-style seduction get much more attractive either.

There are few compensations for the nightmare of the drive from Don Muang airport to the centre of this great city. When I first came here in the 1960s, as an upwardly mobile, overpaid, arrogant puppy earning my City bonus, I too headed for the Oriental Hotel. Bangkok in the 1960s was a vision of hell, unbearable humidity, snarled-up traffic, insufferable exhaust fumes, honking madmen, massive pollution. Forty years later it has changed for the better in some respects. It has become yet another Asian miracle where prosperity abounds but an ancient kingdom, never conquered by Western imperialism, has now entirely surrendered to Western capitalism. The people of Bangkok are slaves to a different master – that is all.

But what is the MUST? You have to stay in the Oriental Hotel on the banks of the Chao Phraya River. Only the Splendido in Portofino can beat it, in a race for the greatest hotel in the whole wide world. You emerge from the horrors of a modern city, growing at some exponential rate, into an old-fashioned haven of peace and tranquillity, from the squalor and bustle of an international airport into the incredible cleanliness and freshness of this unique hotel. Every few steps a beautiful Thai girl in immaculately pressed Thai costume flashes you a lovely smile and, hands clasped in greeting, welcomes you with the faintest bow.

So, the limousine from the Oriental Hotel awaited me holding a placard saying Monsieur Jean Nut. I am he. My sleeping partner had no baggage, except for one of those folding canvas bags that holds one pressed suit, two shirts, toothbrush, condoms and the other necessary accoutrements for a business stopover. It was slung like a parcel across his shoulder and no sooner had we stepped inside this air-conditioned carriage than it began to happen.

Ting-a-ling, ting-a-ling – Beethoven's Symphony No. 6 filled the car. 'Hi, yes, on the road. What's doing with markets mate? Great. Forty, yes. Sorry. No. Dunno. You're breaking up. Ring back.' Ting-a-ling, ting-a-ling. Beethoven. 'Cheers, mate. Hang on a sec. Lovely. Nah. How much? Do it. Cool. See ya. What. Can't be right. Wait. Try ten thousand. I'll wait. Yes, six-fifty bid. You're kidding. Ring back. On way to centre. What's her name again? OK. How many? Two. Great. Cool. Conference call. What time. Christ. Tokyo. Call back, arrived.'

God, the awful man, I think. How could I have given him a lift? We part in the hotel lobby with a friendly goodbye. And I thank my lucky stars that I shall never set eyes on him again. As on every previous occasion, I don't know why, I am upgraded into a suite overlooking the river and I collapse upon the bed, savouring the frangipani in a little vase, a bowl of fruit and a book advertising the more exotic services provided for oriental pleasure.

I decide to patronise the Health Club across the river. A fleet of motorised sampans criss-cross the River Styx to what the expectant passenger anticipates will be a session of heavenly sin. 'Miss Pretty Girl welcomes you Sultan Turkish Bath. Massage put you in dreamland with perfume soap etc., etc.' The Health Club is certainly like none other. It is rich with acres of sandalwood floors, walls and ceilings which give out a sweet relaxing perfume. The architecture is traditional Thai with hidden gardens, silent pools, gravel paths and silence everywhere. No one, absolutely no one, inhabits this silent heaven:

In Xanadu did Kubla Khan
A stately pleasure dome decree.

There is a reception desk inhabited by an enormously elegant lady of middle years, who enquires what pleasure sir requires. Sir would like a massage, please, to relax sir after the flight from London. We have twenty different types of massage, the lady says – you can have a Japanese, Swedish, Burmese, Abyssinian, Vietnamese, Mongolian, Finnish, Amazonian, Nigerian, Russian but I don't advise a Russian, Indonesian; I interrupt her very politely, or so I hope, because she is clearly an aristocratic lady, probably a cousin of the King with a first-class honours degree from Oxford. I will have a Thai massage, I say, not knowing the error of my choice.

Tinkle, tinkle, tinkle, the aristocratic lady rings a little bell and as from nowhere there appears a young angel, so pretty and slender that you would think a puff of wind would knock her down. How is it possible, I wonder, that such a delicate little waif immaculately clad in the whitest, cleanest costume can pass her delicate fingers across a horrible old man like me. Oh, the anticipation is almost too wonderful to bear. 'You come now, Miss Pretty Girl want you, massage you from tippy toe to head top, nice clean, to enter Gates of Heaven.'

So I am led away to a luxurious cubicle where I am invited to take off my clothes, have a shower if sir would like it and then lie face down on a massage table with a towel across my bottom, not a pretty sight. I follow her instructions while she absents herself. I begin to wonder if this joint is not a whiff too high class for me. But I dream about those delicate little fingers, smoothing themselves across my crinkly, wrinkly skin.

Then it begins. My little flower returns. The first pressure of those little fingers into my sagging flesh is agony. She prods, she digs, she pushes, she pressures my body as if I were a lump of dough. These delicate fingers have the power and persistence of a pneumatic drill. This is no heavenly sin; this is a transport into Hell... Her fingers, her arms, her strength is akin to the seventeen-stone Russian shot-putter who won gold at the Athens Olympics. I lie there utterly exhausted but don't dare say a word because, however great the agony of it all, I don't want to offend my pretty flower. She might lose her job. Satan forbid that I would jeopardise her career. When it is all over I climb off the rack, my head spinning, and collapse into a chair. Pretty flower smiles sweetly at me; she is proud of what she has achieved. My God, she is pretty but a fiend.

Around lunchtime, still suffering from trauma, I am collapsed in the lobby sipping a whisky sour, when who should appear but my young sleeping partner from the BA flight. He approaches me with a revolting bonhomie, rather like the sort of welcome that you get from an acquaintance in a suburban golf club. 'How are you?' I say, praying that he will not seat himself beside me, but of course he does. A great smile spreads across his face. 'I have had a sensational time,' he says. 'What about you?' I tell him about my visit, across the River Styx where I was directed by St Peter (the aristocratic lady in disguise) into a torture chamber run by Saddam Hussein where the torturer was disguised as a pretty little flower.

'God,' he says in a patronising way, 'why do you have one of those Thai things? They are part religion and part pain. A Thai massage is to be avoided at all costs. What you should have,' he says 'is a Bangkok-style Bath and Soap massage.' I am interested.

'Ting-a-ling. Ting-a-ling' Beethoven's No. 6 again. 'Hi, Trevor. Great. Two. Yes. Really cool. Camilla. Nah. Butterfly. Love. Remembers you. Cool. Ha! Ha! Hollywood. FTSE. Down. Nah. Tiny little tits. You're kidding. Shell. Buy. Sell BP. Nah. Soap. Yeah.

Soap. Yeah. Ha! Ha! Coke. Nah. Drink. No wait. Thirty-nine kilos. Less. Brazilian. Yeah. Giggle. Yeah. How much? Great. Caio. See you. Tokyo. Cheers, mate. Gotta go.' Click, shutdown.

When this is over and I catch the drift, I ask, 'What is a Bath and Soap massage?' 'You don't know?' he says. 'I thought every City type came to Bangkok on business to get a Bath and Soap. You've come all this way for a Thai massage, you must be joking.' I feel marginally humiliated, but curious all the same.

Ting-a-ling. Ting-a-ling. Beethoven. 'Hi, mate. Thai Railways. Nah. Phuket construction. Tomorrow. Butterfly free. Tonight. A thousand baht. Prefer dollars. FTSE up. Yeah. Dow down. OK buy. Nah sell. Up yours too, mate. Pretty flower. Soap. Off balance sheet. Why not?'

'Can we concentrate on Bath and Soap for a moment?' I suggest. 'Sorry, mate, have to keep in touch, you know the form. Emails chase you around the world. Get calls. Market is up. Always happens when I'm here. Hard work in Bangkok. Work hard, play hard, you know what I mean. Ha! Ha! Yes, of course, they take any age, the older the better, less hassle. You'll be fine. Don't worry. Saw an old Japanese, must have been ninety. The girls are not particular. But one word of advice, never choose a pretty girl. They are tough. The old ones know the form, have to try harder and want to please.'

'Thank you,' I say, 'but what actually happens at Bath and Soap?' 'You don't know?' he says. 'It's all on the internet. Where's your laptop? Haven't you got one with you? God. How do you survive? I get over a hundred emails each day. Mostly joking. Taking the piss, that sort of thing. Always copy jokes to Alice on the next dealing booth. She keeps a record. Nice girl, Alice, big tits, unlike Camilla and Butterfly at Bath and Soap.'

'Well, the thing about Bath and Soap,' he says, 'is that everyone has a splendid time. It's not like a Jacuzzi in Holmes Place which is a single-sex experience and very boring. In the unisex Bangkok version there is more giggling, steam, laughter, soap, bubbles and general entertainment that you would ever get back home.

'I have never been invited to a Buckingham Palace investiture or a Lord Mayor's Banquet, but Charlie, our head dealer, who got the MBE last year, tells me that he would swap either experience for a Bath and Soap any day.'

Ting-a-ling, ting-a-ling. Beethoven. 'It's my partner,' he says, and snaps the infernal machine shut.

'When you arrive,' he carries on, 'you are ushered into a big foyer and all up one wall there are rows and rows of giggling, chattering girls behind a glass window with numbers on their chests. You choose a number and, hey presto, number forty-two appears from nowhere, takes your hand and leads you into a room with a large bath and a tiled floor. Charlie told me that two girls are less exacting as they keep each other entertained, so I selected number eighty-five as well. I would advise you, at your age, to go for the two-girl option.'

Naturally I am tremendously shocked at this story. I am easily shocked, of course. 'Do you realise?' I say, 'that you are participating in the sex trade? In my day respectable young bankers like you always set a good example to foreigners, stiff upper lip, fly the flag, show how the Brits behave etc., etc. How do you expect to do business abroad if your behaviour is discovered?

'Well,' says my sleeping partner from the BA flight, 'I would never do any business at all in the Far East unless I did Bath and Soap with my Thai clients and Kee Sang parties in Seoul with my Korean friends. Anyhow, as far as I can see the girls are free to come and go as they please. If they were exploited in the way you say why would everyone have such uproarious fun? Is it all invented?

'Grow up,' he says, 'would the girls have more fun planting paddy or sitting all day in front of a screen with a hundred other Oxbridge graduates in Canary Wharf? My man,' he says in an insulting way, 'you don't know what slavery is like until you have sat in a dealing room in London with a hundred other sods. No right-minded girl would swap the Bath and Soap profession in Bangkok for a dealing room in Canary Wharf. After six months in front of a screen, we lose all our best girls, particularly those with first-class honours degrees, to lap-dancing in Puss in Boots and Spearmint Rhino.' Who would want to work for Americans in Morgan Stanley or Goldman Sachs when you can earn more money and have more fun in a London club?'

I can see that I am at the losing end of this discussion, so I ask him, 'What happens next in Bath and Soap?' 'Oh,' he says, 'an old bag comes in with drinks on a tray, we have a chat in pigeon English and then everyone takes off their clothes and piles into the bath. Huge giggles, much splashing around, head massage etc., until the old bag returns with a rubber mattress, lays it on the tiled floor and covers it with washing-up liquid, or some other soapy concoction. We climb out of the bath and Camilla gives me a massage by sliding up and down my soapy body. It is not exactly erotic, but it's much more pleasant than your Thai thing.'

'What would your wife, or should I say your partner, have to say about all that?' I ask. 'Oh, I tell her all about it,' he replies, 'but she doesn't want to waste the washing-up liquid so I have to come to Bangkok now and again, on business you see. Times move on. Anyhow, my partner has a moonlighting job in Puss in Boots in the evenings and she is not a bit fazed about taking off her clothes. I can understand it if you don't approve of our lifestyle, but your Dave Cameroon knows that he has to "connect" with people like us. He understands our modern lifestyle and we will probably vote for him.'

By this time I am really taken with Dave, my sleeping partner from the BA flight. The age gap between us has led to all sorts of misunderstandings. I like his lifestyle, too. I am so glad to have met him that I offer to set him up in Patagonia where, with modern communications, he can trade in Treasury strips and Japanese warrants just as easily in Punta Arenas as in Canary Wharf. He has also offered to recruit a team from Bath and Soap to staff my proposed health clinic and unisex spa. I shall exercise my seigniorial rights of course when I inaugurate the Punta Arenas Bath and Soap. The initial launch will obviously involve a team of celebrities. However, Jordan and her new spouse and Elton John with his civil partner will be joining me in Patagonia, so I anticipate substantial revenues from the *Daily Mail* and Channel 4.

23

A Gay Hostel

Last time I was in Sydney, with a weekly pass that took me everywhere on trains, ferries and buses, I had set off north on a journey of adventure. I wanted to get out of the city to see suburbia and the rather beautiful sea inlets which carve into the coast north of Sydney. So I took the train north and alighted at a suburban station. It is a delightful spot with a busy marina, the odd commercial fishing boat, a post office and the odd café or two selling seafood. By the time I had seen around this little community it was six o'clock in the evening and, as I had brought my little haversack, I thought I might find somewhere to stay the night. The local store said that there was nowhere much to stay, but I could try a largish house at the top of the hill. 'I don't know what you will think of it,' they said, 'but there is really nowhere else.' They wished me the best of luck, with the faintest smile I thought, but sent me on my way.

I tramped to the top of the hill and found a largish house in a very good position overlooking the estuary. The proprietor said that he was pretty full, but that there was still one bedroom available if I would like to take it. I therefore checked into a comfortable room with a large double bed and was shown a sarong and slippers in case I wanted to use the pool. I was hot and sticky, so, donning my rather flimsy sarong, I climbed the stairs and introduced myself to the other guests; three couples – two girls together from Adelaide, two youngish men from Sydney and two rather more elderly men from Fort Lauderdale in Florida.

I noticed that all four men were wearing similar rather skimpy costumes as they lay around the pool. The costumes were somehow all made in identical style, but were of differing colours of the rainbow. The men were all reading magazines with titles like *Flesh, DNA, Blue* and *Jock* as they thumbed through them in a desultory way. I did notice from some distance that the cover of each magazine seemed to contain young lads also in the same skimpy-type costumes, with bare, shiny chests and wide come-hither smiles. Then the Americans climbed into the pool, took off their costumes, threw them on the side and started embracing one another. I even saw one American apparently kiss the other.

It began to dawn on me that I had intruded on a hostelry for gays and, testing the water, I turned to one of the girls beside me and asked her very politely if she would mind if I discarded my sarong and had a swim as well. 'Not a bit of it,' she said, with a very friendly smile. I thought her rather large lady partner looked at me in a rather sullen way, but she too raised no objections – although my request seemed to raise her from a sort of mid-afternoon stupor and she grabbed her girlfriend's hand and started stroking it.

I am going to see this whole thing through I thought. I had never been in a gay hostelry before, but I anticipated that it would be enjoyable and very educational. I have a late developing interest in education of various kinds. By the time the proprietor's partner had joined us – he was a bank manager in the local town – it was suggested that we should all gather together at six o'clock for tapas and drinks before a barbecue. Everyone disappeared to change and shower. Was I nervous? Yes. I could not quite imagine how the evening would develop, not least because I had been told, even warned, that gay people were very promiscuous.

Anyhow, on gathering for drinks, everyone was in a very gay mood; or should I say in a very cheerful mood? They could not have been nicer or more polite to me, a simple stranger who had arrived out of nowhere into their company, but I was conscious that, in due course, I would be subjected to an interrogation as to my nationality, reason for being in this particular hostelry, my sexual predilections and other personal details which I had not the slightest intention of disclosing. I scented danger and I knew that I was on my own. Self-preservation was the watchword.

The girls asked for beer, which they drank out of the bottle, but all the men requested white wine in a glass. One of the Sydney guys announced that he liked red wine, 'but it turned him wild and uncontrollable', so he gave it a miss whenever he could resist it. Small talk about the weather, the heat of the pool, the next day's activities and general pleasantries took us through the drinks session without incident.

As soon as we sat down to the barbecue, however, without more ado the conversation quickly dissolved into a discussion about human sexuality. The more elderly of the two Americans had studied biology at Harvard, but had quickly been diverted into the profession of itinerant lecturer into the corners of human sexuality. He was clearly a very great expert on the subject, showing himself to be a master of Masters & Johnson, the definitive study of human behaviour. He wanted us all to know about his lectures and gave us a vivid description of the demonstrations, exhibits and visual aids with which he spiced his lectures. He was not very amusing, but he thought his rather disgusting stories were extremely entertaining; he laughed loudly at his own anecdotes and jokes, so we all laughed with him. I laughed very loud indeed, as I was very nervous that my sexual predilections would be discovered.

The young, prettier of the two girls aged thirty-four – her girlfriend was forty-four – was tremendously impressed by the academic-type distinction of the itinerant lecturer and announced that she was just finishing her Master's in psychology at Adelaide University, but she was shortly going to move to Brisbane to read for her Ph.D., also in human sexuality. Her future provoked great interest among the dinner guests and there was universal agreement that the world had cast off its inhibitions in the sixties, seventies and eighties to bring us into a much happier, freer, liberal world but that, horror of horrors, the student community had now become boringly conservative and really showed very little interest in sexual issues. The American deplored the fact that his lectures, once packed by avid listeners, were now all but deserted. Everyone made sympathetic and expressed great concern at the disapproving nature of the young.

Very foolishly, I piped up and advanced the theory that young people had so much sex on the internet that it was hardly surprising they were not entranced by lectures on sexual practices, mores, deviations, techniques etc., etc. This observation did not go down at all well and, although everyone remained very charming and friendly towards me, I had a distinct sense that I was being judged as a potential member of the enemy classes – a heterosexual, a straight.

One of the Australians, an airline steward with Qantas, asked me if I had ever slept with a man. The crisis, long anticipated, was upon me. Eight pairs of eyes fixed upon me in anticipation of my answer.

The eyes of the senior female looked particularly menacing. I knew that my integrity as a resident in a gay hostelry was under severe test and I decided that the truth would subject me to unknown torment – and abuse. So, I answered, 'yes, of course, I often sleep with men', although I added that I had in fact been married for forty-three years. I put in this piece of irrelevant information to salve my conscience for having told a whopping lie. It seems that I had more or less surmounted the first obstacle on the assault course because three out of the four men all answered that they had once been married and had slept with a wide variety of women before they had been converted. The younger girl then announced, without invitation, that she had her fair share of men before she had fallen for the attractions of Ruth.

Now Ruth did not raise a smile, but gradually Ruth began to grow on me. She was quite ugly and very butch, but her love for Sarah, the younger girl, was really rather touching. She told us all that she had been supporting Sarah's academic career for the past five years – and the only way she could pay the fees and meet the mortgage was to work the night shift at her factory. She went to work at eleven o'clock at night and came home at seven in the morning. She hated it because Sarah was away at study when she came home and worked in a bar in the evenings to make a contribution to the household expenses.

It slowly dawned on me that all three couples, including the bank manager and my landlord, were in love with one another. They were all very touchy-feely with their partners and exhibited far more affection than I had ever seen at a social gathering of married couples. I thought it was like spending an evening with eight gay bishops, two of them having overcome the furious antipathy of the Synod of the Church of England, to become pioneer Lady Bishops.

The problem was that I found the younger female, Sarah, rather attractive and intelligent, but I knew that if I became too friendly with her her butch lover would thump me – and I found Ruth both endearing but frightening at the same time.

As the evening wore on I felt myself to be more and more of an intruder, a voyeur indulging in an illicit peepshow. When the discussion turned to where to stay in various capital cities around the world, the Qantas air steward being an expert, it became clear that none of them ever stayed in what they described as a 'straight' hotel. To be found in a hotel patronised by 'straights' was a particular embarrassment – evidently they travelled with a particular book which listed all the accredited gay establishments.

This topic brought out all their militancy about their sexuality.

It didn't bother me to find myself in a gay hostel among rather strange and different people, but clearly they seemed to have an instinctive dislike, almost a hatred, of 'straight men and women.' They inhabited a very special world of their own and their contempt and suspicion of straights was very evident. The Americans were the most militant and boasted how Fort Lauderdale had become a sort of Mecca, or gathering place, for the gay community. Gays had abandoned placed like Key West because the cruise lines disgorged a whole lot of cruising people who had intruded on their private world.

One of the Sydney boys, the Qantas airline steward, then recited all the 'mile-high' incidents he had tackled in the Qantas loos. This provoked his partner to tell us about all the extraordinary people he encountered in the condominium he managed in Sydney. You can't believe what all these married people get up to, he said.

He said that as soon as one partner in a marriage went to work all sorts of shocking things went on, the parking lot being a particular favourite place for misbehaviour by straights. He had a very low opinion of heterosexuals generally and their conduct, although all my fellow guests seemed to admit to several same-sex relationships in odd corners, in the backs of cars, in parking lots and Qantas loos. Apparently dissolute behaviour by gays was normal and understood, but similar practices by straights distressed them greatly.

I checked out the next morning to return to the Holiday Inn, a viper's nest of bourgeois straights if ever there was one, but I have to admit that I found the gay hostelry much more interesting, stimulating and intellectually absorbing than the Holiday Inn in Sydney. This may not be surprising. But the crucial difference was that the inhabitants of the Holiday Inn seemed to be gaining limited degrees of pleasure and exhaustion from their tourist antics, but none of the straight couples there seemed to show any genuine warmth and interest in each other. My fellow gay guests on the other hand seemed to be genuinely fond of each other and displayed great affection – almost love – for their partners. It was nice to see; not offensive in the least. They reminded me of an evangelical group of militant Christians who wanted to convert the world to their way of thinking.

24

New Zealand

I can think of nothing, absolutely nothing, to say about New Zealand that is either funny or entertaining. It is just a very quiet, well-organised, rather dull but wholly splendid place with marvellous people. The South Island seemed rather private but beautiful, except for Christchurch, rather as I imagine England must have been before I was born. The North Island is more commercial and it is where I went to stay the previous year; around Hawkes Bay, it is a marvel of vineyards and orchards, evident prosperity and class. But I am in the south.

Ron spent Sunday slaughtering sheep for his landlady, an elderly farmer's widow in Springs Junction, an isolated hamlet in the Southern Alps of New Zealand. He cut their throat, hoisted them up on the tractor's forklift, skinned and gutted them and then put them straight in the widow's deep freeze for the winter.

Ron was one of nature's gentlemen. He had never had a regular job. He had been a fisherman in the Chatham Islands between New Zealand and Antarctica, as well as a logger, and had worked in a slaughterhouse and on several farms as a hand. Now, during the summer months, he was a fishing guide. I decided that if I was ever to be in a slit trench in a nasty bloody punch-up, Ron was the sort of man I would like beside me. Although he had no compunction about killing an animal for food, he was devastated when we hit a chaffinch on the road to the river. We stopped the car to see if we could find and help it. On the river he hated to see a bumble bee floating upside down and a great smile spread across his face when he successfully waded out to rescue it. As we stalked a big trout, we were visited by a bush robin, a fat little bird with a white breast and a black head that had this amazing friendliness towards man. We had to break off fishing so that Ron could demonstrate the remarkable instincts of these birds. He lit a little twig with his lighter, we stepped back, and, sure enough, the robin came along, shook the stick and put out the flame, making sure that the fire did not spread in the bush. Ron was St Francis of Assisi disguised as a slaughterer. He was monosyllabic, but he helped me over boulders, through impenetrable scrub and beech forests, held me in fast water, pulled me up and down cliffs and mountains, changed my fly and advised me what to do. I had not had such childish attention since I parted from my Gurkha orderly in the jungles of Malaya sixty years ago.

I was staying at a place called the Western Rivers Lodge, in the central spine of the South Island, somewhere between Christchurch and Nelson. We fished the Grey, Boyle and Lewis rivers. My host, Barry, and his partner Ali, had looked after me last year, and I had crossed the world a second time, partly to fish in those wonderfully clear NZ streams, but also to admire the company of men like Ron and Barry. I will desist from describing my fishing experiences, the big trout and screeching reels – they are hardly interesting, even for the aficionados. More interesting are the men. Barry had two passions. Clearly, like all country people living in the wilderness, it was the rivers, streams and mountains, the glaciers, the sun, the moon and the stars that transfixed him – and the extraordinary understanding that goes with living next to nature was what made the man.

I have experienced it before, but only in the company of ghillies and stalkers, whose conversation can often be riveting because these people have the time to contemplate, speculate, muse, ponder and understand. Barry had a wisdom that one's country forefathers possessed, but which millions living in towns have lost; even worse, they have never known that such wisdom existed.

Barry's other passion was exploration. His lodge was hung with photographs of *Endurance* caught in the Antarctic ice, pictures of Elephant Island, of the little sailing boat – the *James Caird* – that took Shackleton eight hundred miles from Elephant Island to South Georgia in its rescue mission for the crew of *Endurance*. The explorers, James Cook, James Weddell, Robert Scott, Ernest Shackleton, Ronald Amundsen, Richard Byrd, the whalers and the early navigators were all his heroes. But his greatest hero was Frank Worsley, a New Zealander from Christchurch. He was the man who navigated the little *James Caird* over hundreds of miles across the worst ocean in the world to land at a chosen bay on South Georgia – and then with Shackleton and one other companion to climb the mountains of South Georgia in their desperate but ultimately successful attempt to reach the whaling station at Grytviken. When the crew of *Endurance* had been rescued, Worsley returned to the First World War, won a DSO when sinking a U-boat in 1917 and then a second DSO fighting the Bolshevik army in Russia. He did a little spirit-running into North America, searched for Inca gold off Costa Rica – and then, possibly one of the great navigators of the century, he became redundant. No one would offer him a job.

When I told Barry that I was planning the following year to go on an Antarctic cruise to South Georgia and Elephant Island, he was quite overwhelmed with enthusiasm on my behalf. 'Why can't you get me on board as a lecturer?' he said. I commented that he knew more about the men who set out to meet these challenges, challenges which made and broke the heroes of the times, than all the professors who would accompany the boat, but how could I help? I couldn't do so.

When my week with Barry and Ron came to an end, I decided to travel as near to Antarctica as I could get. There were no flights to the Campbell and Auckland islands and a sea voyage would take too long. So I set off for Stewart Island. Here I had a great experience. For the first time in my life, out in a boat, I saw the wandering albatross, which can live to the age of eighty – and has a wingspan ten feet across. Two albatrosses glided around our boat with a grace and beauty that could only be equalled by a prima ballerina dancing the White Swan.

I remember being taught at school 'The Rime of the Ancient Mariner' by Coleridge:

At length did cross an albatross
Through the fog it came
As if it had been a Christian soul
We hailed it in God's name.

The Ancient Mariner shot the albatross with his crossbow: 'God save thee Ancient Mariner from the fiends that plague these times'.

I am going to enjoy my time in Stewart Island. Is this the place to end my days, away from all the dangers, pollution and endless scares in the country of my birth?

25

Stewart Island

When I heard of the Christchurch earthquake on 22 February 2011, I wondered whether my adventure to the end of the Southern Hemisphere made sense. Here was I in the South Island of New Zealand to investigate as part of my survival project, only to learn that one hundred buildings had been destroyed and there had been more than 2,500 earth tremors over the proceeding year. My hotel lay in ruins. My trip to Punta Arenas had also proved a failure. Would I not be safer in Spitsbergen, the most northerly island in the world, within reach of the North Pole, rather than these southern extremities of New Zealand and Chilean Patagonia? However, I had been invited to fish in Invercargill, the most southerly town in New Zealand, so I decided to keep to my Southland programme.

The area around Invercargill, now a Scots enclave, had first been visited by European sailing ships in the late 1700s and by the whalers around 1830. The Maoris had been there six hundred years earlier and had established themselves at Bluff on the coast, which is at the head of a storm-tossed channel called the Foveaux Strait. Across the strait lies Stewart Island. I had to investigate Stewart Island because, apart from the small population in the Chatham Islands, it was the nearest populated island to Antarctica, hence its interesting history as a base for the whaling ships. Captain Cook had seen the island but mapped it as a peninsula in an appendage to New Zealand proper.

I flew from Invercargill to Stewart Island in a very small, cramped aircraft, a Britten-Norman Islander, with six other passengers. It was a short hop across the Southern Ocean as we were buffeted by the heavy storms for which the Foveaux Strait is famous. The Strait is well down in the infamous Roaring Forties.

Stewart Island has great beauty with most of the island in a primeval state, forest-clad to the water's edge. It is about forty-five miles across from coast to coast with a large bay called Paterson Inlet, which gave sanctuary to the whale chasers in the nineteenth century, the small boats that caught the whales down in the Antarctic seas and remained there for overhaul in the winter. Seventeen chasers had their base in the local shipyard.

The chasers were the real rovers of the world's oceans. Their task was to hunt and capture animals that were up to fourteen times the size of an elephant. The whaling ships were under 120 feet in length and, between 130 to 250 tons, hardly bigger than a blue whale which might average 80 feet and weigh 100 tons. Killing a blue whale was an intensely hazardous business. We can detest the cruelty and greed of the whaling fleets but we cannot ignore the bravery of the men who manned the chasers, liable to be dragged under water with their boat as the whale plunged deep into the sea, or be smashed by its lashing tail.

In the 1920s, much later than the early expeditions, Paterson Inlet became the Norwegian Antarctic Ross Sea Whaling Company's refitting base and coaling depot for their fleet of whale chasers. After the season the mother ships went home to Europe with the whale oil, leaving the chasers on Stewart Island. The Norwegian fleet, comprising five Norwegian factory ships and one British, made nine expeditions to the Ross Sea in Antarctica.

The depletion of whale numbers in the South Atlantic through overexploitation led to the decline of South Georgia and the transfer of activity to the Ross Sea. However, by 1932 there was a glut of whale oil on the market and a worldwide recession led to the closure of the base in Paterson Inlet. Bits of old iron and derelict quays are all that remain.

Many families on Stewart Island, with its population of around five hundred, are of part Maori descent, for in the whaling days in the nineteenth century the whalers came ashore and married the local Maori girls. Scotsmen who settled there named many of the coves from memories of the Highlands and Oban became the main settlement. Two dozen Shetlanders settled in the port but even they found the place so remote that they departed after a few years for civilisation in Invercargill.

It is difficult to capture the spirit of these remote places without recourse to the personal memories of those who lived there or visited them. There are several books about Stewart Island and its natural history, archaeology and ornithology but I could find no descriptions of what it was like in the whaling days until I contacted a resident, a friend called Bruce Storey. He was the person who took me out on the fishing trip mentioned at the end of the last chapter and with whom I stayed on my visit. 'You must read the *Foveaux Whaling Yarns of Yankee Jack*,' he said. I tried everywhere to obtain a copy but it was unavailable on the second-hand market and, unusually, there was no copy in the British Library. Bruce kindly sent me his copy from New Zealand.

Why Yankee Jack? Because in the nineteenth century the British government offered money for whaling in order to contribute to the training of seamen for the Royal Navy – and it enticed Americans to join the whaling fleet. It also wanted cargoes for the convict ships on their return to England. Many of the men in the whaling ships were escaped convicts from Australia and it was a rough and dangerous trade. An advertisement in a Sydney paper on 9 April 1809 read:

Wanted immediately 6 seaman for the ship Pegasus about to proceed to the River Derwent and from there on a sealing voyage, after which to England… sailed with provisions and upwards of 50 male prisoners on board to be distributed among the settlers removed from Norfolk Island thither.

Mr William Stewart was the First Officer on board the *Pegasus* and he surveyed the island and the Foveaux Strait. The island seems to be named after him but it is not clear why. He reported that the island was then found to be uninhabited, abounding in wood fit for shipbuilding and all other purposes, containing several excellent harbours and runs of the purest water.

Yankee Jack was born on 25 April 1826 in a poor farming community in Connecticut and at sixteen worked his way to New York with a young friend; there he saw a sign reading 'Whalemen Wanted'. He joined the bark *Tenedos*, one of twenty-one whaleships that left the East Coast of America during 1844. On a three-year voyage the *Tenedos* took 75 barrels of sperm oil, 1,625 barrels of whale oil and 1,400lb of whalebone. The cargo was worth a modest $22,399. Jack was meant to earn a dollar a day but was hardly ever paid and was entitled to a share of one barrel in every two hundred. According to the *Whalemen's Shipping List* the *Tenedos* was only at Stewart Island from February to August 1845, by which time the conditions were so unbearable that Jack deserted at Hobart Town in Tasmania, but was apprehended and served three months on a treadmill rather than return to the ship. During the three months when he earned his nickname as a 'lagger', or convict, he had a miserable time, always hungry and devoured by lice and bedbugs, until he met a Scots deserter 'who de-loused them and let them earn their keep clearing his land'. He then joined another whaler, the *Baltimore* and deserted again at Paterson Inlet, making a successful escape. This is when his adventures on the island and on further whaling trips began. Interestingly, the *Tenedos* eventually went to the popular Arctic whaling grounds around Spitsbergen, about which I have written earlier.

Jack – his real name was Burr Osborn – recorded his story about his time on Stewart Island in a personal memoir that he wrote in his old age. Needless to say it is full of exaggeration and inaccuracy but it is truly authentic. He describes the area around Invercargill and Stewart Island in 1845.

> In the north part [Invercargill] there were a number of settlements made by Whites. They were convicts, ex-convicts and runaway sailors from American whalers. At Stewart Island where I resided nearly all the time there were 42 whites on either side [of the Foveaux Strait] made up of convicts who had escaped New Holland or Van Diemen's Land. They had married native women and were making clearings. There were 6 white men on this island.

Jack's exploits on the island are described in his memoir: fights with the Maoris, escape from the ships' search parties, foraging in the tangled jungle, attacks by feral cattle and kindness from a settler who gave him food in exchange for labour.

But more importantly for this chapter is his description of his whaling exploits around the southern coast and towards Antarctica.

Much of my story in this book takes place in Iceland, Spitsbergen, Arctic Russia and the Canadian Arctic – all of them engaged, and some dependent in earlier times, on the exploitation of the whale, walrus and seal. The products from these rather wonderful animals are numerous and range from the workaday to the exotic: tusks from the walrus and the sea unicorn, the narwhal; whalebone or baleen from the whales mouth used in the making of corsets and for whips; sperm oil used for lubricant, tanning leather and smokeless candles; whale oil for soap, heating and lighting; and, the most valuable, a product taken from the whales' large bowel as ambergris used as an aphrodisiac and a base for perfume. As the population of Europe grew in numbers and wealth from the sixteenth century onwards, so the demand for all these products increased – they became a form of black gold, as valuable as real gold exploited by the Spanish conquistadores of America.

So I conclude this chapter with Yankee Jack's description of a whale hunt. The more sensitive reader should probably skip these paragraphs, but remember that the species known as a 'human' continues its greedy, selfish exploitation of the animal kingdom. Jack describes a whale hunt in 1845:

Well, the second day out we raised a school of sperm whales and lowering our boats, the six man crew pulled directly for the school. The sperm whale is from eight to one hundred and twenty five feet in length. A hundred foot whale will make about one hundred barrels of oil. The old bull whales which are very intelligent keep themselves on sentinel duty on the outskirts of the school while they are feeding – normally on squid. The whale is discovered by its 'spout' when the masthead shouts out 'there she blows'. Care and skill are required in making the approach to the whale before he goes down which he does as soon as he has had his blow out. This is generally accompanied by running the bow of the boat directly upon the animal when the harpoon is buried in his back. As soon as the harpoon is fastened, the command is given 'stern all' and the boat moves rapidly astern till out of reach of the flukes, or tail, which lying flat upon the water, enables him to dive almost instantly. This is a moment of danger. The men and boats are exposed to instant destruction by a violent blow from his flukes. The whale now moves on the surface almost with the velocity of a rail road train, dragging the boat and crew with him. As he 'sounds' going down sometimes to the depth of a mile, the utmost care is required on the part of the crew as the line (attached to the harpoon) is running out. The harpooner stands with a hatchet in his hand, ready to cut the line the moment there is a foul or a kink in the line. In such a case if the rope is not instantly severed the boat and her crew would be drawn to the bottom.

The whales remain down from five to thirty minutes. The longer they remain under water, the greater their exhaustion when they rise. When the animal comes to the surface a lance is used for killing him. In a short time he goes into a death 'flurry'. At this time he lashes the ocean into a foam of blood but sometimes moves about for miles and continues through the day and into the night when the boat's crew have to cut the line and let him go.

The dead whale is then dragged to the mother ship where the blubber is cut from the body, the valuable parts of the body separated, the carcass dismembered and eventually placed in huge potash kettles where it is boiled down to oil.

I warned my readers of the bloodthirsty nature of a mid-nineteenth-century whale hunt which slaughtered hundreds of thousands of whales all over the world to provide oil and other products for the human population. How can I absolve myself from telling this story? This is how. It is hardly mitigation but at least I am having a go.

When I was Secretary of State for Trade I proposed a ban on the export and import of whale products into the EEC, which came to fruition in 1981, as a Commission Regulation No. 3786. This prohibited the use of whale products for commercial purposes throughout the Single Market. Maybe it was not a ban on whaling but it had a major impact on whaling worldwide – the number of whales is now increasing.

So I ended my visit to the Southern Hemisphere. It is time that I returned via Christchurch and Sydney to more familiar ground in the Northern Hemisphere at the other end of the earth. I had found that Darwin's experience in Terra del Fuego more than justified my trip to Patagonia, but the investigation into Punta Arenas as a location for my survival project had proved a total failure. There was nothing to hold a group of TV celebrities like Jeremy Clarkson and Edwina Currie. I think that Ann Widdecombe, a truly adaptable lady, would have been happy dancing away her years in a Punta Arenas bar but the casino man from Barclays Bank, my friend from the BA flight, would have found the time zone inhibiting when it came to gambling depositors' savings in New York, Tokyo and London.

Madame Carla Bruni-Sarkozy, now that her husband is unemployed, needed to return to her earlier career as a Parisian crooner to supplement the household income. Jordan's career had escalated since she won a debate at the Cambridge Union and was now in increasing demand for 'exposures' on ITV2 and Channel 4. Personally, I would have been happy in Punta Arenas so long as there was a Temple of Health nearby run by ladies from the Bangkok Bath and Soap.

It was sad. The concept had been a good one. Nevil Shute had given me the idea of going south as an escape from the menu of calamities illustrated by Martin Rees. I could have located in Stewart Island as an alternative to Chilean Patagonia to breed among the Maori girls, but all the most attractive ones had been snapped up by English convicts and deserters from the whaling fleets in the nineteenth century. I would have been satisfied working out the last days of my life fishing for cod in Bruce Storey's boat – and dreaming of heaven by watching the wandering albatross floating around me above the masthead.

But in the last resort, the idea of locating myself with a survival community in the Southern Hemisphere was a fundamentally selfish act. Surely there was an altruistic way of spending my final days. How could I make a contribution to humanity? The answer is obvious. I must examine how man and animal can adapt to climate change, not by covering the landscape in wind turbines but by working with nature, rather than against it.

I had gathered useful impressions of how man had adapted

and survived in extreme conditions in Greenland, Spitsbergen and Murmansk and now I was shortly to see how man and animal had survived in Alaska and Arctic Canada on my trip along the Northwest Passage. On my visits to Mongolia, Saudi Arabia and Chile I had seen how the camel had diverged in three directions to meet climate change. The Bactrian camel had survived in the subarctic temperatures of the Gobi Desert in Mongolia, while the dromedary camel had adapted to unbearable heat in the deserts of Arabia. The guanaco, the third member of the camel family, had survived in its millions in the Patagonian uplands before man decimated its numbers.

Now I had an opportunity to study how the polar bear would face up to the challenges of the retreating ice. The journey that I shall be making in *The World* along the Northwest Passage would have been impossible a few years ago – and presumably the polar bear, hunting the seal on ice floes, will be threatened, or will it revert over time back to its forbear, the grizzly bear, to hunt on land? What will be the impact of the retreating ice on the whale, walrus, seal and narwhal? Certainly vast areas of the northern oceans had been shut to them by the ice, where no light penetrated the sea and therefore made it devoid of plankton and other life. Would we see whales where none had been seen before the ice retreated?

My forthcoming trip will help me to form a judgement on all these things and, in particular, how the Inuit are adapting to the arrival of Western civilisation with its mining and oil pollution; that is transforming the traditional lifestyles of the Inuit. For the better? Who can say?

It is ludicrously short-term to think of mankind's future in the context of whether average world temperature rises or falls by 3° Centigrade either way. We would not be here if the dinosaurs had not been eliminated sixty-five million years ago. We owe our existence to the extinctions of the past. And why should anyone believe that today's climate is the best climate for mankind? There will be upheavals, migrations, problems, but nothing on the scale that has faced mankind before.

26

Christchurch – Sydney Flight

On the flight back home from Christchurch to Sydney I realised why I love New Zealanders. As I entered the cabin, clutching my boarding card for Economy Class seat 23D, there she was. Six feet tall, definitely with lashings of Maori blood, eyebrows halfway up her forehead, legs like a giraffe's, skirt up to her midriff, high heels the height of the Empire State Building and big Maori boobs bursting out of her black Air New Zealand blouse. Was she a trainee hostess? Was this her first flight, or her last before they dumbed her down to look like an efficient, dowdy attendant, like the rest of them? Surely she would be allocated to Economy Class seat 23D and I could say a few endearing words to her about the comfort of the flight and the tasty salmon and spinach pie that she would hand to me in a cardboard box?

Seat 23D was an aisle seat, allocated to me on the first leg of my flight back to London, and they must have known that I always ask for a window seat, but on this special occasion I was happy with seat 23D for it meant that I could peep at her legs in those Air New Zealand black stockings as she pranced up and down the aisles like a kangaroo.

I recollect being told the story of an innocent young Aussie lad who had never seen the local town, and when he ventured there for the first time he picked up a girl and took her back to his lodgings. She excused herself and went to the bathroom, as girls tend to do; when she returned our Aussie yokel had moved all the furniture to the side of the room: chest of drawers, cupboard, bed and carpets had all been shifted into a pile. 'What on earth have you done that for?' enquired the girl. To which our Aussie country bumpkin replied, 'Well, if it's anything like a kangaroo we'll need all the room that we can get.'

All right, this has very little to do with my flight from Christchurch to Sydney as I stuck my neck out into the aisle to monitor her progress as she offered herself 'body and soul' for the comfort of the passengers on the three-hour journey to an alien culture called Australia. And then disaster struck. She was spoken for! She handed me the spinach and salmon pie in its cardboard box and there, on her long, slim finger was a diamond rock, an engagement ring the size of the Kohinoor.

Could it be true? Surely she had got herself into all this kit, made a silk purse out of the sow's ear that is the Air New Zealand uniform, in order to attract, seduce, capture, entrance a rich, landowning businessman in Business Class, seat 2A, even an elderly English geriatric in Economy Class seat 23D?

Maybe attraction is a mystery between man and woman; just maybe she would prefer an elderly English pensioner in seat 23D to a rich, handsome businessman in Business Class seat 2A. Life is full of surprises and the mysteries of mile-high phenomena are manifold.

Wow! She passed me again a moment ago, wheeling her trolley, flashing her Maori eyes at each passenger from left to right – and a great whiff of perfume – something like kangaroo musk – passed across my sensitive nostrils. And here she was again: back to seat 23D to retrieve my cardboard box with the remnants of about half of my salmon and spinach pie, which I was going to praise.

Then disaster struck again, not for me this time, but for our trainee hostess. Two seats down from me sat a very old man and as she gathered up his coffee cup I caught her eye and she was distracted for a moment. She fumbled with the cup and the coffee dregs fell into the old man's lap, with loud exclamations of surprise and disgust from the nearby passengers. She grabbed a damp cloth from the trolley and bent down to wipe his trousers. Dab, dab. 'Never mind, never mind,' muttered the old ingrate who was obviously enjoying the girl's administrations. As she bent down to finish the job, the trainee hostess's skirt, or what there was of it, rode up to reveal two pink cheeks divided by a red thong. Why couldn't she spill coffee on my trousers, I thought? Dab, dab.

The other end of the trolley was manned by an efficient looking Kiwi in a black skirt and white blouse; she had made no attempt whatsoever to display her charms. She was the back end of the circus horse. She clearly thought her trainee colleague was incompetent and would probably report her to the authorities for her sartorial taste and extravagance. At this point a huge great Kiwi weightlifter-type female pushed herself past the trolley to get to the loo. She was wearing a blue t-shirt on which was emblazoned the slogan 'Don't call me a cowgirl till you see me ride'. This must be the mufti fashion for my beautiful air hostess when she visits her Aussie lover in Sydney – the lucky wretch who gave her the Kohinoor.

27

Admiral Frobisher, the Spanish Armada and His Expedition to Find the Northwest Passage

My grandmother always claimed that we were descendants of Admiral Frobisher who led the first official expedition to explore the Northwest Passage in 1573, hence my desire to travel it. When he was seen off by Queen Elizabeth, it was the first official attempt to find a new way to exploit the treasures of the East without encountering the belligerent Spanish and Portuguese who dominated the southern route to the Pacific, first discovered by Magellan. I describe below Frobisher's unsuccessful attempt to find the passage past Greenland and Baffin Bay. It was never breached until Amundsen made the crossing in 1903–6, more than three hundred years later. It would be remiss, however, not to describe Frobisher's part in defeating the Spanish Armada, which arose ten years after his exploration of the Northwest Passage.

Frobisher and Drake were contemporaries and seafaring privateers who made their fortunes and reputations by robbing Spanish ships on their way back and forth to the Caribbean. They were aggressive and greedy competitors – capitalists before their time. This piratical practice ensured that when King Philip of Spain despatched the Armada to conquer England his fleet was met by skilful seafarers, with a strong contempt for the Spanish. They also knew how the large, lumbering, overgunned Spanish galleons could be outwitted by the more nimble English ships.

It was on 20 July 1588 that the Spanish Armada lay off the Lizard, with the wind south-west. Philip of Spain had ordered the Duke of Medina Sidonia not to provoke the English before he had linked up with the Duke of Parma, who was bringing an invasion party of 17,000 soldiers from the Netherlands to join the 125 Spanish galleons which had 19,000 soldiers on board with 8,000 sailors. As the Armada sailed east from the Lizard it stretched along a front of two miles.

On the same date, Lord Howard of Effingham, Lord High Admiral and notionally in command, together with Drake, beat out to sea and cleverly got in behind the Spanish fleet with the wind to their advantage. Contrary to some local mythology, Drake was never bottled up playing bowls in Plymouth Sound.

There is very little reliable documentation of the sea battle. As in the twentieth century Falklands campaign, the ships' captains were too busy with their commands to record the detail of what happened. Indeed, most information has come from the Spanish records of the battle.

In the first two contacts with the Spanish galleons off Plymouth and Portland Bill, there was little coordination among the English – private initiative was in the ascendant. It was unsatisfactory and Howard decided to order the English fleet to divide into four squadrons. Frobisher in the *Triumph*, the largest ship in the English fleet, was ordered to take the inshore position, Howard and Hawkins stood in the middle and Drake commanded the seaward squadron of the fleet. Even then the squadrons acted independently and there was limited coordination.

In the early stages Frobisher got into deep trouble; Howard had withdrawn, exposing Frobisher to the Spanish ships which moved against Frobisher with four big fifty-gun galleons. Frobisher was in danger but the wind saved him: it shifted to south-south-west, enabling the rest of the English fleet to counterattack. Drake, who had been out to sea, threw himself into the battle – and he was not slow to record how he had rescued Frobisher.

At this stage neither fleet had sunk or crippled its enemy. If anything, the Spanish were in the ascendant because they sailed on to link up with Parma. On the other hand the Spanish had not been able to secure the Isle of Wight and their principal objective, to clear the Channel for the Duke of Parma's invasion barges, had been frustrated. Howard, Drake and Frobisher had not been neutralised and were still able to grapple with Parma's seaborne army as it crossed the Channel. The Duke of Medina had failed to clear the passage for Parma, who showed great reluctance to embark his army in unseaworthy barges, with the threat of the English ships still present. The invasion of England had failed and the Armada steered for Calais.

After the neutralising of the Armada much of the glory went to Drake, and Howard and Frobisher were dismayed; no one was more virulent than Admiral Sir Martin Frobisher who said in public:

> Sir Francis Drake reporteth that no man hath done any good service but he, but he shall well understand that others hath done as good service as he, and better too, he came bragging up at the front, instead, and gave them his prow and his broadside; and then kept his luff and was glad that he was gone again, like a cowardly knave or traitor – I rest doubtful but the one I will swear.

Frobisher was enraged and fulminated with unbridled passion against Drake's good fortune. He said:

> Drake thinketh to cozen us of our share of fifteen thousand ducats, but we will have our shares, or I will make him spend the best blood in his belly, for he hath had enough of those cozening cheats already.

Drake and Frobisher were, it is worth emphasising, both pirates and greedy capitalists, like their English descendants in the City of London today who rob the struggling middle classes of their savings.

Nott's Navy Cuts.

Anyhow, my grandmother's claim to our descent from Admiral Frobisher caused a certain amount of scepticism among the younger members of her family. The Stephens of Eastington, the family name, were wealthy landowners, seafarers and divines and the later generations normally served in the Royal Navy. A descent from Admiral Frobisher was obviously a cause for pride and prestige in the Royal Navy, and several members of the family bore the second name of Frobisher. My grandmother would have been appalled had she known that her grandson was later accused of sinking the Royal Navy!

So, how did Frobisher come to command the largest English ship in the Armada? How did he acquire his reputation as a leading seafarer of the times, and also his reputation as a greedy capitalist? It was established largely as a result of his three famous expeditions to the Northwest Passage which had taken place more than ten years before the defeat of the Armada.

For sixteenth-century Europeans, the Arctic was like another planet: alien and mysterious in the extreme. It was seen as a place of impenetrable ice and perpetual daylight from which early travellers brought back tales of huge white bears and the horns of the unicorn – in actual fact the narwhal. The principal map of the area had been drawn up by Mercator in 1569 and it had been assembled from a range of travellers' stories starting in classical times, and the earlier voyages of Pytheas the Greek, a trader who first named a place called Thule. The North Pole was depicted as a huge mountain surrounded by an open sea. Arctic explorers in later years claimed that sailors not only knew of Norse Greenland, which had been deserted and forgotten by 1500, but had access to actual Norse sailing directions.

Surprisingly there was a suspicion that, in spite of frozen seas in the far north, some believed in the concept of habitable land based on the warmth of the Arctic summers. There were iron mountains, giant whirlpools, pygmies (the Inuit) and perpetual day, but land awaiting development; it was a nonsense, of course.

John Cabot had discovered Newfoundland in 1497 and English cod fishermen, slavery traders and pirates had frequented the coast of Iceland since the early fifteenth century. Basque whalers were very active off the coast of Newfoundland but nothing was known, apart from stories of Norse settlements in Greenland, of Arctic Canada and Labrador.

The spark that led to interest in the Northwest Passage was probably sown by earlier attempts to find a way to the East along the Northeast Passage, past the northern coast of Norway and Siberia. It was sponsored by the Muscovy Company whose forerunner had obtained its charter in 1551. In the reign of Queen Mary some regard was also paid to the Papal Bull that awarded sovereign rights over the Americas to Spain and Portugal. Hence the eastward explorations of Hugh Willoughby, which ended in disaster in the Barents Sea, and that of Richard Chancellor who got as far as Archangel and then travelled overland to meet Ivan the Terrible and open up a profitable trade with the Russian Kingdom.

When Queen Elizabeth came to the throne, the Papal Bull was largely ignored by a Protestant Queen and interest in the likely success of a passage to the East along the Siberian coast had waned. Moreover, there was a growing band of restless English pirates and seafarers – Drake, Hawkins and Frobisher among them – who had cut their teeth undermining the Spanish prerogative in the West.

Much of Frobisher's career is rather hidden in history. He was a Yorkshire-born orphan and was placed with his guardian, a London merchant, who sent him to sea. His biographer wrote of him:

> He was sent to sea because they could do nothing with him ashore. At sea he remained for forty years, with scarcely any rest, and in action he died.

Frobisher's inability or unwillingness to acknowledge the fine line between legal privateering and illegal piracy had led him to successive fines and periods of imprisonment. The transformation from prisoner and pirate to naval officer is a mystery. He seems to have come to the notice of the Queen as a skilled mariner and a competent leader in hazardous circumstances. The obvious starting point was to seek assistance from the Muscovy Company but they turned Frobisher down. However, Michael Lok, its agent, had been involved in Frobisher's repatriation from Africa to a Portuguese prison and eventually to England. Lok reminisced in his memoirs that he renewed his acquaintance with the adventurer in 1574 and that...

> ...finding him sufficient and ready to execute the attempt of so great matters, I joyned with him, and to my power advanced him to the world with credit and above myne own power for my parte furnished him with things necessary for his first voyage lately made to the northwestward for the discovery of Cathay and other new cuntries to thirutent the whole world might be opened unto England which hitherto hath byn hydden from yt by the slowthfulness of some and policy of others.

Frobisher set off on the first expedition with two small ships, the *Gabriel* and the *Michael*, with a tiny pinnace. The two ships were about the size of the Norse boats that had undertaken the Greenland trips some five centuries before. The *Gabriel* weighed thirty tons and was about fifteen metres long and had a crew of thirty-five. The *Gabriel* was nearly lost off Greenland but carried on; the *Michael* turned back to England and the pinnace was lost. The *Gabriel* reached Baffin Island and explored a strait which they called Frobisher Strait, 'like as Magellanus Straits at the Southwest end of the world', and they deluded themselves that this was the route through the passage to the East. Inuit people came on board to trade but five crew were lost with the Inuit – and Frobisher took an Inuit hostage back to England to prove his discovery – and also a piece of black rock for assaye. After several assayers decreed the rock as worthless, Lok and Frobisher found a devious Italian assayer, one Giovanni Agnello, who claimed that the rock contained gold at £240 a tonne, indicating a financial return of 2,400 per cent on the expenses of a second visit.

Now the second expedition had royal support; the Queen invested in the next trip by providing a much larger vessel called the *Aid*. It was a two hundred-ton ship that was to have a crew of forty-five. And the ship was to have a gang of convicts on board (burglars, highway robbers and horse thieves) who were to be marooned at Frobisher Strait with supplies to overwinter and establish an English foothold on these shores.

Wow – even Queen Elizabeth, Francis Walsingham, her Secretary of State, and several courtiers invested in the expedition; it was a classic case of greed overcoming all common sense. It was ever thus with finance – and the whole enterprise became a sort of forerunner of the South Sea Bubble, Madoff and swindles down through the ages. Frobisher's fleet was to have a complement of 120 men, of whom thirty were miners and assayers, specifically employed to dig and load gold ore. Frobisher had ceased to be viewed as a freelance privateer and adventurer, and had become a mariner engaged in the services of the Queen.

After a stormy crossing of the Labrador Sea, the mariners found the northern entrance to Frobisher Bay – and, more importantly, they recognised the island where the previous landing party had found the black rock. Frobisher went ashore through the ice with two pinnaces accompanied by the assayers, but they could not get 'in all that land a piece so big as a walnut'. The second boat, however, visited nearby islands and found them well supplied with ore. The first task was to claim the newly discovered country and its potential riches for England. The procedure for claiming sovereignty over land not already possessed by another Christian ruler was well established by medieval concepts of authority. Frobisher raised a cross and claimed the land in the name of God for England and its monarch.

By late August the men had loaded two hundred tons of ore and both the miners and the equipment were badly worn by their labour. The fleet set sail for home on 23 August as the ice was beginning to close in. After several serious mishaps, Frobisher rode to London to be received by Queen Elizabeth who commended his accomplishments and gave the name 'Meta Incognita' to the new land that had been claimed on her behalf. The precious ore was unloaded from the *Aid* and held under heavy locks at Bristol Castle.

The leading partners in the voyage began to take stock of their venture. The passage to Cathay had not been discovered, no Englishman had settled in the new lands, nor had friendly relations been established with the Inuit; all hope lay in the value of the two hundred tons of rock. Several assayers were appointed and came up with conflicting but largely negative results.

Even Giovanni Agnello, whose original tests had really initiated the quest for gold, could find no evidence of it. Michael Lok, the financier, began to get desperate, and Frobisher's temper deluged all the assayers with abuse. Francis Walsingham, urged on no doubt by the principal investor, the Queen, then appointed a German, one Bernard Kranich, who had opened silver mines in Cornwall, unsuccessfully. Kranich possibly felt, coming from where it did, that his assignment brooked no other choice and pronounced he had found 13½ ounces of ore per ton, although suggestions were made that he had introduce some of his own gold into the assaye. This was a turning point. The investors were required to pay up what they owed, particularly to the crew who had received no wages – but much worse, substantial sums were required to build a new and very expensive smelter in Deptford.

By this time the Queen was very much in charge and decided that a major mining and freighting expedition was warranted by the assays. The third expedition took shape under the Queen's command.

She proposed that a much larger expedition of ten ships, under Frobisher, should be despatched to Meta Incognita. The investors were required to provide a 135 per cent investment over the stock already committed in order to outfit the new fleet. If there had been what today is described as transparency, it would have appeared odd that Michael Lok then sold £1,000 of his stock to the Earl of Oxford. Yes – it followed the course of all later financial disaster.

The members of Queen Elizabeth's court realised that they were now inextricably involved in a political as well as an economic project. It began to take on a colonial slant and the Queen's new lands were to be properly established with a colony of one hundred Englishmen in Greenland and Meta Incognita, the first English attempt to people the New World, albeit with convicts. The project had acquired overwhelming momentum.

In May 1578, the Privy Council decreed the mining and colonisation party should assemble at the Port of Harwich and the largest fleet of ships ever sent into the Arctic before the twentieth century set off. The Royal Commission established to oversee the venture issued Frobisher with detailed instructions regarding the objectives of the voyage. It was a good example of the incompetence of all governments since Adam and Eve departed the Garden of Eden. Concorde, High Speed Rail, aircraft carriers, the euro... all come to mind and other prestige projects will surely follow in quick succession, not least the development of our nuclear future under the threat of blackmail from France and China. The only human activity that succeeds is known as Private Enterprise. As Adam Smith wrote two hundred years later:

> It is the highest importance and presumption in Kings and Ministers to pretend to watch over the economy of private people, and to restrain their expense. They are themselves always, and without exception the greater spendthrifts in the Society.

The third expedition was no more of a success than the other two. In fact, it was a disaster.

Week by week the enterprise increased in scale and ambition and in the end it involved fifteen ships. On board now were four hundred men, soldiers, miners and convicts and the materials for a large barrack-like building which was to provide winter quarters for the hundred men to be left behind.

The ships had an uneventful voyage to Greenland, now renamed West England as part of Queen Elizabeth's 'new world' Empire, but ran into terrible conditions as they approached Frobisher Strait. The *Denys's* sank with part of the prefabricated barracks on board, making it almost impossible to leave a winter party behind, as had been planned. Geoffrey Best, the most famous recorder of Frobisher's exploits wrote:

> Some of the Shippes, where they could not find a place more cleare
> of the Ise, and get a little berth and sea room, did take in the sayles
> and there lay adrift. Otheres fastened upon a great island of ise
> and rode under the lea thereof, supposing to be better garded from
> the outrageous windes, and the danger of the lesser floating ise.

The mariners tried to strengthen the sides of the ships by lashing beds and planks to the wooden hulls against the crushing ice. Frobisher sailed on and came upon the 'Mistaken Straits' which were later found to be the entrance to Hudson's Bay and, although believing this to be the Northwest Passage to Cathay, he was forced to turn back to Frobisher Strait – the mining area – because of fog and heavy snow and ice. Geoffrey Best reported:

> There fell so much snow, with such bitter cold air, that we could
> scarce see one another, nor open our eyes to handle our ropes
> and sayles, which did so wette our poor mariners' clothes that he
> had scarce one drie threade to his backe.

Towards the middle of August the ships had loaded over a thousand tons of ore in terrible conditions, and it was decided to head for home before the ice closed in. Strangely, 'grain and other seeds were sown ashore to prove the fruitfulness of the soyle'. Evacuation was not an orderly process – forty men were lost and two ships foundered on the way back.

On return, the assayes produced miserable results – and it became obvious that the only metal being shovelled into the new and very expensive furnaces at Dartford was 'fool's gold', or iron pyrites. Within a year the furnaces at Dartford were abandoned – and today the ore is still to be seen in some walls in modern Dartford. Frobisher and Michael Lok blamed each other for the disaster – and Lok eventually died a bankrupt. Frobisher died from wounds in 1594, in the service of the Queen, when he led a successful assault on a Spanish fortress in Brittany.

Did anything come out of this failed adventure? Maybe it established the first English presence in Canada and North America and, more immediately, the discovery of Frobisher Strait influenced Francis Drake's voyage around the world in 1577–80. Drake had known of Frobisher's first two voyages and, after plundering a Spanish treasure galleon near Panama, he sailed up the west coast of America, probably as far as British Columbia, seeking the 'Strait of Anian', the rumoured Pacific entrance to the Northwest Passage.

And it is to the Strait of Anian that my next journey takes me. I plan to explore the Northwest Passage in *The World*, going from west to east; the opposite directions to that of my supposed ancestor's exploits in 1573. And I hope that I will have a more comfortable time on my trip than my supposed ancestor Martin Frobisher.

A Letter from the Editor

Dear John,

I am very sorry to write you this letter but, with regret, I have decided that I must offer you my resignation as your editor. It was a privilege to edit two of your former books, both of which met with some success. But this book has gone completely haywire, and the only honourable course for me to take is to resign if I am to maintain my reputation in the publishing industry.

I was prepared to overlook a number of very odd chapters because I had appreciated that you are something of an eccentric iconoclast. For instance, the rewriting of our nation's great history by placing Napoleon on Nelson's Column shocked me, but much of that chapter was written in bad French, so I concluded that most readers would have passed it by, anyhow – I described that chapter as 'completely bonkers', and I have not changed my opinion.

Imagining Prince Charles as a vegetarian I found interesting, and your attendance at Jordan's wedding was, I assumed, completely made up and thus did no harm.

If you found it amusing to have your sperm preserved at the Millennium Seed Bank in West Sussex, I overlooked it too because it was, rather uniquely, relevant to the title of the book.

But I am now two-thirds of the way through your text and I just cannot manage to make sense of the chapters 'The Nation's Favourite Stockbroker' and 'The Election for the President of the United Kingdom'. Where exactly do they fit in?

When I accepted the mandate you told me that you had written a 'travelogue with incidents'. There is indeed a lot of travel to the far corners of the world. But I found the travel rather tedious in parts and it does not come up to the originality of Herodotus, or the incident-packed story of The Wind in the Willows. You strike me as something of a Mr Toad yourself; or are you more like Ratty?

My problem is that the book has no central theme. Where exactly are you travelling, and what exactly is your destination? Do you intend in the final chapter to tell me that you have discovered immortality?

How can I be expected to rework your book to make it acceptable to the publishing industry? As you know, the industry is in great trouble partly from self-publishing and Kindle. It publishes huge numbers of books every week in a desperate attempt to capture 'the bestseller'. It means that retailers are hopelessly overstocked, which, in any normal business, would be a sign of looming bankruptcy. As for the great publishing houses of the past like John Murray, they have all been collapsed into conglomerates with a hundred titles. Your own publisher, Random House, has merged with Penguin. In your former profession of a merchant banker you would know that huge mergers of this kind, dictated by financial reasons, normally lead to failure. I tell you this to warn you that it will be very difficult to find a mainstream publisher for this book of yours.

Now you ask me to agree to a chapter headed 'The Nation's Favourite Stockbroker'. What, may I ask, has this to do with a travelogue? You pointed out that the British nation is greatly in favour of competitions, indeed they take up a large portion of broadcasting time on the BBC.

Take the Booker Prize. There does not seem to be much point in continuing with this competition if Hilary Mantel wins it every time. I know that you found her books good reading but I found it quite difficult to understand her grammar. Is it just me? Perhaps that is a qualification for success in the literary industry.

And take the annual competition in the film and television industry, where all the media types get into evening dress and congratulate each other on their mutual brilliance. It is, of course, a great British tradition to love failing institutions like the BBC, but is it necessary to take up weeks of viewing time for incestuous jamborees of this kind? Of course most sophisticated viewers have abandoned the BBC for the hugely superior Al Jazeera, but I doubt if the guardians of public taste are aware of what is happening to our bloated public service broadcasting which can soldier on indefinitely with public subsidy regardless.

You write about the competition for the Nation's Favourite Stockbroker. The finalists were David Cameron and Nigel Farage. I understand that, when it became known that Farage was likely to be an unchallenged winner, the government called a meeting of COBRA, where it was agreed that Farage must be stopped. The Chancellor declined to stand; and on the basis that Farage was achieving too many triumphs and publicity, David Cameron agreed to step in and put a stop to his progress. This was deemed essential before the European elections in the spring of 2014.

In the final, David Cameron came across as charming, intelligent and honest with an excellent financial pedigree. No one was expecting success with his investment policy or his stock picking, just whether he would make a better stockbroker than Farage.

Farage has become something of a cult figure. There are now large numbers of 'Farageists', City types and former Tory supporters. The 'Farageists' are becoming similar in status to the 'Thatcherites'. In the competition, he had substantial financial backing from investment bankers, traders, the Royal Bank of Scotland and former directors of the banking industry like Lord Stevenson and (Sir) Fred Goodwin.

But Farage came across as being quite dodgy. When the question was put 'whom would you prefer to trust with your money?' Cameron won the contest overwhelmingly.

I found your description of this competition irrelevant to the rest of your book, but not offensive in any way. I could not, however, come to the same conclusion about your chapter 'The Election for the President of the United Kingdom'. The outcome was shocking for me, although I am neither a Republican nor a Royalist.

One finalist was Lord (Chris) Patten of Barnes, the favourite of the British Establishment. He eliminated another former European Commissioner, Lord (Neil) Kinnock, in the semi-finals. Chris Patten was proposed by the Prime Minister and seconded by the Secretary of the Cabinet. He had enormous financial backing from the European Commission (unaudited) and there was great support from Oxford University where he's Chancellor, of course; and great media hype from the BBC, where he is Chairman, of course. The liberal establishment were wild with enthusiasm for him. No one actually imagined that he would not be elected President of the United Kingdom.

I should explain that the competition implied no criticism of the Royal Family. The Duke of Cambridge, with his aristocratic mother, Lady Diana Spencer, and his middle-class wife Kate Middleton, looks like securing the monarchy into eternity. Prince George may bear the family name of Spencer-Middleton, instead of Mountbatten-Windsor, in recognition of changing taste, but these changes have happened before. But nothing is certain in this changing world and provision must always be made for Revolution.

The other finalist in the competition for President was none other than the defeated candidate for the Nation's Favourite Stockbroker. One Nigel Farage. It is simply impossible to put him down; he pops up everywhere challenging daily the government's PR machine.

It turned out that he had overwhelming support. He was proposed by the newly formed Association of Swivel-eyed Loons, otherwise known as the Association of Defectors from the Tory Party. Every pub carried his posters. He had enormous financial backing from the tobacco and brewing industries, whose combined wealth far exceeded the dodgy finances of the European Union (unaudited). The European Central Bank panicked at the prospect of a victory by the leader of the UK Independence Party – and printed vast amounts of new currency, so much so that hyper-inflation took hold of the euro, which began to resemble the paper Mark in the 1920s.

Farage's victory was overwhelming. He had huge popular support. As your Editor, John, I found the result – and the whole chapter – absolutely unacceptable, hence my offer of resignation.

*   *   *

Dear Richard,
I had not appreciated that you would feel so strongly about these chapters. I do not want to lose you as my editor. I therefore agreed to withdraw both of them from my book.
Yours ever,
John

*   *   *

Dear John,
Really?
So there's no escape?
Damn.
Yours ever,
Richard

28

Iceland – Viking Country

The discovery of Spitsbergen by Dutch whalers in the sixteenth century, and exploration west and north towards Novaya Zemlya in Arctic Russia by Willoughby and Chancellor (1553) and Barents (1596); and to the west by Frobisher (1573–7), Davis (1585–7), Hudson (1607–10) and Baffin (1616) brought the Arctic into clearer definition, but nothing was more astonishing than the discovery of Iceland and Greenland by Irish monks and the Vikings over five hundred years earlier. I therefore decided to stop over in Iceland on my journey to Alaska because here was a nation that had shown astonishing resilience for over one thousand years. It had overcome volcanic eruptions, earthquakes, disease and hunger that made today's hysteria about climate change seem ridiculous. These are the people who first discovered America – some five hundred years before Columbus – and occupied Greenland for many generations until the Little Ice Age drove them back to a more temperate climate in Iceland and Norway.

This amazing Viking saga was fed by social needs in ninth-century Scandinavia and by advances in military technology and shipbuilding.

The first example that we have of a Viking ship was the discovery in Gokstad near Oslo in 1880. The hull of the Gokstad ship was twenty-four metres long and five metres wide; it would have drawn less than a metre of water. The single midship mast would have supported a large square-sail and there were sixteen ports for oars on either side. When fully loaded with supplies and animals it would have had a crew of twenty-five and could travel at speeds of twelve knots across the North and Atlantic seas with relative security. This was a miracle of design and enabled the Vikings to occupy Ireland, England, Scotland and Normandy and much else in Europe. These ships enabled King Canute, one of England's greatest kings, to conquer England and rule it with compassion and good sense, in contrast to the savagery and destruction meted out to the English by the Norman conquerors in 1066.

I described Iceland in my memoirs as my favourite country, home to 320,000 Icelanders. I always find them cheerful and friendly, and my opinion of them is constant because I do not visit the streets of Reykjavik on a Friday or Saturday night when drunkenness, with all its disgusting consequences, seems to take hold of them in a sort of Scandinavian madness. However, unlike in many British towns the streets are all clean and tidy by the morning.

Every year I go to Iceland to fish for salmon. It is the best salmon fishing in the world, and still the best ocean fishing since the Icelanders imposed a two hundred-mile limit against the furious opposition of the British fishing industry.

To an outside observer Iceland still exhibits a fair degree of prosperity since it went bankrupt in 2008. The locals tell me that life is a perpetual struggle but their lifestyle, hugely more comfortable than in any northern English city, is now kept afloat by the International Monetary Fund. The Icelanders are expert at living high at the expense of foreigners, be they tourists or the IMF!

Is it because of my Viking heritage that I feel so comfortable – almost like coming home – when I visit Iceland, Norway and Denmark? It is partly the people, but more the atmosphere, the remoteness of much of the country and the detachment from urban anxiety. They are right not to repay their debts to the British and the Dutch; the whole world is living off debt; Iceland is no different.

Of course, I have no certainty that I am the descendant of Viking invaders in the mid-tenth century, more than a thousand years ago. It was the same time that Viking ships and seafarers founded the first known settlement in Iceland. But there are too many signs to question my genealogical instincts. The names of Nott, Knut, Cnut, Knut still appear in the Icelandic telephone book.

And when England was devastated by the Norman Conquest and Anglo-Saxon Saxon culture was largely destroyed, strangely enough the descendants of the Danish Vikings still prospered in the City of London. Much of the Scandinavian merchant class which was founded in the hegemony of Canute's reign – he was King of England, Denmark and Norway – carried on regardless of the Normans. One John Nott, Mayor of London in 1363, just after the Black Death, was of Viking ancestry, as were many of the other prominent and wealthy citizens of the City of London.

When the English Civil War came along Sir Thomas Nott, the son of Roger, 'a wealthy citizen of London' (*DNB*), bankrupted himself in the royal cause – that finally eliminated any pretensions that we might have had and we became part of the common fold where we remain.

It is perhaps ironic that, as Minister of State in the Treasury during Mr Edward Heath's administration, I attended a meeting at No. 10 in 1972 to consider British policy during the Icelandic Cod War. It was attended by the First Sea Lord and a bevy of uniformed and bemedalled admirals. The Prime Minister asked, very aggressively, why the Royal Navy seemed unable to resist the Icelandic gunboats, mainly adapted fishing vessels. 'Have we your permission, Prime Minister,' said the First Sea Lord, 'to sink the Icelandic gunboats?' 'Certainly not,' said the Prime Minister, 'we are not at war with Iceland.' 'Then I do not think,' said the First Sea Lord, 'that we have an answer to the problem.' 'The country is being made to look ridiculous,' said the Prime Minister. 'We are spending hundreds of millions of pounds a year on the Royal Navy, the third largest navy in the world, and you tell me that you are unable to beat off a few minor gunboats, who are hazarding our frigates and destroyers by ramming themselves into their flimsy hulls.' The meeting broke off with bad tempers all round.

This 'war' sealed the fate of the huge British fishing industry, which was finally destroyed when Heath, in his passion for the European Economic Community, signed away our own fishing limits to the rapacious French and Spanish trawlers that have all but destroyed our fishing grounds.

Now it must seem strange that my first choice for my survival community did not lie back home in Viking country. At least if I got bored with my celebrity collection I could have bedded down with a lovely blue-eyed Scandinavian blonde from healthy farming stock. But it made no sense because the whole ridiculous idea had been to ensure the survival of my genes in association of whatever totty became available. And I did not believe that northern Europe was going to survive the machinations of rogue scientists. I thought that northern Europe was doomed and the only hope was to escape in the farthest corners of the Southern Hemisphere like Patagonia or Stewart Island. The project was grim but any reader of that book by Nevil Shute that I have alluded to so frequently [Editor's note: John, at least four times. Is it still in print?] would understand how I came to this conclusion. But the project was altogether a failure; I could not handle the isolation and the griping of my survival community. They had no discos, no newspapers or television, no drugs, no *OK!* or *Hello!*. The totty abandoned me.

This book is about adaptation and survival and nowhere was it more stark than in Iceland where the people deserve their special place in history for their resilience.

Iceland is a barren volcanic island with limited resources except for fish. It is no longer covered in the forests that the first discoverers found – sheep and horses have turned it into something of a barren wilderness. The lack of wood became an increasing problem in Iceland's history until it was imported from elsewhere.

It is likely that the first visitors were Irish monks at the end of AD 700 – and they probably settled there until the Norsemen arrived around AD 870. In the fifth and sixth centuries Ireland was the centre of high culture in Europe. Its monasteries were a refuge for intellectual thought and spiritual practice. Under pressure from Rome to bring their traditions into line with Christian orthodoxy and pressed by barbarian Vikings, the monks moved north and west to the Faroes and Iceland where they built monastic cells. Tradition holds that they went west to Greenland ahead of the Norse, even to Labrador and Newfoundland, but there is no certainty of this.

An island called Thüle where the sun shone all night in the summer was held in European myth and geographical treatise going back as far as the voyages of Pytheas the Greek in 300 BC.

The first Norse arrivals may have been blown off course on a passage between the Faroe Islands and Norway, but the Norwegian Vikings had already established settlements in Ireland around this time and they must have arrived with many Celtic wives and slaves obtained by raiding the British Isles.

An estimate in the National Museum of Iceland in Reykjavik, which I know well, reckons that the men were predominantly Norse, but that half their women were of Celtic origin.

The world is fortunate to have the record of St Brendan in Irish folklore and the more authentic history of Iceland in the two Books of the 'Icelanders' and the 'Settlements' written in Old Norse, not Latin. The author was Ari the Wise Porgiksson writing two hundred years later when he chronicles the Viking settlement between AD 870 to AD 930.

What possessed these Norsemen, often accompanied by their Celtic wives and slaves, to make these hazardous journeys is a mystery.

It is known that Norway was going through a violent and uncertain time in the ninth century. But in setting out across an unknown sea with no picture of the far shore when they departed is remarkable; they possessed no developed tools of navigation, no maps with any geographic authority. All that they could do was to steer by the moon and the stars, and in spring and autumn follow the migrating geese. Shipwrecks were so frequent that no record exists of deaths at sea and as they sailed they suffered fatally from the weather, scurvy, starvation, Inuit hostility and thirst. There is a running exhibition in Reykavik which shows the literally thousands of shipwrecks around Iceland's shores between 1850 and the present time. They were held together by a sense of achievement and a regard for each other. At that time there were no notions of a road to Cathay and a corridor to vast wealth at the other end of the Northwest Passage. All they needed was land for their animals, peace and food and housing for their families. It is a truly wonderful idea – and it precedes the driving ambition, lust for recognition and fame of the later explorers.

The western progress of the Norse in the Viking age did not cease in Iceland. Before long they observed empty land further west and in late AD 900 an Icelander known as 'Eric the Red' had established a settlement on the west coast of Greenland. According to Ari the Wise, the Greenland settlement took place around AD 985 and people of Norse origin lived there in Greenland for five centuries with a population thought to number around three thousand men and women.

Apparently the settlement survived by trading walrus tusks, gerfalcons, polar bear hides and sealskins in exchange for iron, grain and manufactured implements. Then, with the rise of the Hanseatic League, the collapse of Bergen from which the ships for Greenland sailed and the removal of the Norwegian capital to Copenhagen, Greenland was forgotten. Without trade there was nothing much to sustain the Greenlanders. The remnants of the Norse population died out, or intermarried with the Inuit, or were abducted by English slave traders in the sixteenth century. No more was heard of Greenland until Admiral Frobisher's expedition in 1573.

According to the sagas 'Leif the Lucky', son of 'Eric the Red', sailed west from Greenland to Vinland (so named because wild grapes and wheat were growing there) where he came into contact with native North Americans. This was some five hundred years before Columbus 'discovered' America. Doubts were raised by historians about this story – historians are very possessive and conservative people – until Helge Ingstad discovered Viking age sites in Newfoundland in the 1960s. It is likely that the passage to the west was in search of forests because the Icelanders had stripped the country of trees for house-building, fuel and smelting and wood had become a scarce resource.

The Iceland story thereafter is a chronicle of slow development and occasional disaster, often brought about by change in climate. The forcible introduction of Christianity by the Norwegian king, the creation of a thriving trade in stockfish exports to Europe between 1300 and 1400 and the development of a mixed agrarian/fishing society typified the Icelandic economy for centuries. Then, between 1400 and 1495, the Black Death struck and the population was decimated. The next blow was famine in 1750 due to cold weather and poor fish catches. This was the Little Ice Age. The population was around 50,000 at this time. It is a story of survival against tempest, fire, disease and storm.

On my return from the volcanic mountains and rivers of central Iceland I had cause to spend the night in Reykjavik. The next morning before the departure of my flight I thought it might be interesting to attend the eleven o'clock Lutheran Matins at the National Cathedral. Iceland had a Reformation and the islands were ordered by their Danish overlords to convert to the Lutheran faith. Many good Catholics refused and were duly executed for disobedience. The congregation was sparse, about twenty persons present, and I found the service all in the Icelandic language hard to follow. It was, however, presided over by a female Viking priest, clad in dazzling and fluorescent bottle-green robes. I had seen the same fancy dress worn by the Archbishops of Canterbury and York at a recent Lambeth Conference – where one third of those invited failed to show up – women bishops, homosexual practitioners and all that. The lady Viking priest arrived alone and unaccompanied by choir or retinue and stood facing the altar with her back to the congregation, where I gazed in spiritual awe at the golden symbols, stars resurrecting, suns that covered her bottle-green robes. As the clock struck eleven, she turned to face us. But nothing happened. We all know that long pregnant silences are riveting and I assumed that this was part of Lutheran ritual. But no – there was a knock on the church door and in rushed a perspiring pianist. The Viking priest and all the congregation had been waiting for the late arrival. Now it would be sacrilegious to suggest that he had a dreadful hangover from the night before, but if that was not the problem he would have been the only sober member of Reykjavik society that morning. We read about the drunken louts and ladettes who pour on to the pavements of British cities on Saturday nights, but it is only the inhabitants of Glasgow who come anywhere near the consumption of alcohol absorbed by the residents of Reykjavik on a Saturday night.

In Reykjavik airport's departure lounge, on my way to America, there was whole gang of pretty schoolgirls, all clad in an electric-blue uniform with their Viking names printed on their chests. There were seven of them sitting on my left and I was asked if I could move up a place or two to make room for an army of other Icelandic fourteen-year-old blue-eyed blondes who were all over the airport lounge. 'Why are you all dressed like that?' I asked. 'We are the Icelandic girls' football team,' they said. 'We are off to Denmark for a major international competition.'

* * *

If I had not been born an Englishman, I would like to have been an Icelander. Sometimes I wonder, as I endure the squalor of the British press, whether I would not rather be an Icelander anyhow.

Most nations have their customs and their rituals; and given the extraordinary history of Iceland it is not surprising that Icelandic rituals involve a rather macho rite of passage for the young. In parts of Africa young men, following the onset of puberty, go through a most unpleasant – even frightening – public ceremony of circumcision. The Icelandic equivalent is a puffin hunt.

In Iceland, fathers introduce their male offspring to a 'blooding' at the age of seven or so. While British sporting magazines are reluctant to show photographs of young riders being blooded when they encounter their first kill on the hunting field, no such inhibition prevails in Icelandic hunting magazines; they revel in publishing photographs of young men's faces being blooded by dead puffins.

The rite of passage for young male Icelanders goes like this. In England when young boys of seven are traditionally sent blubbing to their boarding school, in Iceland fathers grab their weeping offspring from their mother and their video games and drag them unwillingly to their monster 4x4s. The young lad, having heard descriptions from his friends of what fate has in store for him, is most reluctant to join his father and pleads to be allowed to stay on his computer in the safety and comfort of his bedroom.

But, no; tradition requires the full ritual so the weeping child is kitted out in his grandfather's traditional hunting gear of heavy, slightly damp tweed and sealskin and thrown into the back of the 4x4 for the six-hour drive on ash roads to the western fjords. As father thrashes through the barren volcanic landscape the car radio booms out a continuous rigmarole of hunting songs combined with stories of the annual Icelandic seabird shoot.

In this annual tradition, whole areas of the western fjords are covered with dead shags, seagulls, razorbills, guillemots, cormorants and puffins, and any other breed of seabird that is foolish enough to be in the area of the seabird shoot. The participants in this annual affair are hardly experienced shotgun hunters and casualties, while not approaching the number of dead seabirds lying on the water, do mount up as the fishermen swing their guns at everything that moves.

The European Union, as part of Iceland's entry talks, is trying to ban this practice, and speaks of its horror at the cruelty involved. It is just one of many examples that convinces Icelanders that they should have nothing to do with the ridiculous bureaucrats in Brussels. No 'Bird Directive' for Iceland then.

By the time our little seven-year-old has heard these stories of the annual seabird shoot and the hunting songs on the radio, he is reduced to a blubbing wreck. But the rite of passage has hardly begun. The 4x4 is parked on some isolated piece of tundra and the long walk begins. It takes the hunters through lava fields and undergrowth to find a puffin colony on the cliffs.

British soldiers are blooded by marching them, at night, through Dartmoor bogs or across Brecon Beacons carrying an 80lb pack, but the seven-year-old Icelanders are only required to carry a puffin net.

By this time, the father's excitement at the hunt is only equalled by the misery of his son who is expected to bear the horrors of this experience like a man. Suffice it to say that the father takes an occasional swig of Brennivin (unsweetened schnapps drunk on special occasions) from a flask so that his excitement is enhanced by this lethal spirit.

Eventually the party arrives at the cliffs, where it may encounter other puffin hunters. Father explains to son that they have to circle the puffins in their lair – and that he will drive a puffin towards his son who must catch it in the puffin net. The young lad misses several puffins and is sworn at by his father for his incompetence but eventually an undernourished puffin is successfully driven into the net. Father, his heart racing now with excitement, brings out his grandfather's hunting knife, grabs the puffin out of the net, holds the bird up by its neck and slices through it with granddad's hunting knife so that blood spurts out everywhere. The little boy vomits and is scared out of his wits, not least by granddad's hunting knife. But the ritual is not concluded until the little boy's face and hair have been covered by puffin blood; he shrieks with horror and runs back to the car where he is photographed for the local hunting magazine.

On the return journey, several puffin hunters meet up, drink themselves silly with Brennivin and celebrate by cutting slabs of puffin flesh, which is consumed as sashimi.

Eventually a great party of friends is called together and, as in a bar mitzvah, a feast is held of boiled cormorants, seagull curry and rotten shark meat (the Icelandic delicacy called Hákarl) while photographs of the bloodied child are shown around, among many congratulations and much jollity. Indeed a great Icelandic custom.

*   *   *

Located just below the Arctic Circle, Europe's most remote nation is also quite bizarre. Every poll shows that the majority of Icelanders strongly believe in trolls, elves, gnomes and fairies. When I suggested to my son that he stayed in our remote fishing hut in a valley between high mountains, he said that he was worried that the trolls would see him as an intruder – and give him a bad time. The most logical explanation for such a large majority being truly superstitious is Iceland's isolation from the rest of the world. Storytelling in the dark winter nights about heroes and supernatural beings has blurred the distinction between reality and fantasy in people's minds. A jagged coastline full of bays and fjords, impressive geysers, high waterfalls and threatening volcanoes are all part of a fairy-tale land that, uniquely still talks in the language of the Icelandic sagas written over one thousand years ago.

Iceland has a remarkable fascination for the historically minded. It is a resolutely modern nation that is devoted to its past. It became the first truly literate country in northern Europe around the tenth century and its sagas are some of the greatest literature ever written. I have been to Iceland many times – and I know of no other country in the world that I find so hard to leave.

29

There's No Place Like Nome

To get to Nome, where I was to join the Ark, the flight from Reykjavik to Seattle had been pleasant enough as I was in Saga Class, terminology presumably employed to remind passengers of how the early Viking settlers suffered on their transatlantic journeys. I doubt whether Eric the Red would have ever sailed via Greenland on his transatlantic crossing if he had been made to suffer the indignities of body scans, computer and toothpaste checks and other generally intrusive searches while transitting an airport. An aggressive Viking, I suspect he would have thumped the overweight body police and landed himself in jail. Vinland (America) would have remained undiscovered for another five hundred years.

I had arrived at this godforsaken spot via Seattle and Anchorage, Alaska, on a perilous flight through tempestuous rain and an Arctic gale. But the journey was made interesting by meeting an air hostess, a clone of Sarah Palin, the former governor of Alaska and one of my heroines. If I had thought of it earlier, I would have invited her to join my survival community in Punta Arenas with Ann Widdecombe. Sarah Palin is certainly the breeding type and has killed and garrotted many a moose with her bare hands. She is just my sort of gal.

I consulted several men in Nome as to why they had elected her Governor of Alaska – and was impressed by the sophistication of their reply. 'I voted for her because she has big breasts.' Now, in Europe people would have mumbled about gay marriage in church, the euro, the state of the National Health Service, taxes and mortgages, but here in northern Alaska they come, instinctively, to the point.

There is no place like Nome. How true. No one could invent such a depressing place. But for a few years around 1900 Nome was the largest town in Alaska, with 20,000 miners, gamblers, card-sharpers, tradesmen, prostitutes, thugs and dance-hall girls all trying to make a fortune from the 'vast beaches of golden sand'.

Just after the Klondike Gold Rush in 1898 three Scandinavians discovered that the beaches and adjoining marshland was full of gold, brought down by the glaciers in earlier times. Today the town with a population of 3,500 presents a scene of semi-decline, but the high price of gold is giving it a second life. It is still a preserve of drunks and chancers although the locals are delightfully friendly.

I would have stayed at 'The Pioneer of Alaska, Igloo No. 1' – an old people's home – but I chose the Aurora Inn from the internet. It was adequate but served no food so I had to go out into the tempestuous rain to eat in the Polar Café, which had a heavy rusting door.

With my predilection for low life, I wandered into the main street alongside a fierce sea and found the 'Board of Trade Saloon – Headquarters of the Sin City of Nome', or so it said. It was an appropriate visit from a former President of the Board of Trade in England – that's me.

The miners all carried guns for their personal protection, and the army moved in to restore order in the streets in 1901. *The Diary of a Gold Rush Prostitute*, published by Mary Newman in 1900, recalled: 'Today I walked around the town and I counted over 100 saloons and gambling houses catering to the gold rush.'

When gold was discovered on the beaches and the $300 million Klondike gold became more difficult to exploit, the 'stampeders' moved into the tented camp beside the beach – and brought with them the prostitutes and forty or so dance-hall girls. Some became famous, adopting names such as 'Black Kitty' and 'Ella the Glacier'.

Had I known earlier I would have recruited Ella the Glacier and the girls to join Ann Widdecombe at her dance hall in Punta Arenas.

Sitting along the long bar were a succession of inebriated locals who held out their hands to me in welcome. But I chose a table nearby and met Kevin, a young self-employed diver. He worked from a small launch and dived in the sea for up to six hours a day when the weather permitted. He puts a funnel down to the seabed and, guided by the diver, it sucks up the sediment into the launch where it is separated from the gold. Kevin knew where to search on the seabed and last year he recovered 100 oz of gold, which, after giving a share to the dredger, earned him around $128,000.

I asked him whether he dived in the winter. 'I do,' he said, 'but it can be dangerous. The sea ice is between one and two metres deep and we have to cut an air hole with a chain saw or a mechanical digger – and we carry a subsidiary supply of air in case we are trapped by a sudden closing of the ice which can happen when the air drops to minus thirty degrees. The seas are quite shallow in the Bering Sea but we can dive to thirty feet without too much danger of the bends.'

Kevin expressed no desire to return to civilisation: he was enjoying life with his mates. I admire these itinerant youngsters, like the Norwegian girls who work the huskies in Spitzbergen. These frontier people are a fascination for me.

Talking of dogs, Nome is famous for the annual dog race from Anchorage to Nome in which sixty to ninety competitors take part, each starting with a team of sixteen dogs. It takes place every March and the competitors must cover a thousand miles in around ten days. The winning 'musher' becomes a local Alaskan hero.

In the local museum there is a glass case which contains a rather handsome stuffed Siberian husky called Fritz. Fritz was discovered in a New York junk shop and was brought to Nome. He is the first registered sire of the Siberian husky breed, registered by the American Kennel Club – some dog.

On my last evening in Nome I fought my way through another storm to pick up a takeaway from the Twin Dragon. Sitting in the corner of the café was a tall young man who beckoned me to his table; he looked to be of Chinese origin. I had the impertinence to enquire whether he had been born in Nome. 'Yes,' he told me, 'my mother is an Eskimo and my father is Caucasian with a bit of Scottish blood, and I am married to a native girl. I am a fisherman and have just returned from a six-week trip in my uncle's thirty-nine-foot boat when we caught, in the forty crab pots which we are allowed, 32,000 pounds of crab. My share of 12 per cent of the gross bought me $26,000 – not a bad return given that we had very bad weather with eight-foot waves.'

At this point the owner of the café, who seemed to be an Eskimo, too, came over and they began reminiscing about the previous winter. Each of them had shot a polar bear on the ice near Nome and had kept the skins. My young friend added that he had shot several walrus and spent much of the winter carving the walrus tusks, the ivory fetching $40 a pound. He explained that being of Eskimo origin he was allowed to hunt the polar bear – and added with a smile that he was also entitled to free dentistry and medicine.

I stopped off on my journey to the harbour to board *The World* and saw the monument to Captain Amundsen who had arrived in Nome with his crew of six in 1906 after three years crossing the Northwest Passage, the first explorer to do so, in his little ship. Beside the statue was the site of the Dexter Saloon where Wyatt Earp had been the proprietor from 1899 to 1902 when he left the town with an alleged $50,000, a considerable fortune at the time. Opposite the Dexter Saloon stood a major resting house called the Nugget Inn and I saw an old notice on the wall saying 'Hot baths – 15 cents, used water – 5 cents'. I must see if *The World* can do better.

30

Aboard *The World* (or Health & Safety Gone Bonkers)

My first impression of *The World* was not a happy one, crossing from the land of Nome to seek Nirvana in the Ark. I was given a taste of purgatory as the ship's tender encountered a force eight gale while we crossed the River Styx. It nearly overturned. Try to avoid a spell in purgatory if I was you.

On arrival at the Gates of Heaven we were greeted by St Peter at the reception desk who told us to renounce all evidence of our sinful past by handing over to him our passport and credit cards. There is no money in the Ark and all our names, preferences, deficiencies and lustful cravings are already known to St Peter's bureaucracy, based in Miami, where we have been checked out by the security services and Wikipedia.

The first shock was that heaven seemed to be obsessed with dress regulations, rather like a suburban golf club in Finchley. I had assumed that our choice of clothing would be informal, relaxed, simple – after all this is the Arctic – but not a bit of it. It took me days to discover what I was allowed to wear in the several restaurants, either 'resort casual' or 'smart casual', whatever that may mean. Then a message arrived by a ship's angel, headed 'Expedition Dress Code' saying, 'Expedition – appropriate attire' will provide a more relaxed option for residents and guests during the Northwest Passage. But it is still quite puzzling: can I transit the lobby in my balaclava on my return from some Arctic experience ashore, or will that provoke a summons to the Committee of Public Safety/Behaviour, elected by the Residents?

There are two classes of persons in heaven: the apartment owners, known as residents, and the ordinary punters, the visitors, like me. I have to recognise that the moneyed aristocracy on board who contribute up to $1 million a year to keep heaven solvent are the upper classes. I am just a paying visitor, not even a guest. Nothing wrong with that. Those seeking survival on the Ark must compromise, and learn to touch their forelocks to Noah and the moneyed aristocracy aboard.

More upsetting was that I had travelled across the world to escape from the European Union and Health & Safety – only to find that here in heaven it has gone quite ape. For instance, I went for a swim in the pool to cleanse my vile body, only to be confronted with a notice that read:

> Elderly persons, pregnant women and those with health conditions such as high blood pressure, heart conditions, compromised or deficient immune systems, diarrhoea, vomiting or fever, or on medication are advised to seek medical advice before entering the pool.

How is it possible for anyone, let alone a healthy geriatric, to avoid at least one of these several conditions? I took myself off to consult a buxom Ukrainian nurse in the ship's hospital, to find out if it was safe for me to have a swim. 'I have several compromised or deficient immune systems,' I explained, 'through overindulgence in the past – perhaps you could check me out in the Jacuzzi?' No – that's the route to humiliation before the Committee of Public Safety. This is an American heaven where 'political correctness' reigns.

Then came the *Titanic* moment. We were requested to attend a safety briefing, followed by a visit to the lifeboats. There is more lifeboat capacity than passengers so it is probable that we will survive collision with one of the many icebergs on the route. A helicopter arrives tomorrow at the Canadian border – and an ice pilot will man the bridge.

Before boarding the helicopter I was required to sign a 'Helicopter Voluntary Release', which read as follows:

> I thoroughly understand the inherent risks of helicopter operations which may result in serious injury or death... these hazards include, but are not limited to, rotor strike, air crash and ditching... especially on the Northwest Passage expedition which will be conducted at sites that are remote either by time or distance or both from medical facilities.

I'll say.

I then completed a codicil to my will, with the help of one of the many American corporate lawyers on board.

I had hoped to put Health & Safety behind me as we approached the Canadian border in a minor swell. Here we had to undergo an immigration check by a group of Canadian officials who had been flown into our anchorage on a float plane. I happened to be on the bridge to overhear the radio conversation between our Norwegian captain and the Immigration Chief ashore.

'Welcome,' said our captain, 'I hope that you had a comfortable night ashore?'

No answer, just a grunt.

'We are looking forward to getting you on board to check the passports and we will send you two Zodiacs to pick you up.'

The answer was slow in coming.

'We are very concerned at the state of the sea,' said the Chief. 'Here on the beach we have six-foot waves and it may be dangerous for us to join you. Several of our team are unwilling to risk themselves in this sea.'

'In that case,' said the captain, 'since our passengers can hardly cause any difficulties or escape from this remote Arctic island [Hershel Island], could we put our passengers ashore in the Zodiacs for a breath of fresh air, pending your visit to check the passports?'

'That would not be possible,' said the Immigration Chief, 'it would be against the immigration rules. Clearance must come first'.

'When do you think,' asked the captain, 'you will be able to get on board? We have four thousand miles ahead of us through the Canadian archipelago and a rather tight schedule before we hit the ice again.'

'It is impossible to say', said the Chief, 'we have a number of health and safety regulations which do not permit us to take to the sea in certain specified conditions.'

At this point radio communications was discontinued.

'Welcome to Canada,' said the captain. 'What are we to do? We can send the helicopter, but it has already cost $15,000 to get the immigration officials here from Winnipeg. I hope the officials are not afraid of helicopters.'

Another official on the bridge remarked that it is possible to travel around Europe without any immigration hassle, but here tension over borders between Canada and the United States is continuous. 'Probably the immigration officials from Winnipeg had never seen the sea before.'

So, the helicopter was unleashed from the deck and the Canadian immigration officers were flow on board and the tedious but entirely pointless check of the ship's passenger lists continued until completed three hours later. The ship was then searched for drugs by a large team of dog handlers.

In the meantime, clearance granted, two teams of passengers, women, children and geriatrics in lifebelts, were shipped ashore in Zodiacs, but the immigration officials still refused to return to the shore by sea – so the helicopter was once more unleashed and carried the officials to safety.

I relate this incident to indicate that government officials through the Western world use rules to protect their jobs and the honour and integrity of their bureaucracy, regardless of common sense and practicalities. This occurred in a place where history is full of the determination and valour of earlier Canadians to open up these frozen wastes.

*   *   *

I had been sent a reading list so that I could brief myself on the Arctic experience before embarking on the Ark. I duly ploughed my way through a collection of Arctic and Antarctic classics, including *Titanic, Moby-Dick, The Polar Bear, Arctic Obsession*, the journeys of Martin Frobisher etc., etc.

But when I explained to an English friend that I intended to explore the Northwest Passage on *The World* he was shocked. 'It is a strange ship,' he said, 'the apartment owners comprise a veritable congregation of the American rich, you will find them lacking in style and culture. The conversation will be confined to "money" and Republican politics.'

'How do you know this?' I asked.

'Because I had a dinner on board when the ship was docked in Greenwich and I was propositioned by my host and representatives of the management to buy an apartment. This would have cost me several million dollars before the annual service charges, which fell not much short of a similar figure. How could anyone enter such a trap, imposing a moral obligation on themselves to endlessly circumnavigate the world in a search for new experiences wrapped in cotton wool?'

I explained that my plan was not just to explore the Passage following the sixteenth-century example of Admiral Frobisher, but also to check out the ship as an escape from Armageddon so determinedly predicted by doomster scientists, obsessed warmists,

Green conservationists, apocalyptic sections of the Book of Revelation.

I had been reminded that the Black Sea, which I had once visited, had been a massively rich fresh-water lake supporting one of the greatest civilisations in pre-history, but, as the sea rose with the retreating Ice Age, the Bosphorus had been breached and the consequent flood had destroyed the civilisation and bequeathed the biblical story of the Ark which, of course, I believed implicitly.

'What nonsense you talk,' said my friend, 'forget your Arctic reading list and prepare yourself otherwise for the journey on *The World*. Consult the internet – where you can learn about the sort of types who inhabit the ship. Try the story of J. Howard Marshall [eighty-nine] and his wife, Nicole Smith, [twenty-six] and her lover, Frederic, Prinz von Anhalt, the husband of Zsa Zsa Gabor. They will all be on board.'

I was sufficiently interested to do so and certainly the internet was full of their antics. In fact, my friend, a typical specimen of all that is absurd about the British upper classes, had got it completely wrong.

I had seldom met so many delightful and intelligent people; that goes for both the passengers and crew on board, and the Inuit ashore. I was wary, however, because I had learnt from bitter experience that humour varies from place to place, and it is most fraught when jesting with Americans, who tend to see the world in black and white. It is a cultural void. What a European would take as harmless comment would be seen by many Americans as an abuse of good manners. Fortunately this ship is a United Nations – without politics – and the heavy weighting of Americans is diluted with a majority community of Norwegians, Australians, Canadians and New Zealanders. Most of them had worked all their lives and built up prosperous businesses; they were an admirable collection of charming and successful people.

It is difficult to describe *The World* in a light-hearted way. This ship is a one-off experience: there is nowhere else quite like it. Many of the passengers have cruised the world for many years. To be such a resident you must be extremely rich. The annual charges are quite outrageous, but the subscribers are motivated to keep their private yacht solvent and afloat, almost regardless of cost.

To an outsider like me, looking in from outside, much of it is strange. *The World* is like a retreat – a Buddhist retreat turned upside down. Spiritual enlightenment is gained through comfort, not abstinence. Luxury is the path to heaven. There is no need for a rich man to pass through the eye of a needle so long as he has a large enough bank account to buy his way into heaven.

The residents live in 165 separate caves (in earlier times they would have been known as troglodytes). It is not exactly a floating hermitage, but some passengers seldom venture into the world outside; they shelter in the privacy of their own cave or apartment, or berth or suite, depending on how much wealth they created in an earlier life. There is a certain class system attached to the residential floors; the tenth floor is nearest to heaven and it declines down to the sixth floor, where I reside. There is a running commentary on the television monitor every day informing each hermit what is on the menu; lobster, caviar etc. The cells are luxurious and are equipped with every convenience, including the service of hovering angels – Filipino angels to be precise – who can be summoned to answer for every need. The angels flutter about cleaning the cells, collecting the laundry and administering to every whim; and they are much the best thing on Noah's Ark.

The purpose of *The World* is to give the community on board a taste of the afterlife; it is immortality of a kind. Having conquered this world with their wealth, the Ark promises a glimpse of what the afterlife can offer. A helicopter is available on deck to take the passengers into the clouds to glimpse the real thing, for a package of five flights, at $3,700. After a few days in purgatory in a force eight gale it is all here: heated swimming pools, Jacuzzis galore, a health centre with personal attention and a spa staffed by beautiful Thai girls. I have seen no evidence that the animals on board (to use a biblical phrase) intend to leave this life as they entered it – naked and unashamed – none of this dust to dust, ashes to ashes nonsense. No – they plan to take with them all the luxuries provided.

I wondered how Noah had organised the embarkation of his animals, his wife and children. Had they all been provided with independent lodgings, or had they all been herded into a single hold? I hesitated to consider the consequences of all these animals and humans being herded into one place, providing unlimited opportunity for frumpy-pumpy during the forty days and nights of the Flood. Just as we can have no idea whether today's climate is the best for humanity until it changes, so we cannot be certain whether today's animal and human species are pure-bred, or the consequence of frantic cross-breeding on the Ark.

I have seen the outcome of cross-breeding between the polar and grizzly bear; their stuffed carcasses are available for scrutiny in several Arctic exhibition halls. On *The World* I can observe the results of cross-breeding in the American race. Inter-breeding between Latinos and Wasps is inevitable and it seems to have produced a hybrid race, aggressive and troublesome maybe but astonishing for its inventiveness and vigour. The Greeks, nearer in time to the Ark than us, observed the consequences of inter-breeding between animals and humans and admired the centaurs, griffins, mermaids and winged genie who made up their mythical world. Did all this happen on the Ark?

It is astonishing to me that David Attenborough, who is on television every night describing animal species from the flea to the mountain gorilla, and their dependence on each other, has never made a programme on the mule, the liger, the grolar bear or your average American citizen. It is probably the reluctance of the BBC to dabble in issues of race. Sadly I have noted no overt sexual activity on *The World* as a result of the apartheid generated by its separate apartments. It has been a disappointment.

Most days, following a lecture by a variety of naturalists, ornithologists, botanists, geologists, geophysicists, etc., we were landed by Zodiacs on some barren shore. Normally it was at a site where there had once been a trading post established by the Hudson's Bay Company. It consisted of a single but derelict hut where the Inuit trappers had collected thousands of musk rat (used for hats), Arctic fox pelts (used for furs) and, in the west, sea otter skins (known as Arctic gold). All this death was exchanged for guns and knives and other products of the so-called civilised world. On 1 September we launched into a bay – to search out wildlife, in a raging snowstorm and a wind chill above the beach of minus 5°.

On 3 September we came to Devon Island, the largest uninhabited island in the world, where I had breakfast beside a massive glacier that came right down to the sea. The barren mountains of Devon Island rise to 2,000 metres and are daunting beyond belief. It was snowing hard; autumn had arrived in the Arctic and most migrating birds had gone.

I conclude this passage by saying how impressed I am by the energy and guts of many passengers – they are the kind who might survive disaster and start again. Bankruptcy and revival. A single day off Devon Island in the high Arctic demonstrated the resilience of the human race.

*   *   *

The helicopter dumped a group of adventurers on a thousand-metre mountain in sub-zero temperatures to scout out musk ox, caribou and polar bears with only coffee, chocolate and champagne to keep them warm. Champagne was available, I believe, on a white tablecloth served by a Filipino butler dressed in Arctic livery.

Another group of intrepid ladies went kayaking single-handed in quite steep waves around the floating icebergs, the kayak being the principal transport of the Inuit.

I accompanied another group which went out in Zodiacs among the floating ice in a force six sea and, yes, hiding behind a massive iceberg was a ship's tender of Filipino girls who handed out champagne and hot dogs!

And to cap it all, the marina platform at the stern was lowered into the sea for an 'Arctic Polar Plunge'. All passengers were invited to take a 'dip' in the icy Arctic waters. And quite a number did. Not me. The ship's doctor and a nurse stood by with oxygen and a defibrillator on deck and a diver and two Zodiacs coasted around the plungers to tend those suffering from shock.

This lot illustrates that if the wealth of the world continues to grow, and it is not frustrated by the pessimism and machinations of the 'warmists', the solution to the problem of climate change will be as easy or as difficult for man as the landing of 'Curiosity' on Mars.

The problem will be solved by man's astonishing ingenuity.

At last the scientists, in desperation at the failures of alternative energy, have been forced to study the options provided by geo-engineering. They do exist, many of them in the realm of science fiction. For instance, putting giant mirrors into space to reflect heat, salting clouds to make them brighter, feeding oceans with iron to spur the growth of plankton, painting white reflecting roads and buildings and capturing carbon in a multiplicity of ways. Man's ingenuity will solve the problem.

The night before our arrival in Greenland we were treated to an evening of karaoke. There were several really terrible male singers on board, but the bar was crowded to watch a particularly wholesome wife who warbled away rather unhappily; her movements, however, were spectacular. She wiggled and dipped and swayed. She could only have learnt such movement as a professional pole dancer – and the delight on her face as she was transformed back to her early career was a pleasure to watch. It is uncertain whether she was on *The World* as a result of the wealth created in her earlier profession or whether she had found her very own billionaire. It is distasteful to say so, but several passengers have undergone more than one marriage; some two, etc. No one as many as Gabor, though. She's one of my heroines, like Sarah Palin, the former Governor of Alaska.

Zsa Zsa Gabor could justly claim to have been the very first 'celebrity'. This was an unknown phenomenon until people like Ann Widdecombe came along. Zsa Zsa is Hungarian and was crowned Miss Hungary at the age of fifteen. She emigrated to the United States in 1941 and became an actress, but she is best known for her wit and her nine husbands.

It must have been because of the karaoke, or the fact that I had consulted the internet after the comments by my ridiculous English friend, that I had a dream.

I dreamt that we had Nicole Smith (still twenty-six) on board who sadly passed away, in the deepest grief, after the death of her husband, J. Howard Marshall, at the age of ninety. Nicole had come back to life on *The World*. She had a distinguished career as a *Playboy* model and centrefold, although she was said to be 'larger and heavier' than the typical *Playboy* model because she was addicted to 'fries'.

She told me in my dream that she met Howard when he was eighty-nine and she was considerably younger at Gigi's (now renamed Pleasure), a Houston strip club (some hope for me yet). It was a real love affair and I believed her. Against my advice, she posted her measurements on the noticeboard – bust 36DD, waist 26 inches, height 5 foot 11 inches – because she is seeking another husband on the ship. J. Howard Marshall left an estate of US$1.6 billion (modest for a resident of *The World*) and Nicole claimed half, which was reasonable enough as she had been married to him for two whole years. The inheritance was disputed and the controversy went to the Supreme Court. She had a baby daughter and many fortune hunters claimed paternity, including Frederic, Prinz von Anhalt, the husband of Zsa Zsa Gabor, who claimed that he had a decade-long affair with Nicole. Poor Zsa Zsa; he was her ninth husband, thirty-six years younger than her, and her longest marriage.

I awoke with a start and wondered what this dream had to do with a trip to the Arctic. A lot actually.

We were there to learn about animal behaviour in harsh conditions. For instance, are the birds faithful for life like the pigeons in Trafalgar Square, or do they stray while the wife is away hunting for fish? There seems to be a lot of questionable behaviour on the cliffs. Some animals, like the polar bear, are known to spread their seed, going from one ice floe to another while the females are in season.

We should translate this into human behaviour, and study Zsa Zsa's skill in surviving in the harsh world of celebrity. Her second husband was Conrad Hilton, the hotel magnate and grandfather of an aspiring celebrity called Paris Hilton. She said of him, 'Conrad was very generous to me in the divorce settlement, he gave me five thousand Gideon Bibles'; and 'I am a great housekeeper. I get divorced, I keep the house.'

If you are rich, this is the kind of information you want from the naturalists and professional behaviourists on board. It is a pertinent lesson to any bored female passenger who finds these endless peripatetic journeys around the world quite tedious. She craves excitement with a new lover; how do you set yourself up for life, with the divorce settlement? Follow Zsa Zsa Gabor's example.

As for the men, we should remember the example of Frederic, Prinz von Anhalt, who is not a genuine aristocrat at all; a bit like Prince, the pop star. Frederic was adopted as a thirty-six-year-old by Princess Marie-Auguste von Anhalt, daughter-in-law of the German

Emperor Wilhelm II. Princess Marie was bankrupt and his adoption was a business transaction, the finance evidently coming from Frederic's son, Prinz Marcus, one of the largest night-club owners in Germany. He has spent some leisure time in jail for trafficking and tax evasion, and has been photographed with his cousin by marriage, one Paris Hilton.

I understand that the organisers of this great journey invited Prinz von Anhalt to come on board as a lecturer. He was to join other distinguished lecturers like our geophysicist who told us that we will all perish under water unless we mend our ways. The Prinz's subject was to be 'adaptation and sustainability'; sadly he declined because he is currently engaged in a court dispute with his step-daughter, Francesca Hilton, over control of his wife's finances.

What I have really learnt from my dreams is how to get on in life. Success is all around me. J. Howard Marshall met Nicole Smith in a Houston strip club and she had a long affair with Prinz Frederic who married an elderly actress with eight previous husbands. It is this merry-go-round of business and human relationships that interests me; some people have consummate networking skills; others do not. 'To a smart girl, men are not the problem; they're the answer' – who else but Zsa Zsa Gabor. Exactly. We have three Russian girls on board and I have been observing their behaviour.

My wife gave me a solemn warning: 'Do not mix with the Russians. They like old men and may assume that you are rich.' These girls are said to be involved with rich Canadians from Calgary, but there is no sign of their men. Are they married? Are they on probation? Have they been hired for the journey? My breakfast companion, who knows them, says they are very high-maintenance and are to be avoided, but how did they get from some Siberian outpost like Kirkutz to the oil fields of Calgary? I don't know!

But, steady; it is the last night on board and I am packing. The telephone goes in my cabin. 'Hello, it is Jenny here. How are you,

John? I saw you last night and I want you to have dinner with my friends'.

I am mystified. Who is Jenny?

'Nice of you to call, but I am packing – when did I meet you, Jenny? There are so many people on this ship that I cannot remember everyone's name.'

'You were photographed with me at the party last night; in fact you had your arm around my waist. We are the girls from Russia, although actually we come from Calgary. We want to meet you because you are famous and worked with Mrs Thatcher.'

Now here's the story. At some point on this trip I was identified as an English politician. No one on this floating United Nations has ever heard of anyone from England; they barely know that England exists. But everyone feels they have a personal relationship with Mrs Thatcher – and all of them have seen the film *The Iron Lady*. So the ship's gossip has it that I am famous. Well, of course, I accept the invitation, out of curiosity.

My sarcastic comments about these ladies prove to be unjustified. I owe them an apology. I recall having seen them at karaoke, but I have never exchanged a word with 'the Russians' on the ship. I am too frightened of my wife.

The four of us gather for 'the last supper' before I embark the next morning. It turns out that, as you would expect, ship's gossip has got it all wrong. The girls are certainly high-maintenance, as illustrated when their husbands delivered them to the ship at Nome in a private aeroplane and then returned to Calgary – and are picking them up at Nuuk in the same manner – while I hang around for three days, waiting to get a connection to Iceland on Greenland Airlines, the cheapest way out of the island. But the 'Russian' girls are delightful.

I have the permission of these three ladies to mention them. It would have been possible, of course, to include a biographical sketch of other passengers but, as I want to return one day, I have decided that discretion is preferable to fame as an author.

For a similar reason, I did not have the impertinence to enquire from the many alumni of Wall Street how exactly they stole the hard-won savings of the middle classes with their swaps, and hedges, and shorts and longs. This is a polite cruise and I do not want to disturb the social equilibrium of a wholly excellent ship which will serve my purposes well when Armageddon – the Flood – sweeps everything away.

31

Adaptation and Survival

Mr Wonderful seeks immortality, of course, by following the Almighty's instruction to Noah at the conclusion of The Flood.

> And God spoke unto Noah saying... be fruitful and multiply... go forth off the ark thou and thy wife, and thy sons, and thy sons wives with thee... I establish my covenant with you and your seed after you... forever.
>
> Genesis, 8.13

It was this compulsion that led me to 'multiply' my genes not just through my grandchildren, as Noah had instructed, but also by taking a group of talented celebrities like Jordan to the safest corners of the earth. I gave Mount Arafat a miss. The experiment failed, not just because my celebrities were jaded, bored and lonely in these far-flung corners of the earth, but because I was not sufficiently 'fruitful' and masculine at the age of eighty; I did not appeal.

I had sought to follow the example of the male polar bear, the cock salmon, the Arctic tern and the leader of the Liberal Party, one Nick Clegg ('I have slept with no more than thirty women'), to spread my seed, as Noah had instructed, as widely as possible. It is, after all, the principal compunction of the male until he comes up against some obstacle, like marriage.

Now, we are all descended from Adam, and I was tempted by Eve but that was an awful long time ago; but perhaps not so long ago.

If we imagine, as did geologist Don Eicher, all of earth's history as events compressed into a single calendar year:

> On that scale, the oldest rocks we know date from about late January. Living things first appeared in the sea in February, and continents began to assemble and drift about the globe in early March. All of the major phyla of marine life had evolved by mid-October, and the generation of petroleum followed soon thereafter. Land, plants and animals emerged in late November and the widespread swamps that formed the great coal deposits of the world flourished for about four days in early December. Dinosaurs became dominant in mid-December, but disappeared on the 26th. Man-like creatures appeared sometime during the evening of December 31st. Rome ruled the western world for five seconds from 11.59 to 11.59-50, and the science of geology emerged just slightly more than one second before midnight at the end of our eventful year of years.

So, on this scale of things Adam and Eve appeared in the world sometime around the evening of 31 December. I like the analogy because it puts this survival thing in a proper context. Having failed in my final years to be 'fruitful', as I had earnestly intended, I decided to examine the experience of certain creatures in the animal kingdom. How will they survive?

It is obvious to me, if not to the scientists of the world, that serious mitigation of the consequences of global warming is impossible. On my trip, a very distinguished Nobel prize-winner, a key member for the 'International Commission on Climate Change', about whom I talk in a following chapter, tried to scare us by projecting that by the end of the century sea levels will have risen by one metre, swamping most of the eastern seaboard of the United States – New York, Philadelphia, Washington – as well as London, Tokyo, much of Holland etc., etc.

But isn't there something insulting here to the wonders of creation – insulting to the Almighty, if you will – for the politicians and scientists to engage in near hysteria because average world temperatures may rise by 3° Centigrade by the end of the century? Ultimately, this hysteria about global warming is about the narrow selfishness of man. OK, so the Maldives may be under water within twenty years and we will have to take our holiday elsewhere; and the poor citizens of Malé will have to move to Kenya or Sri Lanka. But if we compress the history of the world, as above, into one year, it seems *de minimus*.

So, set out below I asked myself, assuming the mitigation of climate change is impossible, apart from dabbling at the edges with wind turbines, photo-voltaic cells and other hopelessly expensive means of alternative energy – what are the prospects for adaptation?

Will the Arctic tern adapt or survive? Will the Atlantic salmon, with a little help from our hatchery, adapt to warming seas and survive? Will the polar bear survive an Arctic Ocean without ice? Possibly not. We will have to introduce the polar bear to Antarctica, maybe. Will the Inuit survive with a new shipping passage and more oil extraction in their homeland – can the poor Inuit adapt *even* further and survive? Can Nick Clegg survive – that deserves an answer!

i) The Arctic tern

28 August 2012 – we entered the Arctic ice this morning north of Cape Barrow, the northernmost tip of America. It is not far from Prudhoe Bay where the Alaska pipeline carries oil south for eight hundred miles to Valdez, which was wrecked in 1943 by a huge tsunami following the second largest earthquake ever recorded at 9.2 on the Richter scale. It also destroyed the town of Anchorage, which I have recently vacated, safely.

As we watched for whales and wildlife, we saw a young Arctic tern resting on an ice floe at the start of its first migration south. I am familiar with the Arctic tern, one of the most extraordinary survivors in the animal kingdom. Older birds have been tracked migrating south in the late summer from Alaska, Iceland and Greenland all the way to the Southern Ocean, from pole to pole.

To track Arctic tern a new device called a geolocator has recently been invented which weighs around 2 per cent of the bird's body weight. The geolocator reveals information on sunrise and sunset and these dates, combined with time recordings and daily geographical positions, track the migration routes of this astonishing bird.

Some birds have been known to fly up to 10,000 feet to catch the air currents, and take around six weeks to travel from Greenland to the Weddell Sea in Antarctica, barely stopping for food or rest. Others take a more leisurely journey, if that is the right description, and seem to have a resting place in the rich feeding grounds in the mid-Atlantic where the cold, productive northern waters meet the less productive southern ones.

The average round-trip distance from Greenland to Antarctica and back for the summer journey is around 50,000 miles, which, given the Arctic tern's lifespan of some thirty years, means that on a lifetime of migration it can cover over one million miles, equivalent to several return journeys to the moon.

The Arctic tern is an aggressive little creature and I have seen flocks of them mugging polar bears in Spitsbergen. I know from my fishing exploits to Iceland each year that these little birds can swoop on an unsuspecting walker, and even draw blood. I always wear a hat in Iceland when fishing near the nesting sites of the Arctic tern.

There is so much more to say about this bird, but for me it is a wonderful example of how natural selection over millions of years has adapted a creature to fly from one end of the earth to the other – and then return again to breed most likely to the same location every summer. To suggest that humankind cannot adjust over the next one hundred years to a rise in average world temperature of 3° Centigrade is an insult to the Arctic tern and our creator.

ii) The polar bear

30 August 2012 – the polar bear is the largest land carnivore in the world. It lives on seals and is therefore at the mercy of the retreating polar ice. While successful in a marine environment, it is not so successful or adaptable as another carnivore, man; man, too, kills for food but also for territory and greed. The polar bear lives for up to thirty-five years and a fully grown male will stand seven foot at the shoulder and be nine foot long. We saw many polar bears on our passage through the low Arctic.

Genome studies date it back for four or five million years and the remains of polar bears have been found in dates as far back as 130,000 years. The current world population of the polar bear is believed to stand at 25,000 and there are probably around 1,500 in the Beaufort Sea in north-west Alaska, where we are now located. Although the origins of the polar bear is barely known, it is probably descended from the land-based grizzly bear, but it broke away and adapted to a marine environment where its only habitat, ice, is under threat.

In contrast, its distant cousin the grizzly bear lives on vegetation but it has a particular relish for lemmings; however, it needs to consume something like 65,000 calories a day, which equals 450 lemmings, or the equivalent of thirty-four American pizzas! If polar bears come ashore in the hungry summer months they are threatened by the grizzlies, which are known to kill them in their weakened summer state. Grizzlies have mated with female polar bears and several of their stuffed offspring are to be seen in Inuit villages. But cross-mating between the species is rare.

The polar bear has survived, apparently, through several earlier warming periods and, now that it is an international protected species, it should thrive in the future. Only the Inuit have controlled permission to hunt the polar bear. But the outlook is grim. The polar bear is completely dependent on sea ice from where it hunts its main prey; it needs the shallow continental shelf to hunt down seals. In spring it indulges in a huge feeding frenzy, building up fat reserves which take it through the barren summer. There are no polar bears in the high Arctic; they are concentrated on the continental shelf in Alaska and the Canadian archipelago.

Arctic sea ice at its present accelerated decline may disappear altogether between 2040 and 2100. According to projections, which may, of course, be false, only a residual group may survive in a remnant population in a small area to the west of Greenland and in a very limited area of the Canadian archipelago.

All of this is extremely depressing because already female bears are finding it difficult to find sites for 'denning' where they produce their young; and if their food reserves are diminishing with the ice they will lack the fat reserves and energy for reproduction and survival.

Unless the polar bear can adjust to hunting on land it seems unlikely that it can survive this century. Polar bears have been swimming up to two hundred miles to find sea ice and seals, but they are drowning with exhaustion – and the land seems to offer them no protection. This has been the most depressing finding of my entire trip. Beside the polar bear, what is so special about man?

iii) The Atlantic salmon

In sheer stamina on its journeys the Atlantic salmon can almost compete with the Arctic tern. Its hopes for future survival as a species must rank somewhere between those of the Arctic tern and the polar bear.

I own fishing on a little river in Cornwall called the River Lynher. Fortunately, except for those living nearby, no one has heard of it. It winds its way between a strip of ancient woodland, which includes some massive beech trees. The river has followed its chosen route to the sea for a thousand years or more, occasionally eroding its banks to change course a little.

The history of the river is described in my memoir *Here Today, Gone Tomorrow*, where I tell how the salmon were prolific in the spring. Now the salmon run up the river in the autumn in their hectic urge to spawn. The eggs hatch into tiny fry and grow for two years or so in the river until they run down to the sea as smolts. There they find their way to the rich waters around Greenland where they grow strong and beautiful before battling their way back, against every peril, to the same stream of their birth.

Recently a group of us set up a hatchery where we catch up to eight cock salmon and hens which spawn in big tanks. Last year we released 60,000 fry back into the river. No one knows whether this midwifery is more effective than natural spawning, but it seems likely that less than six hundred salmon will survive to return home, there to breed and contribute to the cycle of life and death.

It is because of this wonder of nature that I have dedicated this book to the Atlantic salmon; it is, after all, about adaptation and survival in the animal and human kingdom and the salmon is struggling as a species.

I realised the other day that my passion for rivers has taken me to the farthest corners of the earth. To Patagonia and Terra del Fuego in South America; to Invercargill and Stewart Island off the far south of New Zealand; to Arctic Russia and Canada, and especially to Iceland and Norway. My final destination is this trip through the Northwest Passage, along the top of the world from Alaska back to Greenland.

At sea the Atlantic salmon feeds mainly off the coast of Greenland and around the Faroe Islands. There it gorges itself in these rich feeding grounds, just as the polar bear gorges itself on seals in the spring. When it returns to the river of its birth, its strength so much depends on where it feeds. I have noticed that the salmon in the east of Iceland seem stronger than the salmon in the west of that great country.

Sadly, habitat degradation in its traditional rivers and overfishing at sea has hugely depleted its numbers. Now it faces a new threat from salmon farms – and most of all from the warming waters of the Arctic. By the year 2000 the numbers of Atlantic salmon had dropped off to critically low levels. Since then the reduction of nets at sea has seen some revival in its numbers.

Are we assisting the recovery of the salmon with our hatchery in Cornwall? Perhaps man, with his predilection for destruction, *can* aid certain species in adapting to a changing climate by rather emotional responses such as our hatchery. I doubt that we will be successful against the forces of nature. As mitigation fails and adaption struggles, maybe we must accept that the history of the world is not just about survival but it is about extinction, too.

iv) The woodcock

Every year, at the first full moon in November, a woodcock arrives for the winter in a small wood at the bottom of my farm in Cornwall.

The woodcock settles itself within a few yards of last year's location in this wood until early spring, when it departs back to its breeding site in Russia. I cannot be certain of the route that my woodcock takes on its annual migration, but, thanks to satellite tracking, its cousin was furnished with a geolocator in the Lizard Peninsula nearby and, as I write in early November 2012, it has already flown 9,041 kilometres since it was tagged on 18 February 2012. I await the return of my woodcock to Cornwall around 28 November 2012, when we have full moon.

After describing the extraordinary journey of the Atlantic salmon to Greenland from my river in Cornwall, I realised that I had to describe the annual migration of Cornish woodcock. Thanks to a truly excellent scientific body called the Game and Wildlife Conservation Trust people can adopt a woodcock and follow its passage in real time as it sets off to breed in one of several places in Russia, Norway and other parts of Scandinavia.

I have adopted Monkey, a male woodcock, which left Cornwall in late February and flew 6,200 kilometres to a place called Krasnoyarsk in Siberia, an important junction on the Trans-Siberian Railway. Having bred in this summer location with a female who is left to incubate the young, he has started on his return journey to Cornwall and was last located on the Polish-Russian border, over 2,000 kilometres from his breeding site near Krasnoyarsk. It looks as if he is following the same return schedule to Cornwall as the woodcock that comes from my farm. He will not have travelled quite the same distance as the Arctic tern, but it is no less remarkable for that.

With these miracles going on around me, I have to protest again. The examples of the animal kingdom that I have selected in this chapter are not just remarkable by-products of natural selection; they are also living examples of how to adapt to climate change. Annual climate change decides their life pattern; their life pattern does not seek to change the climate. Nor can we. But we humans do have the intelligence, inventiveness and wealth to adapt, instead of imagining that we can change the world to meet our selfish lifestyle. Who can say that today's climate is the best for us until it changes.

v) The Inuit people

How can one do justice to the Inuit – a broad description of a people who embrace many family groups and tribes that first arrived from Siberia more than a thousand years ago and spread across the far north from Alaska to Labrador and Greenland? Their story is a triumph of adaptation to the fiercest climate in the world and then survival against the Westerners who really only gave them disease, iron tools and guns.

I had several talks with our Inuit representatives on board *The World* and several conversations with the Inuit ashore. It was their cheerful acceptance of their lot that I found so admirable – they talked of education and jobs and new technology. Yes – they are adaptable, but it all seems so sad. Now greedy Westerners – who killed their whales and seals; their walrus and their bears; their Arctic fox and their sea otters for skins – are invading their privacy and way of life again with oil and tourism, and most of all their ice. In the winter their fishermen and hunters could traverse the whole vast area across the ice; now even that is being taken from them, so their territory and birthright is threatened once again.

We stayed at an uninhabited harbour called Herschel Island, which had been 'discovered' by John Franklin on a land expedition in July 1826. He reported 'a great many bow-head whales' and by the 1890s American whalers had arrived from San Francisco. It became a winter station when the ice closed in and the local Inuit exchanged meat of all kinds for guns, knives, cigars, chewing gum and American clothes. The effect on the local Inuit population was catastrophic. Syphilis, measles and influenza were brought to the island and spread quickly. The men of the whaling ships, bored with the long, dark winters, tried to make life more interesting with alcohol and women. Henry Larsen, the great explorer, described Herschel as 'the Sodom of the Arctic'. Within two decades 90 per cent of the Mackenzie River Inuit, a famous tribe, were dead. The Canadian Royal Mounted Police arrived and pulled down the American flag. Herschel became a fur trading post.

A few days after we came to Cambridge Bay, the largest town in this huge wilderness. It has a growing population of around 1,700 people and is visited by shipping supplies twice a year. The town is three-quarters Inuit and a quarter Canadian; the whole place is kept alive by Canadian subsidy and welfare. There are three principal activities, the main one being government employment – teaching, utilities, administration – the second being fishing, mainly for Arctic char, and the third hunting for musk ox and caribou.

Until the Second World War, traders and missionaries circulated in the more accessible locations. Missionaries developed an Inuit script and the local newspaper in Cambridge Bay is in English and Inuit script. Alas, it is full of politics: are the Inuit being fairly represented in Quebec and the Federal government? Are sufficient financial resources being divested to these lands? It is the same debate that can be heard among all displaced native peoples from the Maoris to the Native Americans. The Cold War made Arctic Canada strategically important and Distant Early Warning Stations are located through the Arctic. The Canadian Royal Mounted Police enforced Canadian criminal law on the puzzled Inuit – and missionaries preached a moral code that was different from Inuit traditions. For instance, the Inuit had not been strictly monogamous: open marriages and polygamy were common; marriages were often arranged in infancy. In the school I saw big notices pleading with the children to report 'abuse' to the authorities in Ottawa. Somehow I found these well-meaning notices repugnant.

Traditional beliefs had inspired an Inuit mythology filled with adventurous tales of whale and walrus hunts. The Inuit believe that all things, including animals, had souls; any hunt that failed to show appropriate respect to animals might release the spirits, which could avenge themselves. These traditional beliefs have much to teach the civilised world, but in our arrogant belief in our own superiority, our greed and our riches, there is no room for compromise with native peoples.

So, the Inuit survive and they are adapting to Western culture; many of the schoolchildren in Cambridge Bay ran around with iPads but, unlike me, they had mastered them; perhaps technology can bring them a future – our future. Have we so much to offer?

vi) Nick Clegg

Man generally may not be an endangered species if he learns to adapt to climate change but the same cannot be said of the Liberal Democrats; they seem to be on a path to extinction. Nick Clegg is threatened, rather like the Chinese panda, which survives mainly in zoos, thanks partly to Ted Heath's influence with the murderous Chairman Mao.

Should we put Nick Clegg in Whipsnade Zoo where he could do less harm to the body politic? There he could breed a more vigorous hybrid version of the Liberal species. By his own admission, he has slept with 'no more than thirty women' and he is clearly keen to multiply that achievement. Let us take him away from the pain he suffers in the Coalition and give him a chance to demonstrate his uninhibited breeding potential. As a descendent of Russian and Dutch parentage and married to a Spaniard, he could impart the hybrid vigour of several races, much admired in his natural environment, the European Commission.

It is remarkable how an endangered species can reinvigorate itself, even from the brink of extinction. Take Etonians. In the 1960s and 1970s, their influence seriously declined following the Etonian-dominated Cabinet of Harold Macmillan. Given the low opinion of Etonians in that era – people found their sense of entitlement unacceptable – they were forced to gather together for mutual support in men's clubs like White's in St James's, where the Bullingdon reunion took place.

In that barren period, Etonians had to become estate agents, stockbrokers, City bankers, members of the Household Cavalry, hairdressers and accountants. No one doubted their charm when it came to marrying well into the moneyed classes, but their contribution to society was limited.

Then something dramatic happened. Some fifty years later there has been a positive resurgence in Etonian influence. The Prime Minister and his coterie of friends and advocates, the Mayor of London and the Archbishop of Canterbury, all come from that same stable. Indeed, because money and good food became plentiful under Tony Blair, this caste has multiplied to an embarrassing extent; they

Clegg and the giant panda.

are everywhere, a veritable swarm of locusts. So much so that there is a growing debate among social scientists of the need for a cull.

Would a cull of Etonians be best achieved by vaccination with the badger cull – or will it be necessary for there to be a selective cull in places like Kensington and Chelsea, possibly with the assistance of a travelling clinic from Dignitas? Unless something is done to cull the Etonian surplus, the whole caste will deteriorate like stags in overpopulated areas of the Highlands.

Young ministers straight from school and university do not understand how the so-called 'Thatcher Generation' came about. It was born to reverse the Etonian inheritance in the Macmillan era, which spawned consensus and a particularly liberal agenda associated with the politics of decline. Young Etonians from relatively privileged backgrounds tend to follow the Liberal consensus of the Whigs. What the country needs is Tories with the bourgeois drive for self-improvement – that is not part of the Eton agenda.

So, as Conservative fortunes come and go – sometimes dominated by Macmillan paternalism and sometimes wrenched back to the harsh world of a self-made Thatcher – gaps in the political cycle open up for the Blairs and the Cleggs of this world. Nick Clegg breeding a new generation of Liberal Democrats in Whipsnade Zoo should not be without hope. Long after he is deposed, his successors will have their day in the sun – and the Conservatives in opposition will recover their Tory instincts. It may not happen in my lifetime, but happen it will.

32

The Explorers

Why should the British in particular have been so determined to find the Northwest Passage, a route from the Atlantic to the Pacific across the top of Canada? Of course there were commercial and historical reasons for such a project, but I suspect more than anything it was a challenge – and fame attached to the later superhuman efforts of a Shackleton or a Scott, and the explorers who preceded them.

Many books have been written about the quest for the Northwest Passage and I have selected only one example to illustrate the history of this search: the Franklin Expedition in 1845. As we know now it was attempted through almost impossible odds, with ice and storms and scurvy.

In contrast, I sailed the Northwest Passage in 2012 in the largest ship ever to do so from west to east, but only because the Arctic ice is fast disappearing; up to two weeks before our departure from Nome in northern Alaska the sea was impassable north of Barrow. The ice cleared just in time.

The Franklin Expedition was special because it spawned a whole raft of rescue missions, seventeen in all between 1848 and 1878, to find the missing ships and crew, and it was these repeated rescue missions over several years that charted the western end of the passage, albeit bit by bit.

Behind it were two rather extraordinary features. First the determination of Lady Franklin to find her husband and, second, the overwhelming pride of the Royal Navy that only they had the ships, the skill and the discipline to find the way.

Lady Franklin was the ultimate pushy, well-connected, wealthy and determined lady. She was in the great tradition of the English memsahib who had arrived in India in the eighteenth century to beat up the mosquitoes, the heat, the disease and her husband. The men got on famously with their sport and their Indian wives and mistresses. The English wife's job was to stay at home to breed the son and heir and not to mess with her husband's sport and pleasure. Lady Franklin was in a great tradition; she had been the wife of Franklin, the Governor of Tasmania, and had lobbied hard to get her fifty-nine-year-old husband appointed to this prestigious but ultimately fatal task. When her husband disappeared she came up against the bureaucratic obtuseness of the Admiralty who tried to block her efforts but in the end surrendered to her influence and drive. The story of her several meetings with the Admiralty, seeking assistance to find her husband, are highly entertaining. When the Admiralty grew bored with her persistence, many years after Franklin disappeared, she personally financed several rescue missions of her own which eventually showed that he had died – and his surviving crew had taken to the ice in sleds only to resort to cannibalism to keep themselves alive.

The behaviour of the Royal Navy was also in a great tradition: as stubborn and obtuse as possible to outside influence. It had to prove its superiority and indicate that its approach should be unquestioned – 'we are far and away the biggest navy in the world' – and Lord Nelson, who saved England, now looks down on lesser mortals from his high perch in Trafalgar Square.

When Defence Secretary, I forced changes on the Royal Navy and they hate me for it to this day. I reduced the number of frigates to fifty ships in order to finance an upgrade in the navy's weapon systems. Because the Royal Navy is obsessed with their aircraft carriers, which we cannot afford and do not need, the valuable frigate force has been reduced to nineteen ships today, and the number of soldiers in the army has also been plundered to assist in the financing of the carriers project.

'I have the right to be blind sometimes, I really do not see the signal!'

History is replete with the Royal Navy being immune to change so long as it kept a great big fleet of ships. When Franklin set off for the Arctic in 1845 it was nearly fifty years after Trafalgar, and, looking at a graph of naval expenditure, there is not much evidence of it having shrunk to more realistic proportions since the end of the Napoleonic War. It had ships galore and would save the nation once again so long as politicians kept their distance: but what in the meantime to do with the ships and the men? It trained its crew by sending some naval ratings to join the whalers for experience – and to accompany the convict ships on their voyages to Australia. After all, the whalers and sealers and the fishermen had three hundred years of experience of Arctic activity in Newfoundland and Svalbard waters since John Cabot in 1497 and William Barents in 1596.

As the world required oil for lighting and lubrication when the population of Europe grew and moved into the towns, the adventurous acquired considerable fortunes hunting the harmless whale, but they had to be brave enough to risk their lives pursuing animals six hundred times the weight of man. The hunt for oil and blubber was a great maritime industry in sixteenth- and seventeenth-century England and it satisfied man's greed for wealth. Fashionable ladies also required the bone for corsets, which was obtained from the baleen in the whale's mouth.

These amateur adventurers were hardly disciplined like the Royal Navy, but they knew the Arctic waters from Newfoundland to Spitsbergen and to Greenland and the approaches to Hudson's Bay like their own backyard. These men had experience, knew about ice and scurvy and its terrible dangers.

But these coarse and greedy whalers were not party to naval tradition, and institutional snobbery held sway. Before the politicians and the treasurers could come along and interfere it was essential to find some way to use the ships and men. There had been embarrassments in the past when the Dutch sailed up the Thames in 1667, but since Trafalgar no one had challenged the superiority of knowledge or bravery of the Royal Navy to undertake a difficult task. And, anyhow, why should fame and glory go to mere fishermen and whalers when the navy would willingly shoulder the burden?

So the elderly Franklin who, to be fair to him, had an impressive record as an Arctic explorer of the Passage on land, was chosen as the leader. He was equipped with two ships, *Terror* and *Erebus*, each weighing 350 tons, which had proved themselves on previous Arctic voyages. Several senior members of the crew had benefited from earlier Arctic experience. Most of the crew were English, Scots and Irish. They were to enjoy a library of one thousand books on board and galley supplies were obtained from the grandest grocer in London, Fortnum & Mason, sufficient to victual the ships for three years at sea. Captain Sir John Franklin was given official instructions on 5 May 1845 'to proceed from the Davis Strait towards the Bering Sea [Alaska] in as straight a line as is permitted by the ice or an unknown land'.

The ships sailed from London with a crew of twenty-four officers and 110 men. The expedition left Greenland – Disko Bay – and met two whalers in Baffin Bay, *Prince of Wales* and *Enterprise*, at which point there was an exchange of news and conversation. This was to be the last word of Franklin and his crew for the next ten years.

Here I should interpose an interesting fact: the passage was not crossed by sea for another fifty years and then it was conquered by Amundsen with a crew of six in his ship the *Gjøa*, which weighed 75 tons!

I don't doubt that the officers and crew of *Terror* and *Erebus* showed great courage in adversity, but what they really lacked was a group of Inuit guides and hunters to accompany them. When the two ships were caught in the ice and the crews took to sleds to find a way of escape, there were no experienced Arctic guides to help them. In contrast, Amundsen had spent his early life in adventure to the two poles, knew about survival with dogs and sleds and benefited from the charts and knowledge gained by the several expeditions sent out to find the Franklin ships and crew.

On our journey through the Northwest Passage we stopped at barren Beachy Island, where Franklin spent his first winter in 1845–6. It has become something of a shrine. Buried there (the first to die) are three crew members of the Franklin expedition, including Seaman Torrington, who died aged twenty. The graves have now been marked by plaques.

I looked at the grave of Seaman Torrington in this entirely inaccessible and unpopulated corner of the Canadian Arctic and I felt deeply sorry for the lad. Not only had they recruited him, or more likely press-ganged him, to join the Royal Navy, but his remains and his soul had been plundered by archaeologists, anthropologists and historians, and for what purpose? Curiosity; or is it called historical research? His body had been preserved, almost lifelike, in the permafrost and tissue samples were taken to conduct an autopsy to deduce why this innocent twenty-year-old had passed away. The latest examination was conducted by an anthropologist, Owen Beattie, in 1984 – more than 130 years after Torrington's death.

I don't doubt that the recovered remains of the woolly mammoth had a soul, just as much as Tutankhamun had a soul in his resting place in the Valley of the Kings before it was disturbed by Lord Carnarvon. We know that Lord Carnarvon had been dealt a mortal blow by a mosquito bite but we had to dig up Seaman Torrington in the permafrost in the cause of historical research.

Surely justice should dictate that Lord Carnarvon's body should have been mummified and wrapped in linen before being displayed in a sarcophagus for public display at Downton Abbey, the popular nomenclature for Highclere Castle.

Seaman Torrington had died. Why was that no enough? No: it had to be known whether he had been eaten by a polar bear or had died from natural causes. In fact, research revealed that he died of pneumonia brought about by lead in the food cans, hastily assembled by a defective canning process, just before the departure of his ship from England. Other research, following further analysis of Seaman Torrington's remains, indicated that the cause of death might also have been lead in the recycled water from the steam engine of *Erebus*, which had come from the London and Greenwich railway.

What all this examination of the lad's remains was meant to reveal was that the crew of Captain Franklin's expedition had suffered not just from starvation, scurvy and hypothermia before they resorted to cannibalisation but also from lead poisoning. The Canadian autopsies had proved a point – or maybe.

Anyhow, we stood before the shrine of these three casualties and offered up a silent prayer for them before returning by Zodiac to the Ark. There, I had a question for myself. Do I want to be dug up by scientists from outer space, or whoever happens to dominate Mother Earth in a hundred years time to prove how I may have died?

It may seem odd that I should have pondered on this fundamental issue while afloat in Noah's Ark. Supposing that they did discover from my remains that I had died from a surfeit of bad Bordeaux, too much sexual indulgence and a lack of exercise; would that mean that the way I had died granted me a form of immortality alongside Seaman Torrington, Tutankhamun and the woolly mammoth; or would it only indicate a high degree of morbid curiosity among the historians and anthropologists involved?

This was the first moment of doubt in my search for immortality. Why should I seek it? Better to be cremated and dumped in some public pit run by Biffa, the refuse collectors, than have my bones reassembled by archaeologists on a table in the British Museum or, more likely, in a derelict garage under some railway arches. It was the first moment on my journey through life that I began to doubt the point of immortality.

So, the Franklin Expedition, famous for all sorts of reasons, had one consequence that was not foreseen. It had raised doubts about my quest for immortality; they built a statue to John Franklin outside the Athenaeum Club in Pall Mall but there is nothing to commemorate Seaman Torrington – except my scribbles in this little book.

33

The West Country Agricultural Show

The Bedford Hotel in Tavistock is my last port of call. It is a truly testing three-star experience – and I love it! I am staying there on my way to the West Country Agricultural Show, which I have to attend as a farmer and a former Cornish MP.

I have stayed in several of the most glamorous hotels in the world – the Splendido in Portofino, the Carlyle in New York and the Oriental Hotel in Bangkok to name but three – but none of them can compare with the satisfying nature of the Bedford Hotel experience in Tavistock.

I returned from the Northwest Passage in time to decamp from Chelsea and stay there on my way to the show, which is just across the border in Cornwall. I stay there every year to fish in the River Lynher – the place where we have the salmon hatchery – and each year it uplifts my spirit.

The younger generation of my family regard the Bedford Hotel with extreme distaste, actually with horror; they will not even accept my invitations to dinner there – 'not in that hotel,' they say. Yet for me the hotel is close to life eternal. Why?

Nearby on the River Tamar, the boundary between Devon and Cornwall, I am a member of something called the Endsleigh Fishing Club. I think I am the only member of the club who does not merit thirty pages in *Debrett's*. I take pride in being a simple landed yokel with a family history that proves that we have never sucked up to rulers, kings or Norman magnates. I know of no ancestor of mine who has been a fashionable urban dandy, a servant of the Crown in return for favours or even a greedy parliamentarian seeking fame; at least until I came along. Humble John, that's me.

I think this awe-inspiring hotel was possibility built with the generosity of the Duke of Bedford, a member of the Russell family, from the proceeds arising from the sacking of the Tavistock monastery by that monster Henry VIII; who was also the benefactor of Trinity College, Cambridge. I return there in the final chapter. I must be careful how I put it because the prolific members of the Russell family, including a dowager duchess, are all members of the fishing club, like me. And from a position of authority in society they are now reduced to zoo-keepers at their modest pile in Woburn.

The Bedford Hotel costs me £130 for dinner, bed and breakfast. Why should I stay in a three-star hostelry when the Endsleigh Fishing Club can boast the Hotel Endsleigh, a five-star establishment now owned by Miss Forte of Trusthouse Forte fame?

Endsleigh was once partly owned by me, a member of the fishing club, and in those days it was delightfully shabby, just like the Bedford Hotel in Tavistock today.

The downstairs rooms had all the best attributes of a Scottish lodge – worn-out carpets, tattered curtains, sofas full of holes extruding springs for the unwary. Several of the beds had hardly been updated since they were slept in by Queen Victoria, as at that time the Duke of Bedford owned this place – he called it Endsleigh Cottage – and the baths were so huge that wooden platforms were needed to get in and out of them. Even without the tartan carpets, the bagpipes and the dead stags hanging from the walls it must have reminded Prince Albert of Balmoral.

And then it all came to an end. The place was lovely and antiquated but it became too expensive to maintain for the fishing club, so along came the glamorous Miss Forte who tarted it up no end. For sheer luxury it can compete with *The World* – and it costs £340 for dinner, bed and breakfast.

The bedroom furniture in the Bedford Hotel is truly awesome, the bathrooms are a festival of brown tiles, the whole place is stupendously out of date and my brass bedstead, with a sort of cross iron erection over my head, reminds me of my granny. But, the atmosphere of the whole place is delightful, Victorian and friendly. The place thrives on Tavistock weddings and meetings of the Rotary. It feels just like that.

The dinner experience at the Bedford is very tasteful. There are no dress regulations for men, most of them dine in short-sleeve nylon shirts, and their well-built wives are dressed up to the nines with the latest Tavistock fashions and hair-dos, piled high. Not one word passes between them from the soup to the coffee, but they gaze at each other in silent adoration.

I wonder as I glance around the dining room – do the men really want life eternal with their fat old women, or are they dreaming of a sexy land girl who squirts milk into a metal bucket? There will be plenty of former Land Girls at the West Country Agricultural Show. Actually, what is so captivating about the customers of the Bedford is that they seem entirely devoted to each other, whereas in the Hotel Endsleigh it is full of fashionistas and rich businessmen snatching a weekend with their mistresses.

When I descended to the Bedford dining room the bar was full of Devon farmers from their subsistence estates on Dartmoor, all enjoying an exciting night out in Tavistock prior to their visit to the show. It is the local art around the walls that grabs attention. There are many excellent photographs of farmyards in the late nineteenth century but the most striking memory is the proliferating portraits of Victorian grannies in lace shawls; there are hundreds of now dead grannies hanging from the walls (like the dead stags at Balmoral) with only one photograph of a startled Duchess of Bedford in a tiara, hanging beside all these common grannies from Tavistock society. How are the mighty fallen.

Unlike at dinner, the breakfast room the next morning is full of weekend visitors about to embark on an exhilarating experience in the enveloping mist and lashing rain of Dartmoor. You can tell ramblers at a single glance: they are upright, calm, austere, determined, fine people – as long as you don't cross them by blocking a footpath, whereupon they set about you with sticks and dogs.

I should recommend the Bedford to the hotel inspectors for full upgrading to five-star status, but, of course, the Bedford is not modern and fashionable and with an upgrading its customers would change for the worse. It would go upmarket like the Hotel Endsleigh. So we have to keep the hotel inspector at a distance – and retain its three-star clientele and the Victorian ambience of the place, for posterity.

The show was due to be opened by the Duchess of Cornwall, but there had been a mix-up in the royal diaries so that a hastily assembled meeting took place between Clarence House and Buckingham Palace to solve the problem. Relations between the two centres of royal power had been somewhat fraught; it being suggested that the Prince of Wales had been impinging on the royal prerogative, and needed to be put in his place. The Court of St James, representing the combined and competing institutions of royal power, named 'P', Philip, Duke of Edinburgh, as the duchess's replacement.

When I arrived at the showground I was invited to stand in line for two hours to meet the arrival of the royal presence. Imagine my surprise when an attractive young lady, dressed in a gym tunic and flip-flops was introduced along the line-up. It was Pippa Middleton – bum and all. A further error had been made by the royal courtiers and it had been assumed at Clarence House that 'P' referred to Pippa Middleton, the famous sister of the Duchess of Cambridge and her train-bearer at the royal wedding.

As the former MP for a Cornish constituency I inspected the pig, cattle and goat enclosures, followed by the chicken, pigeon, hamster and badger tents. I had entered my tame badger, Tarquin, in the competition and I was delighted that he won a third prize in spite of the mange on his hindquarters. I had saved Tarquin from the repulsive murderers from the ministry when they arrived on my farm for the badger cull. He had slept upstairs in my bedroom until my wife complained of the smell from my socks. It had caused problems because I could not accommodate him in the kennels, which was the home of my Springer spaniels, trained hunting dogs.

The morning proceeded according to form and I met several farmers with their beautiful spouses whom I had seen at the Bedford Hotel the previous evening. Then I was accosted by a charity worker who insisted that I visited the Donkey Trust. I had not quite sloughed off my habit of visiting anything for a vote.

The Donkey Sanctuary occupied the largest and richest pavilion in the show, even larger than the tent of the Royal Society for the Protection of Birds (RSPB). Like my badger, one donkey had serious mange to demonstrate the appalling state of donkeys in Africa, and the other had a glistening coat of burnished Cornish gold. Before and after, as it were. Money was pouring into a bucket at the entrance. The Donkey Trust was very rich, but rather short of donkeys, so vets were on hand to perform IVF on the mangy donkey in the hope that the donkey population – and hence the charitable contributions – might be enhanced.

This took me and my granddaughter to the official luncheon. The President of the Show, Sir Evelyn Gormsby Bt, presided and after we had consumed slabs of local beef and boiled Cornish cauliflower, he rose, slightly pissed, to make his speech. There was polite applause from the local landowners; my farmer neighbour mumbled under his breath something like 'bloody toffs', but I may not have heard him correctly.

Sir Evelyn was of the opinion that 'upcountry' the nation had gone to the dogs. Why anyone should want to cross the Tamar to pollute themselves in Britain's multi-cultural towns was beyond him. Better to stay in the Duchy. He pulled his speech out of his pocket to welcome the Duchess of Cornwall, whereupon Lady Gormsby hacked him under the table and whispered rather loudly that the official guest was called Pippa Middleton. It caused a titter from my farmer neighbours.

Sir Evelyn had decided to treat us to a sociological appraisal of life in our 'upcountry' towns.

'Mother leaves £5 on the table. Mother goes out to work. Son gets late out of bed. No mother; Father does not exist. Mother gets back late. Son goes out. Spends £3 on a Big Mac and a beer.'

This is the modern family, explains Sir Evelyn. 'On my estate in Scotland we keep tight control of the "servants". The ghillies and stalkers are prone to consume an excess of Scotch, so we have to have strict discipline on the estate family.' The RSPB has no idea, Scottish heritage is bonkers, the Woodland Trust is an obstacle to progress on the estate – and so on, and so on.

He sits down to polite applause, and asks my farmer neighbour, the local chairman of the NFU, to make a contribution.

He is also pissed after drinking many glasses of Cornish wine. The farmer rises rather heavily to his feet. He says that we do not have any 'fancy' food at this show. We only eat 'wholesome' local produce. The beef and lamb come from local farms. If the government had any sense of patriotism they would order the local Ministry of Defence, all state schools and other public institutions to serve only Cornish produce. The supermarkets are greedy bastards (or some such word) serving only cheap food from countries that ignore British standards, rules and regulations.

'We farmers, single-handed, put the Conservatives in power

and now we want it back for small farmers like us, not for the rich farmers with big estates. I am nearly...' says the farmer, 'at an end,' shout the toffs, as he slumps down in his seat.

After a short time for recovery he notes that my granddaughter has not touched the local produce; the slab of beef lies untouched on her plate. 'Don't you like our local produce?' he asks. 'I am a vegetarian,' says my granddaughter. 'I only eat things that are grown in the ground.' 'I suppose you live on tofu and lemongrass water and I imagine you are a badger hugger,' says the farmer.

Fortunately the dialogue is interrupted by a hunting horn. 'Thank you,' says Sir Evelyn Gormsby Bt, 'we are summoned to a display by the local foxhounds from our several hunts. We must hurry to the stand.'

34

The Last Days of the Arctic

No course of action will freeze today's climate. Change is under way and is certain to continue because of inertia in the global industrial economy and the climate system; we have already emitted into the atmosphere since the Industrial Revolution enough greenhouse gases to extend far into the future. Population growth and the energy consumption that accompanies it has become a dominant factor.

Europe is situated on a latitude rather similar to that of central Canada and Central Asia, which have much harsher climates than Western Europe. Many of the places that I have visited on this trip, not least Murmansk, Iceland and even southern Spitsbergen benefit from the North Atlantic current which I discussed in and earlier chapter. The whaling industry in Spitsbergen in the early seventeenth century would have been unthinkable without the ocean currents which brought plankton and crustaceans to this northerly extremity of the polar world.

Ice and snow reflect solar energy back to space. More ice promotes a cooler planet and a cooler planet encourages even more ice. The reverse is also true. Diminishing ice cover in the Arctic will mean that less solar energy will be reflected back into space and the surface will grow warmer, including the temperature of the sea. The Arctic Ocean is warming and, as also described earlier, this is causing more precipitation on the Greenland Ice Cap, which in turn is leading to the glaciers sliding at an accelerating pace into the sea. Vast quantities of fresh water are being released; the Greenland Ice

Cap is said to contain *300* billion tons of ice, or fresh water.

To this release of fresh water from the glaciers is added the thawing of the Arctic permafrost. Thawing across the vast expanse of Canada, Alaska and Siberia is underway. This is happening via the Mackenzie River, which drains much of western Canada, and the Lena, Tanesi and Ob rivers that drain northern Asia – and flow into the Northeast Passage across Siberia. Eventually all this added fresh water will dilute the Arctic sea water and make it less likely to sink, impacting on the circulation of the tropical sea water from the Caribbean.

The changes resulting from the melting of the Arctic sea ice are also proving very destabilising as the balance of temperature between the Arctic and the Tropics is affected. The polar jetstream in the stratosphere is being pushed south, causing colder air and summer rains in the United Kingdom and, in 2012, the worst drought in the United States since the 1930s.

My farm lies at Land's End and the Gulf Stream passes within one mile off the north coast near St Ives and within three miles of the south coast near Penzance. When we grew daffodils on seventy acres of the farm, we benefited from some of the warmest winter land in Western Europe. Indeed, only the Isles of Scilly produced earlier crops than us. Now I have noticed that our advantage for early crops in January and February is being eroded. Has the transport of heat to us from the Gulf Stream been affected? Is our winter land no longer warmer than elsewhere in western England? Has the Gulf Stream already changed our climate, albeit marginally? With a slower oceanic transport of heat from the Tropics to the high latitudes of Western Europe, the increase of greenhouse gases may compensate and reduce the cooling that might otherwise occur.

We are all overwhelmed with scientific opinions on this topic, but in the end it is simple observation that provides the answer. I do not need computer projections to tell me that Arctic ice is disappearing;

I have seen it with my own eyes. We cannot arrest it; it will prove impossible. We can mitigate it marginally here and there, but the solution, if there is one, will come from the astonishing inventiveness of man. To make invention and adaptation possible, we have to foster the creation of wealth. And that means fossil fuels. No viable alternative to fossil fuels is in prospect. The capital cost of nuclear power is prohibitive. Alternative energy sources are an expensive mirage. With greater wealth, the world will have the financial means to assist the poorer nations to adapt through scientific progress and inventiveness. The central dilemma for humanity remains: are we to be 'warmer and richer, or cooler and poorer?'

35

Advice for No. 10

The telephone goes. I have just got back from travelling across the top of the world, I am jet-lagged and weary, but I pick up the wretched instrument just the same.

It is Chris. Oh my God, no, not her again.

'Can I help you?' I say politely.

'Yes,' she replies. 'I must come and see you. Thank God you are back. It is important.'

'Look,' I say. 'I know nothing about politics, I have not read the newspapers for five weeks and in that respect I am reinvigorated by my trip. Can we meet in a few weeks' time, when I will have brought myself up to date with the sex scandals, corruption, cock-ups and personal failings of everyone, except of course the failings of journalists and their proprietors?'

'No,' says Chris. 'The Prime Minister has asked me to see you urgently. I am now working with other pollsters in his Private Office at No. 10. I have been appointed Deputy Director of Strategy and Implementation. It is about implementation that I must see you. Surely, John, you will help the country?

'I cannot talk on the telephone,' she says, 'everything I say here is recorded, monitored by the Security Services and subject to a Freedom of Information requests. I am besieged by prying eyes, political gossip and the fear of being exposed.'

So Chris arrives and I take her to my secure room which is built on stilts and is swept daily for bugs and listening devices. I learnt how to build a room like this when I was in government and discussing our national secrets in the MoD. Admittedly I could read a summary of the Top Secret Red Book in the newspapers most days, but it was nonetheless important to keep the Security Services in business. We are a tribal society. It's all about jobs and territory. I learnt that such a room was essential to my integrity when Dave rejected the recommendations of Lord Justice Leveson for the control the worst excesses of the media.

'Well, how is it in No. 10?' I ask Chris.

'Dave is a real gentleman,' she says, 'He doesn't heave telephones around the room like Gordon Brown. He is extremely equable in a crisis. And, of course, his job is overwhelmingly about crisis management. The poor man has hardly any time to think about the future. He is charming and intelligent, perhaps that is his problem.'

'The reason I am here – and it has to be kept a secret because it would be damaging to Dave's reputation if it was ever known that he had consulted an eighty-year-old maverick and troublemaker like you. He does consult a grammar school boy called Kenneth Clarke, particularly on European matters; otherwise he keeps to his own tight circle of school friends who share lifetime experiences with him.'

'Anyhow, I showed him the report about your own experience in government. It is described in your earlier book *Mr Wonderful Takes a Cruise.*

'You must understand that the poor man is beleaguered by advice from all sides. Everyone wants to lobby him. Civil servants sidle up to him, flatter him with praise, seeking to persuade him that they, and only they, can help him. 'Keep away from politicians,' the civil servants advise, 'they are trouble.' 'Yes,' says Dave, 'but I am a politician myself.' 'No,' they say, 'you are not a politician, you are Prime Minister.'

Sir Humphrey Appleby, the head civil servant, sums it up

extremely well. He says: 'Prime Minister, your proposals would work well in practice, but they won't work in theory. Let me take your ideas to Committee. It will first be discussed at the weekly meeting of Permanent Secretaries, and then in an inter-departmental committee, and then with government lawyers, and then with our advisers in Brussels.

'We don't want you to go to prison, ha! ha!' (Civil Service joke).

'I am depressed,' said Dave Cameron to me the other day. 'I pull a lever and nothing happens. I put an idea to my Cabinet and every one of them has a different view; they actually quarrel around the Cabinet table. All I can do is behave in a pragmatic way and seek consensus. Of course this satisfies no one. I ask my Chief of Staff, Mr Ed Llewellyn, an Etonian like me, what can I do? Mr Llewellyn learnt his trade working for the liberal Lord Patten in Hong Kong and in the European Commission, for the Liberal Lord Ashdown in Bosnia and alongside Lord Britten, a Euro Commissioner in Brussels. Like all Etonians, Ed is a very civilised man,' said Dave.

'Speak to Sir Humphrey,' Ed says, 'you have no other option.' 'So I pull that lever and bugger-all happens. I ask Sir Humphrey what has happened to "x" and "y". 'I will enquire says Sir Humphrey, be patient it is in Committee, we are considering your proposals in theory, to see if they are possible'.

'Look,' I say to Chris, 'it is always like this in government. I served in the Treasury, Trade and Defence, and it is sometimes impossible to get anything done. The Civil Service with "due process", has no sense of dispatch. You have to repeatedly ask your Private Secretary what has happened to "x" and "y". Chase, chase, chase. The Civil Service is there to protect their service, their jobs, their prejudices – they are there to give "advice".'

You don't want to go to prison, do you Prime Minister, ha! ha!

'It is not their job to implement anything – that is for outside consultants and tame businessmen. The Civil Service was at its best in the 1960s when it was managing national decline – then they had the misfortune to have a Prime Minister who rose roughshod over their advice, and look what happened to her; then the Tories had a nice man called Major, he did his best to proceed by consensus and look what happened to him. Anyone who wants to be Prime Minister must be bonkers. It is not a proper job when you get there; it is an aspiration before you do so. Being PM is an aspiration, not a job. The whole thing is impossible.' Chris seemed satisfied with what I told her. She might pass it on to the Prime Minister.

I did, however, give her a signed extract from the first *Mr Wonderful*. It is hopelessly out of date, but still relevant, I think.

*   *   *

Extract from *Mr Wonderful Takes a Cruise* (pages 161–2):

> When I was Trade Secretary, I announced on 20 August 1979 a 'Burn a Form a Day' campaign. I had discovered that the Board of Trade boasted over five hundred separate forms for compilation by hapless British business. My initiative dominated the headlines for forty-eight hours. The number of forms continued to rise and Trade now boasts over a thousand forms, but my initiative [my press release] was an undoubted success.
>
> How things have changed in the political life of modern Britain... Walter Bagehot's seminal work, *The English Constitution*, was written in 1867 and it may be in need of substantial revision.
>
> Indeed, things have moved on since I was in government in 1979... All initiatives are reserved for the Prime Minister himself [at that time I was referring to Blair]. Ministers have become what Bagehot described as the 'dignified' part of the Constitution, together with the monarchy and Parliament. Ministers and Parliament no longer matter.
>
> A schedule of forthcoming initiatives and announcements

is drawn up weekly for the Prime Minister by the Department of Public Relations who pass their recommendations to No. 10. This is the tactical arm of government.

The strategic arm of government which conducts 'blue skies thinking' is under the control of a businessman with experience of running a slim, efficient, commercial enterprise – he is Lord John Birt formerly of the BBC. Other advisers joining the presidential suite, all with desks at No. 10, known 'thinkers' with strong ethnic credentials, are Madonna, Ali G, Steve Coogan and Geri Halliwell. No one knows quite that they think about but the announcement of their appointment was met with universal acclaim.

Given my observant nature and long experience and knowledge of government, I have been invited by advisers at No. 10 to plan, reform, modernise, edit and relaunch *The English Constitution* by Bagehot…

Of course the team at No. 10 has changed, but the number of forms and the number of Prime Ministerial announcements has multiplied. Walter Bagehot would be amazed.

36

Return to Cambridge

It all ended in Cambridge, where it began. Several years have passed and I have returned for the Annual Luncheon at Trinity, my old college.

I described my last visit in the opening chapter of this book, and once again my visit has coincided with the Alumni Weekend, when former inmates of this closed institution return to hear lectures from the professors and fellows of this other world.

Last time I was much taken by lectures on 'The Big Bang' and 'Why Life Needs Death'. This latter lecture, readers will recall, covered the subject of 'Cell death in the development of a mouse's paw', followed by 'Cell death in a mouse's mammary glands'. I was following this lecture about cell growth and its replacement when our speaker put up a diagram headed 'Phagocytosis of Apoptotic Thymocytes by Macrophages', whereupon I began to lose him.

Imagine my surprise when I learnt that the new Master of Trinity, who made the speech at luncheon, was a protein engineer, renowned for his experiments on mice; his retiring predecessor, Martin Rees, was, as I have said, Astronomer Royal, an expert on the stars. This combination of mice and the stars gave me all sorts of ideas – to which I shall return – but first I must explain briefly how Sir Gregory Winter, the new Master of Trinity, made his great reputation.

He is a pioneer of therapeutic antibodies. It was explained to us that the cells of the immune system can detect foreign invaders like bacteria and viruses. Antibodies can be turned against human cancers. The arrival of DNA technology offered Winter a solution. If mice are immunised with human cancer cells, the immune system makes antibodies that attack and kill the cancer. Winter used genetic engineering techniques to humanise the mouse antibodies – and, hey presto! – he was the instigator of new pharmaceutical drugs like Perceptin and Avastin.

So the new Master is not only a scientist, but an entrepreneur and a miracle worker. He is the sort of man to have on your side, particularly if you are dabbling in the concept of immortality. And we have to thank the mice, creatures of the animal world whose survival was not covered in my chapter on this subject, but clearly they are important to man's survival. And man, with the assistance of mice, becomes cleverer every day, with a profound leap in knowledge from when I last attended Cambridge to hear a lecture on this subject.

Given my recent trip along the top of the world to observe nature and the animal world, I decided to fit in one discussion session on 'Nature' before I attended the Trinity luncheon. It was a mistake, and perhaps an example of how grant-aided academics live in a separate world to people like me struggling to help nature in a multiplicity of ways.

There were six 'experts' on the subject of 'Conservation and Sustainability'. They mumbled their way through the fashionable jargon on this topic. Can someone please tell me what 'sustainability' means? And while they are at it, can they also define 'biodiversity', 'the agri-environment', 'habitat' and 'the Eco-systems Task Force' (EMTF)? I am sure that my granddaughters in their primary school are fully conversant with this jargon, but it means nothing to a poorly educated eighty-year-old like me. When it comes to sustainability I think it means that I, as a farmer, must put back on the land some good farm manure in return for what I take out in crops and vegetables.

I understand the point, but do I need to be bored by the likes of a

Guardian journalist, a representative of Greenpeace, an environmental economist who is an adviser to Prince Charles, a chaplain from some minor college who never mentioned God and an RSPB educationalist? In fact, I have a lot to teach the RSPB, as I shall explain in a moment. These are the sort of people who promote theme parks, write acres of reports and debate in their closed world whether we should put an economic value on nature. What price nature? Does price represent value? I want to shout out rudely from the back, 'Get out on the land and get your hands dirty' and 'Save the trees' by asking George Mombiot to consume less *Guardian* newsprint.

I propose that the Cambridge Conservation Initiative, which is what they call themselves, decamp from their desks to spend, like Chairman Mao's victims, six months working on a dairy farm. There they could help to pour milk down the drain when the supermarkets refuse to buy it at an economic price – that is modern sustainability for you.

I could also teach the RSPB why there are no songbirds on my farm when I spend a fortune on wild bird seed, winter stubbles, conservation headlands and the rest. It is because corvids, sparrow hawks, foxes, grey squirrels and particularly badgers (all loved by conservationists) wreck every attempt that I make to provide feeding for songbirds and protect the nests of the robin, the chaffinch, the blue tit and other of God's small creatures. Bring back the gamekeepers, I say; they kept nineteenth-century nature in proper balance before upstarts like the RSPB and other conservationists started persecuting them.

Anyhow, I escaped to the luncheon held under the portals of the beautiful Wren Library and the new Master gave a little speech. He said that, as a newcomer to his great office, he did not have much to say except to assure us that Trinity was solvent. This statement was met with a minor cheer and much laughter. If Trinity ceases to be solvent, then the rest of the world will be bankrupt, because since Henry VIII exercised his generosity it has grown into one of the richest institutions in the country. And much good it does, keeping poorer colleges afloat with handsome transfers.

I hope that among its missions will be to ignore the oft-expressed desire of government to widen its franchise by recruiting inadequate candidates from state and other schools. This anti-elitist rubbish is much propagated by ex-Cambridge liberals and retired Oxford members of the Bullingdon Club, less, I suppose, the heretical Boris Johnson.

Isaac Newton, perhaps the world's most famous scientist, started at Trinity as a servant in hall and was recognised for his intellect. How else can the Isaac Newtons of the future be recruited except by intellect rather than background? Trinity would not boast more Nobel Prize-winners than France if it were ever to take a blind bit of notice of political fashion and correctness.

If the new Master, Gregory Winter, were to form a partnership with his predecessor, Martin Rees, they might together solve my future. Sir Gregory might extend my life in perpetuity by ever more life-saving drugs and Martin Rees, the Astronomer Royal, might send me to the stars; a partnership formed out of Sir Gregory's experiments with mice and Martin Rees's probing of the stars.

Martin Rees has told us that what astronomers call the Universe is the space extending more than ten billion light years around us and containing billions of galaxies, each with billions of stars and maybe billions of biospheres.

If this is the case – and I have no reason to doubt it – it is not asking much that I be granted immortality. Surely with his responsibility for the Universe the Almighty can find some space for me somewhere?

Immortality comes closer for the human species in decade-wide leaps. Medicine advances ever faster to sustain, and then lengthen, life.

The actuarial profession is exhaustingly redundant. It can never catch a static moment to do its sums; one day the predicted lifespan of a man is four-score years and ten – and by the next time they apply their pagan practices to the calculation the lifespan has extended to five-score years and more. It can only be a question of time before some cure arrives to arrest the process of ageing altogether, and Sir Gregory Winter's mice will chart the way.

There is no need any more to repeatedly cross the International Date Line backwards or escape to Mars with the Astronomer Royal. The progress towards immortality on Mother Earth is happening right here anyhow.

Unusually, I have been waiting all my life to reach the age of eighty. It is a wholly satisfactory state of grace, even if it creaks a little. If I have to be immortal, please stop the clock at eighty; certainly it would be more acceptable than being immortal at the age of twenty, forty or sixty with all the 'blood, toil and tears' that accompanies these lifetime markers. I have arrived here largely without the help of medicine because I was born with good genes which I had wanted to extend more widely. If some mechanism can be devised to keep me out of hospital – a visit to an NHS hospital would surely kill me – I can wait around for Sir Gregory's next invention. Yes, I'm nearly there.

Early in this book I considered breeding some kind of super-race in a survival community with succulent victims like Jordan/Katie Price or Carla Bruni-Sarkozy. The idea was to go to a scare-free zone safe from global warming and other multiple disasters. But the celebrity victims did not play my game – and, looking back on it, it was actually for me about the entrepreneurial attraction of building a temple of health in Punta Arenas with the help of the girls from the Bangkok Bath and Soap that grabbed me. And when I encountered the prejudices of the gay community in suburban Sydney with their contempt for 'straights' like me, I wondered whether Sir Elton and Lady John would accept me as a friend and neighbour. Life seemed full of doubt.

Then I realised that I was being entirely selfish; did I not have something valuable to offer to the human race? I had encountered Lady Vyvyan and her camper van, and her experience with her plastic man. Her story had profoundly affected me. It was clear that men were on the way to extinction, women did not need them any more and male impotence was getting completely out of hand. Shortly, men might be kept alive, but with no capacity for procreation; they were becoming useless and redundant.

It was while these thoughts were in my mind that I received an urgent call from the Millennium Seed Bank at Wakehurst Place; they said that I had missed my appointment as a donor and expressed their growing concern at the absence of virile young men. Could I still perform at eighty, I was asked; they had given up on the twenty- to forty-years-old generation. The hospitals were overcrowded with partners seeking IVF treatment – and the queues were lengthening while the sperm bank at the Millennium Seed Bank was diminishing; they were on alert to my generation to perform a national service. I said earlier that my generation might still have some role to perform – and so it seems. But what was the point of extending life towards immortality if men had lost the ability to f*** successfully. Did we really want a human race that was dependent on the artificial creation of life through the formula 'Mycoplasma JCVI – syn1.0 cells'; cells which can be fruitful and multiply…? It raised all sorts of ethical issues.

But joy of joys. I am still needed here on earth to help the human race going forward. Maybe a role as an immortal sperm donor is not everyone's cup of tea, but eighty-year-olds should know their place. It is quite an ego boost to know you are wanted. You've done your stuff on earth; put your children through expensive institutions, put your grandchildren through expensive schools, provided a house for them to live in, suffered the whingeing grandchildren while their parents go on holiday abroad and spend their inheritance in expensive restaurants; suffer, too, the patronising comments of your offspring about your attitudes and general carefulness with money; all these acts of generosity may give you a very short period of immortality in their memory but it is nothing compared to being stored to infinity in the vaults of the Millennium Seed Bank.

Then I began to wonder why I should have sought immortality in the first place. I came to the conclusion it was all the fault of institutionalised religion. The Jesuits pointed out, many centuries ago, that if you could capture a lad for his first seven years and ply him with all sorts of religious mumbo-jumbo he would be yours for life. It was otherwise called religious instruction.

It was what happened to all my generation. We were snatched weeping from our parents and dispatched in short trousers to an Anglican boarding school at seven. There we were bludgeoned into a life of muscular Christianity, made to say prayers at bedtime, shiver in a cold chapel every morning and absorb the ritual and superstitions of the Christian church. It did not occur to a boy of seven that all this traditional palaver was actually to keep archbishops, popes and cardinals in business. It was a power play on their part. Unless they could imbue their followers with a vision of the afterlife and of how an obedient, disciplined, practising Christian would go to heaven, the whole edifice had no purpose. This kind of teaching was the foundation of all organised religion. It was about power, jobs and territory and whether it was the Archbishop, the Pope, the Metropolitan, the Rabbi or the High Mufti it was much the same. To keep the mullahs in business they had to convince the suicide bomber that he would wind up in the bosom of fragrant virgins.

It was the common foundation of all the Abrahamite religions. To keep themselves in business the priesthood had to convince its followers of the resurrection story. There must be something good, something better to follow, if you stay with us. Abstinence is one route to heaven, another is to give money to the Anglican establishment, or to the Vatican; another is to build a mosque. It is about the glory of organised religion.

The Eastern tradition seems infinitely more appealing. It is not about power. The Buddhist and Hindu religions are not institutionalised. The Buddhists do believe that an essential part of you survives the body in order to be reincarnated with the law of Karma. But there is an undercurrent of recognition that the individual mind cannot continue without the body. Nirvana means extinction, blowing out the candle of life. The Dalai Lama believes in the continuation of 'an awareness' that does not depend on the brain. Can the mind, the brain, the soul, consciousness, be independent of a living body. The early Jews and Christians realised that immortality could only be promised through the reassembly of the complete living man or woman, hence the need for the doctrine of resurrection of the body.

I found it infinitely depressing that I had been misled like this since my early youth. It is hardly surprising that with my education I had grown up to believe in the resurrection; although the resurrection of the body had been a step too far for me. But I had never had any doubts about the resurrection of the spirit, the soul. I had always believed that my soul would survive independently of my body. And I had mapped out another life for my spirit with more sex, more fishing, more travel on *The World* and repeated visits to the Bangkok Bath and Soap, now in Punta Arenas.

But now the neuroscientists with the aid of modern brain imaging techniques had proved quite convincingly that without having a body, the mind, the brain, the spirit, the soul, consciousness, could not survive. Either I had to become a born-again Christian and believe implicitly without question in the doctrine of the resurrection; or I had to convert to Buddhism where I could follow the teaching of the Dalai Lama that 'awareness' could be separate from the brain.

I was fearful of this latter course because I would have no say in my reincarnation. I would not mind coming back as an Arctic tern, a polar bear, an Atlantic salmon, a woodcock, or even of one of Sir Gregory's mice, but what about reincarnation as a Liberal? Supposing I was brought back like Nick Clegg, a Liberal – that would be a step too far – a truly horrific end. It was decisive for me; I could not become a Buddhist.

So back to immortality again: what would life be like if it became one interminable Sunday afternoon? It had been this thought that led me to taste the afterlife with journeys on *The World* – the waiting room for Paradise. But what pleasure would there be in steaming indefinitely on journeys from one place to another? Having seen Baffin Island once it was a revelation, but how would it seem on a second visit? How many tropical beaches or glaciers would it take to satisfy a troglodyte before he never wanted to see a tropical beach or a glacier ever again? The first time it would be a pleasure, the second time a pleasant reminder, the third time a tedious repetition. I would shut myself away in my cabin as a troglodyte. So there was only one answer left. Immortality offered nothing but tedium. Reincarnation offered uncertainty, and a total loss of control. It has taken all these journeys around the world, these dalliances with celebrities, these multiple experiences, to teach me the glory of mortality. All I want is Nirvana, extinction, and the snuffing out of a candle at the appropriate time.

THE END – *or is it?*

Afterword: Mr Wonderful Has a Makeover

Readers of my earlier book will be aware that I acquired the name of Mr Wonderful as a result of my regular attendance at Mr Wonderful tea dances in Bromley, Battersea and Dartford, and other godforsaken places in the suburbs.

The average age of the participants was around seventy-five, but the idea that an eighty-year-old might participate raised a sense of despair in the charming Indian who is the compère of these events.

'We are not against ancients,' he said, 'but are you sure you are sufficiently virile and athletic to accompany a seventy-two-year-old princess in an American "hot" [one of Ann Widdecombe's triumphs]? We are nervous about gaining a reputation as a geriatric clinic for the residents of our local retirement homes. We had heard that you had been rejected by Katie Price [Jordan] at your survival community in Punta Arenas – and had been known to spend a lot of time in the Punta Arenas Bath & Soap with your young Thai friends.'

'I assure you,' I replied, 'that this is the sort of tittle-tattle and rumour that I suffered in my political days, and it is quite untrue. I am fit and good-looking for my age; indeed, I have been accepted on several websites for elderly people seeking companionship, with maybe "more".'

The reluctance of the Indian maestro to accept me as a regular participant in the tea dances led me to examine how I might undertake a makeover, similar to the transformation that Mr Berlusconi had undergone in advance of his bunga bunga parties for young models and actresses at his home in Milan.

Mr Berlusconi had already had a major operation on his hair – and had been transformed to look like Andrew Neil, the famous journalist who now comments daily on the antics of prominent, and not so prominent, politicians.

Andrew fills the airtime, as he used to fill his newspapers, with a huge quantity of stuff. Indeed, his former organ, the *Sunday Times*, is now so heavy with stuff that my beefy Aussie carer has to collect it while I hurry, with my Zimmer frame, to what the Church of England now call their Eucharist.

I pray that Biffa will collect my ashes and dispose of them anonymously so that archaeologists are prevented from disinterring my remains for historical research.

My loyal readers will recall that, in earlier years, I was the proud possessor of a white van. But one day I read in *The Times* that 'white van man is commonly regarded as suffering from every social disability, so much so that white van man has evolved [Darwin again] into silver van man'.

Accordingly, I took my white van to a clinic for a complete makeover: colour change, facelift, breast enhancement, Botox injections and bikini waxing with a Brazilian. It gave me the idea of a makeover for myself.

I have always been impressed by my friend George Clooney from Hollywood. He appears almost daily with a different lady on his arm. His grey hair sparkles and shines like Mr Berlusconi's former bald head. How does he achieve it? I got in touch with George by Skype, the method that I use to keep myself abreast of developments in Hollywood. 'George, how do you do it?' I asked. 'What clinic would you recommend?'

'Well,' he answered, 'there is the Jordan Clinic in the King's Road which specialises in breast enhancement. It is mainly patronised by actresses and glamour models, but I understand that President Putin uses it before he appears in a glamour pose for *Pravda*.'

I replied that, unlike Putin, I was not interested in breast enhancement at my age, although I expected it in my female dancing partners at Mr Wonderful.

'Well, as an alternative,' said George, 'you could try the John Prescott Clinic which is run by a girl called Tracy. It specialises in bikini waxing and Brazilians. It was formerly located in Hull, the City of Culture, but it has moved to small premises near the House of Lords. It is patronised by many life baronesses seeking bikini waxing and Brazilians.

'Then,' said George, 'there is the Wendi Murdoch Clinic in Wapping. Frequent flying is bad for the skin and her clinic specialises in Botox and wrinkle creams.

'Finally, my favourite is the Bruce Forsyth Clinic in Portland Place, which offers Pilates and yoga stretching for the maintenance of suppleness and libido in senior citizens.'

'That is definitely for me,' I said, 'Brucie is a wonder.'

Well, I appeared at the next tea dance in Battersea, looking as young as Mr Berlusconi. There were several senior citizens present and they doted on me. The makeover had been a triumph. I invited them over to my next bunga bunga party, but they all expected a payment of €10,000 to participate.

I realised, at last, that the ladies were not interested in talent and good looks; they were only interested in money. It reminded me of the punters on Pampellone Beach. The models came 'on board' the yachts for cash, not for conversation.

Clearly I have to solve this problem in Mr Wonderful Part III.

Acknowledgements

I owe this book to several people, but especially to Richard Collins, my Editor. He edited two previous books of mine, and if he had listened to my reluctance to publish this one it would never have seen the light of day. I had doubts about the essential silliness of several chapters but he persisted: 'you must publish,' he said, so here it is.

Penny Cooper typed and retyped many versions of the script. Even on my trip along the North West Passage, with intermittent communications, I sent her faxes from the ship which she translated into readable prose.

Both Richard Collins and Penny Cooper showed remarkable patience with me.

I realise that a series of separately written episodes based on my travels and fishing exploits around the world do not add up to a conventional book. I pulled it all together into a 'search for immortality'. This idea came to me while I was reading *Our Final Century: Will Civilisation Survive the Twenty-first Century?* by Martin Rees (Lord Rees of Ludlow). I am grateful to him for allowing me to quote from his fascinating book.

The *Daily Telegraph* allowed me to republish Garland cartoons from my political days, and I found it very easy to work with the excellent illustrator, Simon Goodway.

I sought permission to quote from Don Eisner's description of the origins of the world, squeezed into a single calendar year, but received no response. Should he read this, I shall be very happy to hear from him. Similarly, on my trip along the North West Passage I tried to contact Robert McGhee who wrote about *The Arctic*

Voyages of Martin Frobisher, but was unable to do so; instead, I have taken most of the material about Frobisher's trip from the first edition of the Hakluyt Society, published in 1869.

I would like to thank George and Pauline Magnus for introducing me to *The World*, and the other owners of the ship who were equally hospitable on my three-week trip along the North West Passage.

Many thanks, too, to Fred and Nancy Tapper, great New Zealanders and fishermen, who were my hosts in Invercargill and who introduced me to Stewart Island across the Foveaux Strait from southland, New Zealand.

Finally, as the book is hardly a conventional one, I did not persist with Random House, who published *Mr Wonderful Takes a Cruise*. Instead, I published with SilverWood Books and I have found their helpfulness and service a real pleasure.

John Nott
January 2014

Lightning Source UK Ltd.
Milton Keynes UK
UKOW03f0623010414

229199UK00002B/52/P